Mastering Chinese

D1400820

Catherine Hua Xiang
Mandarin Chinese Coordinator at the Language Centre & Centre for East Asian Studies, University of Bristol, UK

Review panel

Shio-yun Kan
Programme Director of the Centre for Teaching Chinese as a Foreign Language, University of Oxford, University Senior Instructor, Lecturer in Chinese, Wadham College, Oxford, UK and Language Coordinator of the British Inter-university China Centre

Huang Dian
Senior Lecturer in Chinese, University of Westminster, UK, and member of the Universities' China Committee in London (UCCL)

Yanwen Liu
Lecturer in Chinese, Faculty of Humanities, Languages and Social Sciences, University of the West of England, UK

Wei Jin
Chinese Courses Coordinator, Language Centre, School for Oriental and African Studies, London, UK, and Executive Committee Member of the British Chinese Language Teaching Society

Maggi McEwan
IWLP Co-ordinator, University of Portsmouth, UK

Mc
Graw
Hill

New York Chicago San Francisco Lisbon London Madrid Mexico City
Milan New Delhi San Juan Seoul Singapore Sydney Toronto

The McGraw-Hill Companies

First published in North America in 2011 by McGraw-Hill under license from Palgrave Macmillan, Houndmills, Basingstoke, Hants RG21 6XS, United Kingdom.

First published in Great Britain in 2010 by Palgrave Macmillan.

10   9   8   7   6   5   4   3   2   1
20 19 18 17 16 15 14 13 12 11

ISBN 978-0-07-176642-5
MHID 0-07-176642-1

Library of Congress Control Number 2010941610

Audio production: University of Brighton Media Centre
Produced by Brian Hill
Voices: Catherine Hua Xiang, Ning An, Charlie Qilin Hu, Mrs. Jin X McMartin, Tuobing Zhao

Produced by Small Print/copyeditor Cheryl Hutty
Illustrated by Shirley Chiang
Typeset by WorldAccent

McGraw-Hill books are available at special quantity discounts to use as premiums and sales pro-motions or for use in corporate training programs. To contact a representative, please e-mail us at bulksales@mcgraw-hill.com.

This book is printed on paper suitable for recycling and made from fully managed and sustained forest sources.

Contents

Preface iv
Acknowledgements ix
Overview x
CD track list xiv
Online resources xviii

Introduction 1
Unit 1 *Getting started* 7
Unit 2 *Greetings and introducing yourself* 22
Unit 3 *Introducing family and friends* 41
Unit 4 *Numbers* 62
Units 1–4 *Review* 83
Unit 5 *Dates and plans* 89
Unit 6 *Time* 114
Unit 7 *Shopping* 139
Unit 8 *Eating and drinking* 159
Units 5–8 *Review* 184
Unit 9 *Transport and directions* 191
Unit 10 *Staying in a hotel* 220
Unit 11 *Leisure and hobbies* 246
Unit 12 *Making phone calls* 268
Units 9–12 *Review* 297

Appendix: *Pinyin sound combinations* 306
Answers to exercises 309
Chinese–English word list 347
Index 362

Preface

Welcome to *Mastering Chinese*, our Mandarin Chinese course for absolute beginners. The aim of this course is to learn basic conversational skills so that you can manage in everyday situations in China. This is the beginning of an exciting journey!

Which Chinese should I learn?

The Chinese that we teach in this book is Mandarin Chinese – the standard official language in mainland China. Mandarin Chinese is spoken by 885 million people as a first language, which is around 70% of the Chinese population. It is also spoken widely in Hong Kong, Taiwan, Singapore and Malaysia. Therefore, learning Mandarin is going to open doors and opportunities across a vast area. There are many good reasons for learning Mandarin, including tourism, business or family. Chinese people will always be delighted that you've taken the trouble to learn their language.

Although there are many different spoken languages and dialects in China (such as Mandarin, Cantonese and Shanghainese) which differ completely in their pronunciation, they all share the same written form. There are, however, two different Chinese character sets. We will teach the 'simplified' character set in this book, which is the standard official form used in mainland China. The 'traditional' character set is used in Taiwan, Hong Kong and Macau, but there is a great level of overlap between the two sets.

Mastering Chinese:
our approach and what's in the course

Mastering Chinese is for everyone. It can be used by independent learners or in a classroom setting. We want you to master the basics of Mandarin Chinese as well as to develop a good understanding of Chinese characters and the rich Chinese culture. Our approach is communicative, carefully paced and cultural.

Master Chinese by getting the pronunciation right
Because Mandarin is a tonal language and its sounds differ significantly from most European languages, we think it is important to help you get the pronunciation right. We do this by introducing and revising Pinyin throughout the book. Pinyin is a romanized phonetic system which enables you to read and pronounce Mandarin without knowing the more complicated script. There is more about this in the Introduction.

Master Chinese by setting priorities
The 'Key expressions' sections of the book help you identify the most useful phrases you need to learn. We have also highlighted the mostly commonly used words and characters in the 'New words and phrases' lists. By doing so, we help you focus your study and make choices about what you spend time on committing to memory.

Master Chinese by engaging in communication
We have carefully designed dozens of listening and speaking activities which aim to engage you in real-life communication. Many encourage you to speak out loud, which is vital in becoming confident in Mandarin.

Master Chinese by understanding: characters and culture
One cannot truly master a language without understanding its history and culture. This is especially true when it comes to Chinese culture and Chinese characters. There is cultural information in every chapter of the book. We also aim to help you build an understanding and awareness of the key language points, and of the components of Chinese characters and words, so that you can apply them in further studies.

How to use this book and the accompanying online resources

The key feature of our book is the choice of routes through it. For example, if you wish, you can skip the pronunciation practice and come back to it when you've heard some words in context. You can study the whole book without learning any script if you prefer. It's up to you to decide what you need or want to learn.

There are a range of symbols to indicate the kind of activities or information you need to study. The 🎧 indicates that the material is on the accompanying audio, for example.

The ⓘ highlights interesting Chinese cultural phenomena or language points which differ significantly from English. Most of the points are also explained in greater detail in the 'Language notes'.

There are online materials you can download for free from our website at www.palgrave.com/modernlanguages/xiang. These include transcripts of all the audio materials, audio of the 'New words and phrases', along with the sounds of all the possible Pinyin combinations (see Appendix).

A note on writing conventions

The speaking and writing systems are separate in Mandarin Chinese. We have to combine both Pinyin and script as we teach you, so that you know both how to pronounce a word and how to write it (if you choose to do so). It is important for you to know the conventions we have used in this book and how the separate Pinyin and character systems work.

When writing in Chinese characters, there is no space between individual characters or words. We have followed this convention in the book. For example, for 'I am Chinese' you write: 我是中国人 with each character evenly spaced. However, if you write the same phrase in Pinyin, you follow the English convention where there is space between the words. So the same sentence in Pinyin should be: **Wǒ shì Zhōngguórén**, which actually combines the sounds of the last three characters

together to form one word: **Zhōngguórén** (Chinese person).
In this book, we will mainly display the Pinyin and Chinese
characters together as:

Wǒ shì Zhōng guó rén
我是中国人

where the script is evenly spaced and the corresponding Pinyin
is placed above each character. This helps you relate the Pinyin
to the character. The Pinyin is therefore not spaced as it would
be if it were written without the characters.

   The styles of printed Chinese characters usually vary from
those of handwriting. In this book, whenever we teach writing,
we demonstrate Chinese character stroke order using real
handwriting. We want to show you a more personal approach
that you can replicate yourself, and to help you become familiar
with both computer-generated and handwritten styles.

Hints on learning

Everyone can master Mandarin. It is very easy in some ways –
no verb endings (as in French, for example), no case endings
(as in German), no genders (as in most European languages!)
What is more difficult is the pronunciation. We have structured
this course so that over time your ear becomes attuned to the
different sounds and you find yourself naturally speaking with
good pronunciation and understanding what is said to you.
The writing system is also more challenging to learn, since the
Chinese script is not based on the Roman alphabet, as most
Western languages are. It is however very beautiful and has an
intriguing history. Again, we have paced the course carefully so
that you can learn to recreate the characters stroke by stroke.

   Studying is always easier in smaller chunks. Both preview
and review is useful. Each unit is subdivided into sections. Try
one section a day rather than a whole unit in one sitting. Try
to find other people studying Mandarin and learn with them.
Check out our online resources section for other ways of getting
practice (www.palgrave.com/modernlanguages/xiang). Offer to
help a local Chinese person with their English in exchange for
some Mandarin conversation!

Thanks and good luck!

I would like to finish by thanking everyone who has been involved in the production of this book. My sincere gratitude especially to my editor Helen Bugler and her colleagues at Palgrave Macmillan, and to the whole production team, who have been wonderful to work with and have been supportive and encouraging throughout my journey writing this book. I would also like to thank the entire review panel for their suggestions, time and expertise in the field of Mandarin Chinese education. My sincere thanks also to friends, colleagues and students who have provided useful feedback and also photos of China. My special thanks to my parents for their love and confidence in me, particularly to my father Mr Jinqiu Xiang for all his handwriting in the book.

I'd like to dedicate the following famous saying written by the Chinese philosopher Laozi (604BC–531BC) to all of you who are about to start a wonderful journey:

千里之行，始于足下。
(**Qiān lǐ zhī xíng, shǐ yú zú xià.**
A journey of a thousand miles begins with a single step.)

I wish you the best of luck with your studies!

Catherine Hua Xiang
January 2010

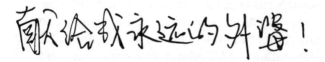

Acknowledgements

The following illustration sources are acknowledged:

Paul Chapman pp 6 (bottom), 57, 93, 102, 107, 201 (top right and bottom right); Clare Hodder pp 144, 180, 201 (bottom left); iStock International Inc. pp 6 (top left and top right), 19, 21, 23, 35, 42, 61, 67, 77, 91, 105, 107 (Terracotta Warriors and City God Temple), 113, 115, 116, 117, 125, 138, 141, 144, 145, 151, 153, 161, 162, 172, 178, 183, 186, 188, 195, 197, 201 (top left), 216, 224, 228, 234, 239, 242, 244, 245, 247, 253, 257, 264, 271, 272, 281, 282, 283, 294, 298, 304 (4–8), 305; Catherine Hua Xiang pp 40, 66, 163, 164, 225, 304 (1–3); Yue Zhang p 107 (beach resorts).

Thanks to Lawrence Lo at www.ancientscripts.com/chinese.html for the use of the handwriting chart on p 17.

Every effort has been made to trace all copyright holders, but if any have inadvertently been overlooked the publishers will be pleased to make the necessary arrangements at the first opportunity.

Overview

	Communication skills	Vocabulary	Grammar	Chinese characters	Cultural knowledge
1	• saying hello, goodbye and thank you	• greetings • goodbye and thank you • titles • times of day	• formal and informal ways of addressing people • use of 们 men to indicate the plural • basic construction of words with 好 hǎo and 见 jiàn	• the history of Chinese characters • how Chinese characters are formed • writing the basic strokes	• meeting people for the first time • typical greetings
2	• asking how others are and answering • introducing yourself	• greetings • nationalities • jobs • simple adjectives	• asking yes/no questions with 吗 ma • translation of 'to be' and the difference between 是 shì and 很 hěn • asking tag questions with 呢 ne	• writing the basic strokes • recognizing and writing characters in the text: 不，好，我，你，是，中国，人，很	• names • polite ways of addressing people in social and work contexts
3	• introducing your family • making simple introductions • describing family and friends	• family members • question words	• indicating possession using 的 de • use of negating words 不 bù and 没 méi • use of the location indicator 在 zài • asking questions with 什么 shénme, 哪里 nǎli, 谁 shuí, 怎么样 zěnmeyàng • use of verb + 一下 yíxià	• basic structures of Chinese characters • recognizing and writing characters in the text: 这，有，爸，妈，住，在，大，叫，儿，子，女，个	• family values • politeness within a family

4	• quantifying things • asking and giving personal information, such as address, age, telephone number	• numbers • measure words • daily objects	• use of numbers • measure words • single and plural nouns	• summary of the general rules of stroke order • recognizing and writing the characters for numbers	• lucky and unlucky numbers
5	• expressing days and dates • talking about birthdays and holidays • talking about travel plans	• the days of the week • the months of the year • Chinese holidays • Chinese horoscopes	• sequence for expressing dates • 是…的 **shì…de** construction • asking questions with 什么时候 **shénme shíhou,** 几 **jǐ,** 多少 **duōshǎo,** 哪 **nǎ** • indicating the future with 要 **yào,** 会 **huì,** 打算 **dǎsuan**	• how Chinese characters are formed (1) • recognizing and writing characters in the text: 年, 月, 日, 星期, 快, 天, 号, 祝, 今, 明, 生, 到, 乐, 走, 回, 从 • writing a birthday card	• Chinese horoscopes
6	• asking for and giving the time • talking about your daily routine • arranging a date • making suggestions	• time expressions • daily activities and leisure activities	• sentence order with time expressions • saying 'yes' and 'no' • use of exclamation words 啊 **a,** 吧 **ba** • verb + 一 + verb construction	• how Chinese characters are formed (2) • recognizing and writing characters in the text: 点, 分, 半, 上, 下, 午, 晚, 去, 吃, 看, 玩, 做, 睡, 买, 要	• traditional festivals
7	• understanding Chinese currency • asking for and giving prices • bargaining	• money • everyday objects • expressions for accepting and rejecting	• asking questions with 几 **jǐ** and 多少 **duōshǎo** • sentence order with money expressions • 大…了 **tài…le** construction • sentence structure for making suggestions	• how words are formed (1) • recognizing and writing characters in the text: 元, 块, 毛, 多少, 贵, 漂亮, 钱, 给, 找, 想, 次, 再, 便宜, 卖	• learning a tongue twister • the art of bargaining

8	• ordering drinks • eating out in a restaurant • reading a menu	• drinks • food • restaurant expressions	• imperative and use of 请 qǐng • verb + not + verb questions • position of adverbs • 那就…吧 nàjiù…ba construction • function of 了 le (1)	• how words are formed (2) • reading a menu • recognizing and writing characters in the text: 酒、奶、糖、醋、茶、菜、鸡、鱼、海鲜、汤、牛、冷、羊、鸭、热	• learning a poem • food culture
9	• taking taxis, buses and trains • describing locations • asking for and giving directions • locating places on a map and reading street signs	• means of transport • buses and trains: travel, tickets, etc. • position and location • buildings and shops	• verbal attributive with 的 de • comparative form with 比 bǐ • expressing position and location • using the prepositions 从 cóng and 到 dào • more on imperatives	• common radicals (1): 口 火 氵 木 心 忄 ⺌ 攵 • recognizing street signs • recognizing and writing characters in the text: 左、右、前、后、东、西、南、北、边、往、坐、拐、远、近、哪儿、面	• learning another tongue twister • transport
10	• checking into a hotel • making requests • describing past events • using simple narrative	• hotel facilities • rooms • time expressions for narratives	• use of the 把 bǎ structure • function of 了 le (2) • use of 能 néng and 可以 kěyǐ • use of …的时候 de shíhou • use of 刚…就…gāng…jiù • use of verb + 到 dào • use of verb + 着 zhe	• common radicals (2): 日 亻 月 车 辶 仝 • recognizing and writing characters in the text: 把、查、能、找、忘、拿、刚、就、房间、单、车、双	• slang and traditional sayings • hotels

11	• talking about activities you like and dislike • making simple comparisons • expressing interest and conditions	• hobbies and leisure activities • expressions of frequency • expressing feelings and opinions	• comparative form with 更 **gèng**, superlative form with 最 **zuì** • expressing conditions with 如果 **rúguǒ**... 就 **jiù**... • expressing frequency • sentence structures: 每...都...**měi**...**dōu**...; 一...就... **yī**...**jiù**...; 既...又... **jì**...**yòu**...	• common radicals (3): 禾 艹 马 犭 夕 • recognizing and writing characters in the text: 更, 最, 聊, 听, 唱, 打, 踢, 因为, 喜欢, 每, 都, 有时	• learning another poem • lifestyle and leisure activities
12	• making a phone call • making enquiries • describing and solving problems • expressing indirect speech	• expressions used on the phone • phone problems	• use of 叫 **jiào**, 让 **ràng**, 请 **qǐng** for imperatives • use of 没 **méi** for incomplete actions • use of 给 **gěi** as a preposition • structures: 会 **huì**...的 **de** • function of 就 **jiù** • resultative complements • function of 了 **le** (3) • expressing present continuous with 在 **zài** + verb • expressing frequency with 次 **cì**, 遍 **biàn** • indirect speech	• common radicals (4): 足 辶 门 扌 力 • recognizing and writing characters in the text: 事, 记, 错, 挂, 声, 清, 请, 告诉, 那, 遍, 还, 慢	• singing a new year and a birthday song • useful phone numbers

CD track list

- Where there is an audio element for an exercise it is marked with a 🎧 icon.
- Every exercise has its own track (and some exercises are further subdivided) so that you can locate the material very easily.
- You can access a transcript of the recordings at **www.palgrave.com/modernlanguages/xiang**

CD1

Introduction

01 1 Introduction – Finals
02 1 Introduction – Initials
03 2 The five tones
04 3 Modification of tones
05 Words from Unit 1

Unit 1: Getting started

1. *Saying hello!*
06 Key expression
07 Exercise 1
08 Key expressions
09 Exercise 3
10 Key expressions
11 Exercise 5
12 Exercise 6
13 Key expressions

14 Exercise 7
15 Exercise 9
16 Exercise 11

2. *Saying goodbye and thank you*
17 Key expressions
18 Exercise 12
19 Exercise 14
20 Exercise 16
21 Exercise 18

Unit 2: Greetings and introducing yourself

22 Getting the pronunciation right
23 Exercise 1
24 Exercise 2
25 Exercise 3

1. Greetings
26 Key expressions
27 Exercise 5
28 Exercise 7
29 Exercise 8
30 Exercise 12

2. Introducing yourself
31 Key expressions
32 Exercise 13
33 Exercise 15
34 Exercise 18

Unit 3: Introducing family and friends
35 Getting the pronunciation right
36 Exercise 1
37 Exercise 2
38 Exercise 3

1. Introducing your family
39 Key expressions
40 Exercise 5
41 Exercise 7
42 Exercise 10

2. Introducing a friend
43 Key expressions
44 Exercise 13
45 Exercise 15
46 Exercise 16b

Unit 4: Numbers
47 Getting the pronunciation right
48 Exercise 1
49 Exercise 2
50 Exercise 3

1. Numbers
51 Exercise 5
52 Exercise 6
53 Exercise 7

2. Measure words
54 Exercise 9

3. Numbers in use
55 Key expressions
56 Exercise 12
57 Exercise 13
58 Exercise 14

Review Units 1–4
59 Exercise 2
60 Exercise 3
61 Exercise 4
62 Exercise 9
63 Exercise 10
64 Exercise 11
65 Exercise 12

Unit 5: Dates and plans
66 Getting the pronunciation right
67 Exercise 1
68 Exercise 2
69 Exercise 3

1. When is your birthday?
70 Key expressions: Days
71 Key expressions: Months
72 Key expressions
73 Exercise 5
74 Exercise 7

2. Talking about travel plans
75 Key expressions
76 Exercise 10
77 Exercise 11
78 Exercise 12
79 Exercise 13b

Unit 6: Time
80 Getting the pronunciation right
81 Exercise 1
82 Exercise 2
83 Exercise 3

1. What time is it?
84 Key expressions
85 Exercise 5
86 Exercise 6
87 Exercise 7
88 Exercise 8

2. Talking about daily routines
89 Key expressions
90 Exercise 10
91 Exercise 12a

3. Making a date
92 Key expressions
93 Exercise 15
94 Exercise 17

Unit 7: Shopping

95 Exercise 1
96 Exercise 2
97 Exercise 3

1. Understanding Chinese currency
98 Exercise 4
99 Exercise 5a

CD2

Unit 7: Shopping (cont'd)

01 Exercise 6

2. How much?
02 Key expressions
03 Exercise 7
04 Exercise 9

3. Too expensive!
05 Key expressions
06 Exercise 12
07 Exercise 14

Unit 8: Eating and drinking

08 Exercise 1
09 Exercise 2
10 Exercise 3

1. What would you like to drink?
11 Key expressions
12 Exercise 5
13 Exercise 6
14 Exercise 7
15 Exercise 8
16 Exercise 9
17 Exercise 10
18 Exercise 11
19 Exercise 12

2. What dishes do you recommend?
20 Key expressions
21 Exercise 15 - a
22 Exercise 15 – b
23 Exercise 15 – c
24 Exercise 15 – d
25 Exercise 15 – e
26 Exercise 18

Review Units 5–8

27 Exercise 1
28 Exercise 2 – a
29 Exercise 2 – b
30 Exercise 2 – c
31 Exercise 4
32 Exercise 9
33 Exercise 10
34 Exercise 11
35 Exercise 12

Unit 9: Transport and directions

36 Exercise 1
37 Exercise 2
38 Exercise 3

1. Beijing Hotel, please
39 Key expressions
40 Exercise 5
41 Exercise 7
42 Exercise 9
43 Exercise 13

2. Where is the toilet?
44 Key expressions
45 Exercise 15 – a
46 Exercise 15 – b
47 Exercise 15 – c
48 Exercise 15 – d
49 Exercise 17

Unit 10: Staying in a hotel
50 Exercise 1
51 Exercise 2
52 Exercise 3

1. I've booked a room
53 Key expressions
54 Exercise 6
55 Exercise 7

2. Can I keep my luggage here?
56 Key expressions
57 Exercise 10
58 Exercise 11

3. I can't find my bag
59 Key expressions
60 Exercise 13

Unit 11: Leisure and hobbies
61 Exercise 1
62 Exercise 2
63 Exercise 3

1. I like swimming
64 Key expressions
65 Exercise 4
66 Exercise 5

2. I'm not interested in Beijing opera
67 Key expressions
68 Exercise 7
69 Exercise 8

3. My leisure activities
70 Key expressions
71 Exercise 10
72 Exercise 14

Unit 12: Making phone calls
73 Exercise 1
74 Exercise 2
75 Exercise 3 – New Year song
76 Exercise 3 – Birthday song

1. Is Liu Hong there?
77 Key expressions
78 Exercise 4 – a
79 Exercise 4 – b
80 Exercise 4 – c
81 Exercise 6 – 1
82 Exercise 6 – 2
83 Exercise 6 – 3
84 Exercise 8

2. You've got the wrong number!
85 Key expressions
86 Exercise 11 – a
87 Exercise 11 – b
88 Exercise 11 – c
89 Exercise 12 – a
90 Exercise 12 – b
91 Exercise 12 – c
92 Exercise 15

Review Units 9–12
93 Exercise 2
94 Exercise 3
95 Exercise 5
96 Exercise 9
97 Exercise 10
98 Exercise 11

Online resources

You can find a series of extra resources at:
www.palgrave.com/modernlanguages/xiang

These include:

- **The complete transcript of the audio material**
  Self-study learners can check their understanding. Teachers
  can adapt the Word document to create extra exercises.

- **Audio for the lists of 'New words and phrases' from each
  chapter**
  Check your pronunciation against the recordings. Test
  yourself on the meanings against the book.

- **The audio for the sound combinations in the Appendix
  on page 306**
  More sound practice to perfect your pronunciation.

- **A list of online resources**
  To complement and further your study of Chinese.

Introduction

Jiǎn jiè
简介

Before you begin this course make sure you have read the Preface, which will offer you pathways through the course. You need to think about why you are learning Chinese and what you need to know. Do you need to learn the Chinese script for example? This course can be used flexibly according to your needs – it is up to you to choose how to use it to best effect.

Getting the pronunciation right

Pīn yīn liàn xí
拼音练习

It is important to get the pronunciation right from the beginning of your study. However, if you would rather get straight into some listening and speaking, skip this section for now, and come back to it after you have been through Unit 1.

The written Chinese language uses characters rather than an alphabet. For example, 水 is the character for 'water'. So looking at a series of Chinese characters gives you no idea of how to pronounce them. If you want to be able to read or write in Chinese, you need to learn some of the characters (there is a section on this in every unit). However, it is possible to read and write Mandarin Chinese using Pinyin, which is a romanized phonetic system. Pinyin will help you pronounce Chinese words whether you want to learn the characters or not. If your learning aim is to focus on conversational skills only, you can speak perfect Mandarin Chinese by just mastering Pinyin.

Pinyin is made up of initials (or consonants, most of which are pronounced similarly to English) and finals (vowels and vowel/consonant combinations). The purpose of the 'Getting the pronunciation right' sections throughout the book is to help you master consonants, vowels and all the possible combinations step by step, so beginning to master the pronunciation of Mandarin Chinese.

1 Introduction to the basic sounds

In this unit, we list all the Pinyin initials and finals with examples of their nearest English equivalents. Listen and repeat each one with the audio. Most of the sounds are very similar to English sounds. There are only a few which are a bit different. You are unlikely to remember all the sounds straight away, but don't worry – this is normal! And we will revise them over and over throughout the book. You can always refer back to this section whenever you need to and go over any sounds that you find particularly difficult.

 Finals. Listen and repeat.

(As accents vary, the words given as guides to the pronunciation of the finals will sometimes be less useful to you, and it can help to add your own words which you think contain similar sounds.

a (as in father)   **o** (as in law)   **e** (between **ear**th and **ill**)

i (as in eagle)   **u** (as in mood)   **ü** (as in German **ü**ber or French l**u**ne)

ai (as in bike)   **ei** (as in baby)   **ui** (as in wave)

ie (as in yes)   **iu** (i + oh)   **an** (as in father + n)   **in** (as in ink)

un (as in look + n)   **ün** (as in French une)

üe (a combination of **ü** + **ie**)

ang (as in father + ng)   **ing** (as in wing)   **ong** (as in look + ng)

Initials. Listen and repeat.

b (as in **B**ob)	**p** (as in **p**olitics)	**m** (as in **m**ore)	**f** (as in **f**og)
d (as in **d**esk)	**t** (as in **t**able)	**n** (as in **n**urse)	**l** (as in **l**etter)
g (as in **g**irl)	**k** (as in **k**ick)	**h** (as in **h**and)	
j (as in **j**eep)	**q** (as in **ch**eese)	**x** (similar to **sh**eep)	

To say the 'x' sound, touch your tongue softly to your lower teeth and let air pass through the channel of your upper teeth and tongue.

z, zi (as in be**ds**) **c, ci** (as in ca**ts**) **s, si** (as in **s**now)

For these three sounds, widen your mouth horizontally and touch your tongue against your lower teeth.

zh, zhi	**ch, chi**	**sh, shi**	**r, ri**
(as in **G**eorge)	(as in **ch**urch)	(as in **sh**ow)	(as in **r**ose)

To pronounce these four sounds, push your mouth forward and let your tongue roll loosely in the middle of your mouth.

y (same as **i**)   **w** (same as **u**)

2 Introduction to the five tones

Mandarin Chinese is a tonal language. It has five tones. The correct pronunciation of these tones is essential, as you can see from the following five characters. Their pronunciation differs only by tone and yet their meanings are quite different!

妈	mā	mother
麻	má	hemp
马	mǎ	horse
骂	mà	to scold
吗	ma	(a word used to indicate a question)

If you do not pronounce the tones correctly, it could cause unnecessary misunderstanding and even offence! The relative pitch patterns of the first four tones are illustrated in the diagram below. The fifth tone is neutral.

1. The first tone (flat or high-level tone) is represented by a macron (¯) added to a Pinyin vowel:

   ā   ē   ī   ū

2. The second tone (rising or high-rising tone) is denoted by an acute accent (ˊ):

   á   é   í   ú

3. The third tone (falling-rising or low tone) is symbolized by a caron (ˇ):

   ǎ   ě   ǐ   ǔ

4. The fourth tone (falling or high-falling tone) is represented by a grave accent (ˋ):

   à   è   ì   ù

5. The fifth tone (neutral tone) is represented by a normal vowel without an accent mark:

   a   e   i   u

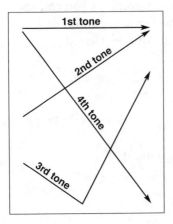

Relative pitch changes of the first four tones

3 Modification of tones

In order to make the pronunciation of some words easier, the patterns of pitch are modified when certain tones follow one another. You will become familiar with this as you work through the book and recording. Listen carefully now, but don't worry about remembering it all. You can come back and refer to it at any time.

The main patterns of tone modification are:

a. When a third tone is followed by a first, second or fourth tone, or most neutral tone syllables, it is pronounced as a 'half third tone', which only uses the lowest part of the voice.

lǎoshī (teacher)   **zǎoshang** (morning)   **xiǎoshí** (hour)

b. When a third tone is followed by another third tone, the first changes to a second tone.

nǐ hǎo (hello)   pronounced as: **ní hǎo**
xiǎojiě (miss)   pronounced as: **xiáojiě**

c. Likewise, when three (or more) third tones occur together, all but the last are normally said as second tones.

yě hěn hǎo (also very well)   pronounced as: **yé hén hǎo**

d. Bù (no, not) is a fourth tone by itself and does not change when it is followed by a first, second or third tone.

bù hē (do not drink)   **bù xíng** (no way)   **bù hǎo** (not good)

But it changes into a second tone when followed by another fourth tone.

bú yòng (no need)   **bú shì** (am/is/are not)   **bú duì** (not correct)

e. Yī (one) is a first tone. But it is pronounced as a fourth tone, yì, when it is followed by a first, second or third tone.

yī tiān (one day)   pronounced as: **yì tiān**
yī nián (one year)   pronounced as: **yì nián**
yī qǐ (together)   pronounced as: **yì qǐ**

And it is pronounced as a second tone, **yí**, when it is followed by a fourth tone.

yī gòng (altogether)   pronounced as: **yí gòng**

Note that the modification of tones is not usually marked. However, some books mark the changed tones of **bù** and **yī**, so we will do that in this book to help you get used to the rules.

Again, you won't remember these rules and sounds all at once, but don't worry. Just as with learning anything, take your time and keep going over it. You will gradually and naturally build awareness and confidence.

 Listen to some of the words that will appear in Unit 1, paying particular attention to the tones and tone changes:

Zhāng (a Chinese surname)   **tā** (he/she/it)   **nín** (you, polite)
tóngxué (classmate)   **hǎo** (good, well)   **nǐ hǎo** (hello)
bù (no, not)   **zàijiàn** (goodbye)   **lǎoshī** (teacher)
búyòngxiè (you are welcome, lit. 'no need to thank')

Shanghai

Open market

Ladies in Qing dynasty (1616–1912) dress

1

Getting started

Dì yī kè   Xīn qǐ diǎn
第一课　新起点

In this unit, you will learn:
- How to say hello, goodbye and thank you
- How to write some of the basic strokes used in Chinese characters
- About the history of Chinese characters
- About greetings in China

Getting the pronunciation right

Pīn yīn liàn xí
拼音练习

If you haven't already looked at the pronunciation basics in the Introduction, you might like to do so now, although it is fine for you to skip it and go back to it later if you'd prefer. From Unit 2 on there will always be a 'Getting the pronunciation right' section at the beginning of each unit.

Communicating in Chinese

Hàn yǔ jiāo liú
汉语交流

Dǎ zhāo hu
打招呼

1 Saying hello!

Key expression: **Saying hello informally**

Nǐ hǎo
你好!   Hello!

1 Listen to some examples of Chinese people greeting each other in an informal setting. They are using the most common expression in Mandarin: 你好! **Nǐ hǎo!**

 Greetings in Chinese are easy. Just say the name of the person you are talking to plus the word 好 hǎo, meaning 'good' or 'well'. The literal meaning of 你好 nǐ hǎo, or 'hello' in Chinese, is 'you good/well', so you are literally wishing the other person well.

2 Try saying hello to a partner or say it out loud to yourself!

 Key expressions: **Saying hello formally and to a group**

To say hello formally:

To say hello to several people (formally or informally):

Nín hǎo
您好!
Hello!

Nǐ men hǎo
你们好!
Hello!

 3 A manager, Wang Ming, walks into his office. Listen for the polite way of saying hello using 您好 nín hǎo and the way of saying hello to a group of people using 你们好 nǐmen hǎo. Note too how the employees address Mr Wang as *Manager* Wang, 王经理 Wáng jīnglǐ.

Staff: Nín hǎo   Wáng jīng lǐ
您好，王经理！

Wang Ming: Nǐ men hǎo
你们好！

你好 **Nǐ hǎo** is used in informal settings, such as with friends or close family members, whereas 您好 **nín hǎo** is used in more formal settings, such as meeting people for the first time in business, or addressing people who are older or more senior than you to show respect.

In Chinese, a person's surname comes before their given name – Wang Ming is Mr Wang. Ming is his given name. A person's surname is also used before any titles, so Manager Wang is 王经理 **Wáng jīnglǐ**.

4 Imagine you are an employee in Wang Ming's office. Greet him as he walks into the office; also greet your colleagues as they greet you.

Key expressions: **Some other greetings**

Zǎo shang hǎo
早上好！
Good morning!

Xià wǔ hǎo
下午好！
Good afternoon!

Wǎn shang hǎo
晚上好！
Good evening!

When you use 好 **hǎo** after a time of day instead of after a person's name, you are not only hoping that they are well but also that this entire period of time will go well for them.

5 Wang Ming is greeting one of his employees, Zhang.

Wang Ming:
Zǎo shang hǎo
早上好!

Zhang:
Zǎo shang hǎo   Wáng jīng lǐ
早上好! 王经理!

 6 Listen to the greetings and decide what time of day it is.

1. morning / afternoon / evening
2. morning / afternoon / evening
3. morning / afternoon / evening
4. morning / afternoon / evening

i In Chinese, the subject is always at the beginning of a sentence. So one says 'morning good' instead of 'good morning'!

 Key expressions: **Using a job title or group name to greet people**

Tóng xué men hǎo
同学们好!

Lǎo shī hǎo
老师好!

Wáng jīng lǐ hǎo
王经理好!

Hello, class!   Hello, teacher!   Hello, Manager Wang!

 7 A teacher greets her students in class:

Teacher:
Tóng xué men hǎo
同学们好!

Students:
Lǎo shī hǎo
老师好!

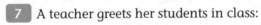

 8 Say this greeting by yourself or with your teacher.

New words and phrases: Saying hello!

In these sections we list all the new words and phrases that have appeared in the unit. As mentioned in the Preface, the Pinyin marked above Chinese characters in this book relates directly to each character. However, when written independently of the characters, the Pinyin elements combine to form complete words. When writing Pinyin yourself, follow the way the Pinyin words are spaced in the **New words and phrases** lists. You can choose whether you want to just learn the Pinyin, recognize the Chinese characters, or even learn to write them. If you want to learn to write Chinese, the highlighted characters are the ones you should focus on. See the Preface for more advice on this.

你	nǐ	you
好	hǎo	good; well
你好!	Nǐ hǎo!	Hello!
早上	zǎoshang	(early) morning
早上好!	Zǎoshang hǎo!	Good morning!
王	Wáng	(a Chinese surname)
王明	Wáng Míng	(a Chinese name)
张	Zhāng	(a Chinese surname)
经理	jīnglǐ	manager
您	nín	you (polite, singular and plural)
你们	nǐmen	you (plural)
同学们	tóngxuémen	classmates/class
老师	lǎoshī	teacher

爸爸	bàba	father
妈妈	māma	mother
下午	xiàwǔ	afternoon
晚上	wǎnshang	evening

Language notes

1.1 Saying hello with 好 hǎo

Saying hello in Mandarin Chinese is actually acknowledging the wellbeing of the person you are speaking to by using the word 好 **hǎo** (good/well). You can replace the 你 **nǐ** (you) in 你好 **nǐ hǎo** with the job title of the person to whom you are speaking or their relationship to you.

Lǎoshī **hǎo**.	*Hello* teacher.
Jīnglǐ **hǎo**.	*Hello* manager.
Tóngxué **hǎo**.	*Hello* classmate.
Bàba **hǎo**.	*Hello* father.
Māma **hǎo**.	*Hello* mother.

When 好 **hǎo** is used after a time phrase, it means the same as in English – that you hope the period of time goes well for the person you are addressing. But unlike English, the subject – the time of the day – comes at the beginning of the sentence.

Zǎoshang **hǎo**.	*Good* morning.
Xiàwǔ **hǎo**.	*Good* afternoon.
Wǎnshang **hǎo**.	*Good* evening.

1.2 Use of 们 men to indicate plural

们 **Men** can be used to mark plurals. It is only used for people and animals, and usually only used with personal pronouns and when addressing people.

wǒ	I	wǒ**men**	we
nǐ	you	nǐ**men**	you (pl.)
tā	he/she/it	tā**men**	they
lǎoshī	teacher	lǎoshī**men**	teachers
tóngxué	classmate	tóngxué**men**	classmates/class

Practice

9 Listen to three exchanges. Which dialogue matches which picture? Write in the corresponding letter.

Dialogue ___   **Dialogue** ___   **Dialogue** ___

1.    **2.**   **3.**

10 What would you say in the following situations?

1. When you greet a friend
2. When you greet your Chinese teacher
3. When you meet your colleagues in the morning

11 Circle the right information based on what you hear in the short dialogues.

1. morning / afternoon / evening
2. you (singular) / you (formal) / you (plural)
3. teacher / manager / students

2 Saying goodbye and thank you

Gào bié hé zhì xiè
告别和致谢

Key expressions: **Saying goodbye and expressing gratitude**

To say goodbye:

Zài jiàn
再见!

Míng tiān jiàn
明天见!

Goodbye!   See you tomorrow!

To express gratitude:

Xiè xie
谢谢!
Thank you!

Bú yòng xiè
不用谢!
You are welcome!

 12 Listen to these Chinese neighbours saying goodbye to each other:

Neighbour 1:
Zài jiàn
再见!

Neighbour 2:
Zài jiàn
再见!

13 Say goodbye to a partner or out loud to yourself!

 14 Now Wang Ming says goodbye to his colleagues as he leaves the office at the end of the working day:

Wang Ming:
Míng tiān jiàn
明天见!

Staff:
Wáng jīng lǐ   míng tiān jiàn
王经理，明天见!

15 Can you respond to Wang Ming's colleagues and say goodbye?

 **16** A teacher thanks her student:

Teacher:
Xiè xie
谢谢!

Student:
Bú yòng xiè
不用谢!

Teacher:
Zài jiàn
再见!

Student:
Lǐ lǎo shī   zài jiàn
李老师，再见!

New words and phrases: Saying goodbye and thank you

再见	zàijiàn	goodbye
明天	míngtiān	tomorrow
明天见!	Míngtiān jiàn!	See you tomorrow!
谢谢	xièxie	thanks
不用谢!	Búyòngxiè!	You're welcome! (lit. no need to thank)
不	bù	no; not
李	Lǐ	(a Chinese surname)

Language note

jiàn
2.1 *Saying goodbye with* 见

Saying goodbye in Mandarin Chinese is actually expressing a wish to see that person again. Thus it ends with the word 见 jiàn (to see). 再见 Zài jiàn literally means 'again to see'. You can replace 再 zài (again, once more) with any time expression to indicate when you expect to see them next.

zài **jiàn**	*see* (you) again/goodbye
míngtiān **jiàn**	*see* (you) tomorrow
xiàwǔ **jiàn**	*see* (you) in the afternoon
wǎnshang **jiàn**	*see* (you) in the evening
míngtiān zǎoshang **jiàn**	*see* (you) tomorrow morning
míngtiān wǎnshang **jiàn**	*see* (you) tomorrow evening

Practice

17 Match each expression with the correct response. One has already been done for you.

Expression

1.
ní hǎo
你好

2.
xiè xie
谢谢

3.
zài jiàn
再见

4.
míng tiān jiàn
明天见

5.
tóng xué men hǎo
同学们好

6.
zǎo shang hǎo
早上好

Response

a.
míng tiān jiàn
明天见

b.
zǎo shang hǎo
早上好

c.
ní hǎo
你好

d.
lǎo shī hǎo
老师好

e.
zài jiàn
再见

f.
bú yòng xiè
不用谢

18 You open the door for your teacher, who thanks you. Play the recording and respond by saying 'you're welcome' during the pause. Your teacher then says goodbye to you and you reply in turn. You'll hear the correct answers after each pause.

Learning Chinese characters

Xué hàn zì
学汉字

The history of Chinese characters

Chinese characters have a long history, starting in the Shang dynasty (1600–1100 BC). Although people from different regions of China may speak different languages or local dialects, the written language has been a way of communicating since ancient times. There are nearly 57,000 characters in total. Knowledge of about 2,500–3,000 characters is necessary for reading newspapers and for most other common purposes. The characters you will learn in this book are the simplified script system, most of which contain fewer strokes per character. This system was made official in 1952 and it is the system used in mainland China. In Taiwan and Hong Kong, people still use the traditional script system.

The art of writing Chinese characters is called calligraphy. Chinese calligraphy has various styles, which also represent the evolution of Chinese characters over time. The following chart shows the most common styles of Chinese calligraphy. In daily life, people will mostly use the regular modern script unless they are being trained in a particular style of handwriting.

	oracle bone *jiaguwen*	greater seal *dazhuan*	lesser seal *xiaozhuan*	clerkly script *lishu*	standard script *kaishu*	running script *xingshu*	cursive script *caoshu*	modern simplified *jiantizi*
rén human								
nǚ woman								
ěr ear								
mǎ horse								
yú fish								
shān mountain								
rì sun								
yuè moon								
yǔ rain								
yún cloud								

Source: Ancient Scripts of the World (http://www.ancientscripts.com/chinese.html)

How Chinese characters are formed

The smallest unit of a character is a stroke. Here is the complete set of 31 strokes. Each kind of stroke needs to be written in a particular direction. You should be able to recognize each stroke in characters.

	bǐ huà Strokes 笔画	
一	㇇	)
丨	ㄴ	㇄
丿	∠	㇄
丶	㇀	㇄
㇆	㇄	㇄
㇏	㇐	㇄
丿	く	㇄
㇆	5	㇄
亅	㇏	㇄
㇆	3	㇄
	㇄	㇄
		㇄

Different characters can be made up with the same strokes. The length of the strokes, their positions in relation to each other and whether they touch or overlap determines the character.

八 eight   人 person   入 to enter

The size and shape of the characters are also important. No matter how many strokes there are in a complete character, it needs to be written within an imaginary square. Therefore, it is essential to balance the different parts of a character to fit it into that imaginary square. The character grids at the end of each unit will help you get used to that.

Strokes grouped together in a certain way to form part of a character are called radicals. Most radicals have a fixed meaning and they bring this meaning to the characters in which they occur. For example, 火 means fire and is a character in its own right. And when 火 functions as a radical, it brings the meaning of fire into the other characters.

烧 to cook   烤 to roast   炼 to smelt

There are around 200 radicals in Chinese writing. Throughout this book, these sections will help you recognize some of the most commonly used radicals, and so begin mastering Chinese characters.

Write the basic strokes

19 Try writing the following basic strokes in the direction indicated.

一	⇉				コ	⇉⤵			
丨	↓				亅	⤵			
丿	⤸				フ	⇉↙			
丶	↘				乛	⇉↴			
ㄱ	⇉↓				ㄴ	↓→			
㇏	↘				∠	↙→			
／	↗				㇄	↓↑			

20 Look at each stroke written below on the left and mark if it appears in any of the characters to its right. One has already been done for you.

丶	一	你	我	他	好
一	二	大	小	上	见
丿	三	王	张	老	晚
㇏	四	明	天	再	们
丨	五	不	用	谢	早
ㄱ	六	同	学	师	您
ㄴ	七	问	中	也	化

Greetings in Chinese culture

Standard greetings in China are very similar to those in the West. You can say 你好 **nǐ hǎo**, or 您好 **nín hǎo** if you are meeting people for the first time, in a formal setting or speaking to older people. In a formal situation you would usually shake hands with both males and females. Kissing or hugging is neither acceptable nor common in China, especially when meeting people for the first time. In Chinese, you can either say the person's name first and then the greeting or say hello first and then add their name. Unlike most Western 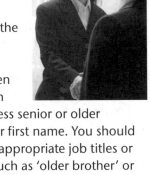 cultures, it is not acceptable to address senior or older members of your family by only their first name. You should either use their surnames with their appropriate job titles or standard family relationship terms such as 'older brother' or 'uncle'. It is acceptable to greet your Chinese friends by just saying 你好 **nǐ hǎo**, without adding their names; however, it would be more polite to greet anyone older or more senior than you using their surname and title, especially in a formal setting or if you don't know them well.

 Apart from asking how someone is, it is also very common for friends to ask about each other's jobs, health or family members to show care and affection. With close family members or when people are more familiar with each other, they tend to greet each other with questions such as 'Are you off now?', 'Oh, are you back?', 'Have you had lunch?' or 'Where are you going?'. These questions are simply ways of opening a conversation and the replies do not need to be specific. You can just say 'yes', or 'I am going out for a walk'.

unit

2

Greetings and introducing yourself

Dì èr kè
第二课

Wèn hǎo hé zì wǒ jiè shào
问好和自我介绍

In this unit, you will learn:

- How to pronounce Pinyin combinations containing a, o, e, i, u, ü, b, p, m and f
- How to introduce yourself
- How to ask someone's name, occupation and where they are from
- How to write the rest of the basic character strokes
- About personal names in China

Getting the pronunciation right

Pīn yīn liàn xí
拼音练习

As before, skip this section if you'd rather learn the sounds as they come up, or would prefer to come back to it later.

In this unit, you will hear and say some basic Chinese sound combinations. First, can you recall how the following sounds are pronounced? Check your pronunciation with the audio.

 a   o   e   i   u   ü   b   p   m   f

 1   Now listen to the four tones with the following sounds and repeat out loud after each set:

bā bá bǎ bà	pā pá pǎ pà	mā má mǎ mà	fā fá fǎ fà
bō bó bǒ bò	pō pó pǒ pò	mō mó mǒ mò	fō fó fǒ fò
bī bí bǐ bì	pī pí pǐ pì	mī mí mǐ mì	
bū bú bǔ bù	pū pú pǔ pù	mū mú mǔ mù	fū fú fǔ fù

22

The tones seem difficult at first because they do not exist in English. However, it is possible for everyone to learn them and all you need to do is listen to them and say them over and over. So keep listening to the audio and speak out loud with it. Come back and listen again when you are further along in the course – you will see how much easier it has become!

2 Listen and circle the syllables you hear:

1. po   bo   mu   fu
2. ma   fa   me   fo
3. bi   pi   mo   pu
4. bu   pu   pa   pi
5. pi   pa   bi   ba

3 Listen and circle the tones based on what you hear:

1. mō mó mǒ mò
2. fū fú fǔ fù
3. pā pá pǎ pà
4. bī bí bǐ bì
5. mē mé mě mè

4 These words were introduced in the previous unit. See if you can remember their meanings and mark up their correct tones. Check them against the word lists in Unit 1 on pages 11 and 15.

1. ni hao
2. xiexie
3. nimen
4. nin
5. laoshi
6. jingli
7. zaijian
8. zaoshang hao
9. wanshang hao
10. buyongxie
11. mingtian jian

Communicating in Chinese

Hàn yǔ jiāo liú
汉语交流

1 Greetings

Wèn hǎo
问好

Key expressions: Asking how others are and answering

To ask how people are:

Nǐ hǎo ma
你好吗?
How are you?
(singular)

Nín hǎo ma
您好吗?
How are you?
(polite)

Nǐ men hǎo ma
你们好吗?
How are you?
(plural)

To say how you are:

Wǒ hěn hǎo
我很好。
I am (very) well.

Wǒ hěn máng
我很忙。
I am (very) busy.

Wǒ hěn lèi
我很累。
I am (very) tired.

Wǒ men hěn hǎo
我们很好。
We are (very) well.

Wǒ men hěn máng
我们很忙。
We are (very) busy.

Wǒ men hěn lèi
我们很累。
We are (very) tired.

Tài hǎo le
太好了!
Great!

Tài máng le
太忙了!
Too busy!

Tài lèi le
太累了!
Too tired!

---

5 Out on the street, Wang Ming bumps into his former university classmate Liu Hong whom he has not seen for a long time. Here's the beginning of their conversation:

Wang Ming:
Liú Hóng   nǐ hǎo
刘红，你好!

Liu Hong:
Nǐ hǎo   Wáng Míng   Hǎo jiǔ bú jiàn
你好，王明。好久不见!
Nǐ hǎo ma
你好吗?

Wang Ming:
Wǒ hěn hǎo　　　nǐ　ne
我很好，你呢？

Liu Hong:
Wǒ　yě　hěn hǎo
我也很好。

6 Have a go at asking 'How are you?' and responding 'I'm fine' alone or with a partner.

7 Now listen to Liu Hong as she greets her neighbour Li Bing whom she sees often:

Liu Hong:
Xiǎo　Lǐ　　　　nǐ　zěn me yàng
小李，你怎么样？

Li Bing:
Bú　cuò　　　nǐ　ne　　Liú lǎo shī
不错，你呢，刘老师？

Liu Hong:
Hěn lèi　　Gōng zuò tài máng le　　Huí tóu jiàn
很累！工作太忙了！回头见！

Li Bing:
Hǎo　　huí tóu jiàn
好，回头见！

> As you saw in Unit 1, when addressing people, it is common to use their job titles (professional jobs only), even in regular everyday speech. So Li Bing calls Liu Hong 刘老师 **Liú lǎoshī** (teacher Liu) to show respect, and Liu Hong calls Li Bing 小李 **Xiǎo Lǐ** (little Li) to indicate that he is younger than her and perhaps does not have a professional job title.

8 Imagine your Chinese friend asks how you are today. Give as many answers as possible. For example, say 'I am well', 'I am busy', 'I am tired', 'Not bad' and 'Work has been too busy'. Then listen to the audio and try to understand the answers that other people give.

New words and phrases: Greetings

刘红	Liú Hóng	(a Chinese name)
刘	Liú	(a Chinese surname)
好久不见	hǎojiǔbújiàn	long time no see
吗	ma	(question particle)
我	wǒ	I, me
很	hěn	very
你呢?	Nǐ ne?	And you?
也	yě	also; too
小	xiǎo	little; small; young
怎么样	zěnmeyàng	how; how about
不错	búcuò	not bad; good
工作	gōngzuò	job; to work
累	lèi	tired
太…了!	tài ... le!	too … !
忙	máng	busy
好	hǎo	OK; all right (also 'good'; 'well')
回头见!	Huítóujiàn!	See you later!
他	tā	he, him
她	tā	she, her
它	tā	it

Language notes

ma

1.1 *Question particle* 吗 *(yes/no questions)*

吗 **Ma** is a question particle. The term 'particle' isn't strictly defined, but particles usually change the relationship between parts of a sentence. They are also known as 'function words'.

The particle 吗 **ma** is added to the end of a statement to turn it into a 'yes/no' question. This is the most common way of forming a question in Chinese.

Nǐ hǎo.	Hello. (lit. you well – a statement)
Nǐ hǎo **ma?**	How are you? (lit. you well? – a question)

Nǐ shì lǎoshī.	You are a teacher.
Nǐ shì lǎoshī **ma?**	Are you a teacher?

Wáng Míng hěn gāoxìng jiàndào Liú Hóng.
Wang Ming is very pleased to see Liu Hong.

Wáng Míng hěn gāoxìng jiàndào Liú Hóng **ma?**
Is Wang Ming very pleased to see Liu Hong?

So, to change a sentence into a yes/no question is very simple in Chinese. You do not need to change the order of the words (subject/verb position) as in English, you simply add 吗 **ma** to the end.

1.2 *Translation of 'to be'*

The verb 'to be' (am, is, are) in Chinese is 是 shì.

Wǒ **shì** lǎoshī.	I *am* a teacher. (noun)
Tā **shì** Měiguórén.	He *is* an American. (noun)

But when you describe someone or something with an adjective instead of a noun, you just need to use 很 **hěn** (meaning 'very').

Wǒ **hěn** máng.	I *am* busy. (adjective)
Tā **hěn** hǎo.	He *is* well. (adjective)

The word 很 **hěn** can also be used to express the degree or extent of something just as in English, but in the examples given it does not indicate as strong a degree as the English word 'very'. If you want to emphasize the degree, other words should be used, such as 非常 **fēicháng** (meaning 'extremely').

1.3 *Question particle* 呢 *(tag questions)*

呢 **Ne** is another common question particle in Chinese. It can be used in various contexts to post the same question back to the speaker rather than having to repeat the whole thing. So, 你呢? **Nǐ ne?** translates as 'And you?' or 'What about you?'

Nǐ hǎo ma?   How are you?
Wǒ hěn hǎo, **nǐ ne?**   I am fine, and you?

Instead of repeating the same question 你好吗? **Nǐ hǎo ma?**, you can just use 你呢? **Nǐ ne?** to ask the first speaker if they are OK.

Nǐ zuò shénme gōngzuò?   What job do you do?
Wǒ shì jīnglǐ, **nǐ ne?**   I am a manager, and you?

Instead of repeating the same question 你做什么工作? **Nǐ zuò shénme gōngzuò?**, it's much simpler to just say 你呢? **Nǐ ne?** to ask the other person what their job is.

Practice

9 First match the Pinyin with the English, and then change the Pinyin sentences into questions using 吗 **ma**.

1. Wáng jīnglǐ hěn máng.
2. Tā hěn lèi.
3. Tāmen shì tóngxué.
4. Liú lǎoshī yě hěn hǎo.
5. Tā shì jīnglǐ.

a. He is a manager.
b. Teacher Liu is also well.
c. Manager Wang is very busy.
d. She is very tired.
e. They are classmates.

10 Match the following:

Nǐ hǎo
1. 你好。　　　　　　　**a.** I am busy.

Xiè xie
2. 谢谢。　　　　　　　**b.** Long time no see.

Wǒ hěn máng
3. 我很忙。　　　　　　**c.** Thank you.

Wǒ hěn lèi
4. 我很累。　　　　　　**d.** Hello.

Tài hǎo le
5. 太好了!　　　　　　　**e.** Great!

Hǎo jiǔ bú jiàn
6. 好久不见。　　　　　**f.** See you later.

Huí tóu jiàn
7. 回头见。　　　　　　**g.** I am tired.

11 Complete the following dialogue in Pinyin using the answers suggested in English:

A: Nǐ hǎo!
B: (1)_____. (Hello.)
A: Nǐ hǎo ma?
B: (2)_____, nǐ ne? (I am fine.)
A: Wǒ yě hěn hǎo, (3)_____. (Thanks.)
　　Zàijiàn.
B: (4)_____. (Goodbye.)

12 Listen to the sentences and decide if the meaning given is true or false:

1. David is very well.	*True / False*
2. See you tomorrow, Manager Li.	*True / False*
3. We are not bad.	*True / False*
4. I am very tired.	*True / False*
5. Mary's job is very busy.	*True / False*

2 Introducing yourself

Zǐ wǒ jiè shào
自我介绍

Key expressions: Asking about names, jobs and where people are from

To ask someone's name and give yours:

Nín guì xìng
您贵姓?
What's your surname?

Wǒ xìng Liú
我姓刘。
My surname is Liu.

Nǐ jiào shén me
你叫什么?
What's your name?
(lit. What are you called?)

Wǒ jiào Liú Hóng
我叫刘红。
My name is Liu Hong.
(lit. I am called Liu Hong.)

To talk about jobs:

Nǐ zuò shén me gōng zuò
你做什么工作?
What job do you do?

Wǒ shì lǎo shī
我是老师。
I am a teacher.

To ask where someone is from:

Nǐ shì nǎ li rén
你是哪里人?
Where are you from?

Wǒ shì Zhōng guó rén
我是中国人。
I am Chinese. (lit. China + person)

Wǒ shì Zhōng guó Shàng hǎi rén
我是中国上海人。
I am from Shanghai, China. (lit. country + city + person)

---

1. When you ask someone's surname, you are literally asking, 'What is your *honourable* (lit. *expensive*) surname?', which is a way of showing respect to the other person and his/her family. This question is commonly used in formal settings or when meeting people for the first time.

2. The location hierarchy in Chinese is the reverse of that in English. It moves from the more general to the specific, thus it usually follows the order of: country, city, town, district, street.

13 Listen to how the following people introduce themselves.

1.

Liú Hóng
刘红:

Nǐ hǎo
你好!

Wǒ jiào Liú Hóng
我叫刘红。

Wǒ shì lǎo shī
我是老师。

Wǒ shì Zhōng guó rén
我是中国人。

2.

Tāng mǔ
汤姆 (Tom):

Nǐ hǎo
你好!

Wǒ jiào Tāng mǔ
我叫汤姆。

Wǒ shì yī shēng
我是医生。

Wǒ shì Yīng guó rén
我是英国人。

3.

Mǎ lì
玛丽 (Marie):

Nǐ men hǎo
你们好!

Wǒ jiào Mǎ lì
我叫玛丽。

Wǒ shì xué sheng
我是学生。

Wǒ shì Fǎ guó rén
我是法国人。

4.

Hàn sī
汉斯 (Hans):

Zǎo shang hǎo
早上好!

Wǒ jiào Hàn sī
我叫汉斯。

Wǒ shì jīng lǐ
我是经理。

Wǒ shì Dé guó rén
我是德国人。

5.

Sū shān
苏珊 (Susan):

Xià wǔ hǎo
下午好!

Wǒ jiào Sū shān
我叫苏珊。

Wǒ shì fú wù yuán
我是服务员。

Wǒ shì Měi guó rén
我是美国人。

6.

Hóu sài
侯赛 (José):

Wǎnshang hǎo
晚上好!

Wǒ jiào Hóu sài
我叫侯赛。

Wǒ shì gōng chéng shī
我是工程师。

Wǒ shì Xī bān yá rén
我是西班牙人。

14 Now it's your turn to speak – introduce yourself with your name, job and say where you are from. Some extra jobs and countries are listed if you need them:

Name: Wǒ jiào _____.
Job: Wǒ shì_____.
Where you're from: Wǒ shì_____ rén.
                       (lit. I am [country and/or city] person.)

律师	lǜshī	lawyer
司机	sījī	driver
护士	hùshi	nurse
教授	jiàoshòu	professor
职员	zhíyuán	clerk
厨师	chúshī	chef
商人	shāngrén	businessman/woman
记者	jìzhě	journalist
画家	huàjiā	painter
秘书	mìshū	secretary
售货员	shòuhuòyuán	shop assistant
家庭主妇	jiātíngzhǔfù	housewife
印度	Yìndù	India
泰国	Tàiguó	Thailand
韩国	Hánguó	Korea
意大利	Yìdàlì	Italy
希腊	Xīlà	Greece

日本	Rìběn	Japan
加拿大	Jiānádà	Canada
巴西	Bāxī	Brazil
澳大利亚	Àodàlìyà	Australia
波兰	Bōlán	Poland
芬兰	Fēnlán	Finland

All the words for occupations in Chinese are gender free. Therefore, the word 商人 **shāngrén** can be translated as either 'businessman' or 'businesswoman' depending on the context. If you want to specify the gender of the person, you need to add 男 **nán** (male) or 女 **nǚ** (female) before the job, for example, 男律师 **nán lǜshī** (male lawyer).

15 Listen to the conversation between Mary and Liu Hong, who meet at a party. Pay attention to how they find out each other's name, job and where they are from.

Mary:
Nǐ hǎo
你好!

Liu Hong:
Nǐ hǎo　Wǒ xìng Liú　jiào Liú Hóng
你好! 我姓刘，叫刘红。
Nǐ jiào shén me
你叫什么?

Mary:
Wǒ jiào Mǎ lì　Wǒ shì Fǎ guó rén
我叫玛丽。我是法国人。
Nǐ shì nǎ li rén
你是哪里人?

Liu Hong:
Wǒ shì Zhōng guó Shàng hǎi rén
我是中国上海人。

Nǐ zuò shén me gōng zuò
你做什么工作?

Mary:
Wǒ bú gōng zuò wǒ shì xué sheng Nǐ ne
我不工作,我是学生。你呢?

Liu Hong:
Wǒ shì lǎo shī Hěn gāo xìng rèn shi nǐ
我是老师。很高兴认识你。

Mary:
Wǒ yě hěn gāo xìng rèn shi nín Liú lǎo shī
我也很高兴认识您,刘老师。

Zài jiàn
再见。

Liu Hong:
Zài jiàn
再见。

New words and phrases: Introducing yourself

叫	jiào	to call, to be called
做	zuò	to do
什么	shénme	what
哪里	nǎli	where
人	rén	person, people
医生	yīshēng	doctor
学生	xuésheng	student
服务员	fúwùyuán	waiter/waitress
工程师	gōngchéngshī	engineer
中国	Zhōngguó	China (lit. middle kingdom)
英国	Yīngguó	Britain

法国	Fǎguó	France
德国	Déguó	Germany
美国	Měiguó	the USA
西班牙	Xībānyá	Spain
上海	Shànghǎi	Shanghai
高兴	gāoxìng	happy
认识	rènshi	to get to know, to meet
汤姆	Tāngmǔ	(a name) Tom
玛丽	Mǎlì	(a name) Marie, Mary
汉斯	Hànsī	(a name) Hans
苏珊	Sūshān	(a name) Susan
候赛	Hóusài	(a name) José
大卫	Dàwèi	(a name) David

Practice

16 You meet a Chinese person at a work party. What questions can you ask him/her? There are some sample answers at the back of the book.

17 Look at the pictures and decide if the statements are true or false:

Liú Hóng   Dà wèi   Tāng mǔ   Mǎ lì

刘红   大卫   汤姆   玛丽

Liú Hóng shì yī shēng
1. 刘红是医生。   *True / False*

Dà wèi shì Dé guó rén
2. 大卫是德国人。   *True / False*

Tāng mǔ shì gōng chéng shī
3. 汤姆是工程师。   *True / False*

Mǎ lì shì Yīng guó rén
4. 玛丽是英国人。   *True / False*

 18 Now you will hear four questions about the pictures in Exercise 17. See if you can answer them yourself after each question, and then listen for the correct response.

19 Free talk: You meet a Chinese friend and his/her foreign friend on the street. Create a conversation between the three of you, either with a partner or by yourself.

Learning Chinese characters

Xué hàn zì
学汉字

Recognize the characters in the text

20 Match the characters with their English meaning and Pinyin:

1. 我	a. I; me	A. Zhōngguó
2. 很	b. very	B. shì
3. 是	c. China	C. wǒ
4. 中国	d. teacher	D. hěn
5. 老师	e. to be	E. lǎoshī
6. 学生	f. no, not	F. xuésheng
7. 不	g. student	G. bù

21 Translate the following sentences into English. Names and occupations have been underlined to help you.

1. 你好。你好吗？

2. 你好。我叫大卫。
   Dà wèi

3. 你好。我叫玛丽。我是老师。
   Mǎ lì   lǎo shī

4. 你好。我叫刘红。我是学生。
   Liú Hóng   xué shēng
   我是中国人。

5. 你好。我叫汤姆。我是医生。
   Tāng mǔ   yī shēng
   我是英国人。

Write the basic strokes

22 Can you remember the basic strokes from Unit 1? Write them here:

23 Here are the rest of the basic strokes for writing Chinese characters. Try writing them in the direction indicated.

L	⌊				㇠				
㇛					㇉				
㇄					㇟				
丶					㇂				
㇈					ㄣ				
㇆					㇋				
亅					㇌				
㇃					㇇				
L									

Write the characters in the text

24 Now have a go at writing these complete characters. Follow the stroke order as indicated.

不 bù no, not	一	丆	才	不				
好 hǎo good	く	乆	女	女了	妁	好		
我 wǒ I, me	丿	二	于	手	我	我	我	
你 nǐ you	丿	亻	亇	伬	伄	你	你	
是 shì to be	丨	冂	日	日	旦	早	早	昰	是
中 zhōng middle	丶	冂	口	中				
国 guó country	丨	冂	冂	冋	囯	国	国	国
人 rén person	丿	人						
很 hěn very	丿	彡	彳	犭	犭	彳	很	很	很

Chinese names and polite ways of addressing people

Like everywhere else in the world, Chinese parents think it is important to give their children nice names. Usually you can tell whether a person is a male or female by their name. It is traditional to use words like 强 **qiáng** (strength), 明 **míng** (bright), 成 **chéng** (success) and 龙 **lóng** (dragon) for boys and to use words like 丽 **lì** (beauty), 佳 **jiā** (nice), 云 **yún** (cloud) and 蕾 **lěi** (flower bloom) for girls. Chinese names can also indicate an important date or location or anything meaningful to the family and child, so they show great variety. Children usually take their father's surname and surnames are very important to families in Chinese culture. When people from different families share the same surname, they often say 我们五百年前是一家 **Wǒmen wǔbǎinián qián shì yìjiā** (We must have been in the same family 500 years ago), to show a certain level of bonding.

In Chinese culture, it is very important to identify social roles and hierarchy. People who know each other well in the work place commonly address anyone younger or junior with 小 **xiǎo** (little, small, young) followed by their surname, and anyone older or senior with 老 **lǎo** (old, experienced) followed by their surname. It's not rude in Chinese culture to call someone 老 **lǎo**; in fact, it shows care and respect. With more and more foreign investment and joint ventures in China, many Chinese people take English first names, while keeping their Chinese surnames. Some are given English names by teachers in school; others choose them by themselves.

'Catherine' is the name that I, your author, chose when I was learning English in China and I have used it in Western society ever since. Chinese people are also increasingly used to Western ways of addressing each other in the work place.

3

Introducing family and friends

Dì sān kè   Jiè shào jiā rén hé péng you

第三课   介绍家人和朋友

In this unit, you will learn:
- How to pronounce Pinyin combinations containing: d, t, n, l, g, k, h, j, q, x and r
- How to make simple introductions
- How to describe your family and friends
- About the basic structure of Chinese characters
- About family values in China

Getting the pronunciation right

Pīn yīn liàn xí

拼音练习

In this unit, you will continue to hear and say some basic sound combinations. First, can you recall how the following sounds are pronounced? Check your pronunciation with the audio.

d   t   n   l   g   k   h   j   q   x   r

1 Listen to the four tones with the following sounds and repeat after each set:

dā dá dǎ dà	tā tá tǎ tà	nā ná nǎ nà	lā lá lǎ là
jī jí jǐ jì	qī qí qǐ qì	xī xí xǐ xì	rī rí rǐ rì
dū dú dǔ dù	tū tú tǔ tù	hū hú hǔ hù	gū gú gǔ gù
lū lú lǔ lù	rū rú rǔ rù	kē ké kě kè	tē té tě tè
nǚ nǘ nǚ nǜ	jū jú jǔ jù	qū qú qǔ qù	xū xú xǔ xù

2 Listen and circle the syllables you hear:

1. da   ta   ha   na   4. he   hu   xu   ru
2. xu   qu   ju   xi   5. ne   te   ge   ke
3. li   ge   ri   qi

 3 Listen and circle the tones based on what you hear:

1. nā   ná   nǎ   nà   4. xī   xí   xǐ   xì
2. rū   rú   rǔ   rù   5. hē   hé   hě   hè
3. dā   dá   dǎ   dà

4 You met these words in the previous unit. See if you can remember the meaning of the words and mark up their correct tones. Check them against the word lists in Unit 2 on pages 26 and 34.

1. ye   2. mang   3. lei   4. gongzuo   5. hen

6. wo   7. jiao   8. nali   9. yisheng   10. Yingguo

11. Meiguo   12. shenme   13. gaoxing   14. zuo

15. renshi   16. haojiubujian

| Communicating in Chinese | Hàn yǔ jiāo liú
汉语交流 |

1 Introducing your family

Jiè shào jiā rén
介绍家人

Key expressions: **Introducing your family**

To introduce a member of your family:

Zhè shì wǒ   de   mā ma
这是我（的）妈妈。
This is my mother.

To say where you live:

Wǒ zhù zài Běi jīng
我住在北京。
I live in Beijing.

To say who is in your family:

Wǒ yǒu jiě jie
我有姐姐。
I have an older sister.
or I have older sisters.

Wǒ méi yǒu dì di
我没有弟弟。
I don't have a younger brother.
or I don't have any younger brothers.

To say a bit more about your family members:

Tā   Tā jiào Lǐ Míng
他 / 她叫李明。
He/she is called Li Ming.

Tā   Tā shì yī shēng
他 / 她是医生。
He/she is a doctor.

Although in Chinese the words 'he' and 'she' are pronounced exactly the same, 他 **tā** (he) and 她 **tā** (she), if you look carefully, you will notice that they are two different characters. The radical in the character for 'he' is the 'person' radical 亻; whereas the radical in the character for 'she' is the 'female' radical 女.

5 In a Chinese family, the different relationships are very precise. There are different terms for each member of the family, depending on whether they are on the father's or mother's side, their age and gender. In Chinese culture, it is not polite to use first names for anyone who's older than you, even with close family members. Look at the family tree and see if you can guess the meaning of the words. Listen to the audio and repeat each word.

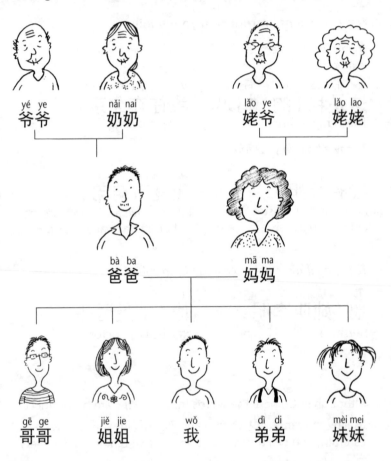

yé ye
爷爷

nǎi nai
奶奶

lǎo ye
姥爷

lǎo lao
姥姥

bà ba
爸爸

mā ma
妈妈

gē ge
哥哥

jiě jie
姐姐

wǒ
我

dì di
弟弟

mèi mei
妹妹

6 Now give a simple introduction for each member of your family and add their names accordingly, e.g.

Wǒ yǒu yé ye
我有爷爷。

I have a <u>grandfather (father's father)</u>.

Zhè shì wǒ de yé ye
这是我（的）爷爷。

This is my <u>grandfather</u> <u>(father's father)</u>.

Tā jiào
他叫 _____。

He's called _____.

Wǒ méi yǒu gē ge hé mèi mei
我没有<u>哥哥</u>和<u>妹妹</u>。

I don't have any <u>older brothers</u> or <u>younger sisters</u>.

7 Here is a picture of Li Ming and his family. Listen to how he introduces himself and his family members.

Wǒ jiào Lǐ Míng shì Shàng hǎi rén Wǒ shì yī shēng Wǒ de gōng
我叫李明，是上海人。我是医生。我的工

zuò hěn máng Zhè shì wǒ de jiā Wǒ de jiā bú dà Zhè shì
作很忙。这是我的家。我的家不大。这是

wǒ tài tai Tā jiào Liú Hóng tā shì lǎo shī Tā shì Běi jīng
我太太。她叫刘红，她是老师。她是北京

rén Wǒ men zhù zài Běi jīng Wǒ men yǒu hái zi yí ge ér
人。我们住在北京。我们有孩子，一个儿

zi hé yí ge nǚ ér Wǒ men de ér zi jiào Lì li tā shì
子和一个女儿。我们的儿子叫力力，他是

gōng chéng shī Wǒ men de nǚ ér jiào Yún yun Tā méi yǒu gōng zuò
工程师。我们的女儿叫云云。她没有工作，

tā shì xué sheng Wǒ hěn ài wǒ de jiā
她是学生。我很爱我的家。

New words and phrases: Introducing your family

爷爷	yéye	father's father
奶奶	nǎinai	father's mother
姥爷	lǎoye	mother's father
姥姥	lǎolao	mother's mother
哥哥	gēge	older brother
姐姐	jiějie	older sister
弟弟	dìdi	younger brother
妹妹	mèimei	younger sister
这	zhè	this
家	jiā	family, home
大	dà	big
太太	tàitai	wife, Mrs
先生	xiānsheng	husband, Mr
住在	zhùzài	to live in/at
在	zài	to be in/at/of (position)
有	yǒu	to have
没	méi	not (only negates 'have/has' – see Language note 1.2)
孩子	háizi	child, children
一	yī	one
个	gè	(measure word) (often toneless when speaking)
儿子	érzi	son

女儿	nǚ'ér	daughter
和	hé	and
力力	Lìli	(a name, lit. strength)
云云	Yúnyun	(a name, lit. cloud)
爱	ài	to love, love
北京	Beǐjīng	Beijing (capital of China)

Language notes

1.1 *Indicating possession using* 的 de

In Chinese, to show something belongs to someone/something, you usually add the word 的 **de** after the subject pronoun:

我 wǒ	I	我的 wǒ de	my/mine
你 nǐ	you	你的 nǐ de	your(s)
他 tā	he*	他的 tā de	his*
她 tā	she*	她的 tā de	her(s)*
你们 nǐ men	you (pl.)	你们的 nǐ men de	your(s)
我们 wǒ men	we	我们的 wǒ men de	our(s)
他们 tā men	they (male)*	他们的 tā men de	their(s)*

tā men
她们 they (female)*

tā men de
她们的 their(s)*

or after the proper noun:

Lǐ Míng
李明 Li Ming

Lǐ Míng de
李明的 Li Ming's

Liú Hóng
刘红 Liu Hong

Liú Hóng de
刘红的 Liu Hong's

Zhōng guó
中国 China

Zhōng guó de
中国的 China's

Měi guó
美国 America

Měi guó de
美国的 America's

* As the words for 'he' and 'she' are pronounced the same in Mandarin Chinese, the meaning depends very much on the context. The same applies to the plural form. When referring to a mixed male and female group, the masculine **他们** tāmen is used.

的 De can be omitted if it's followed by a person who's very close to you, such as a family member or a close friend rather than an object.

wǒ bà ba
我爸爸
my father

wǒ mā ma
我妈妈
my mother

wǒ ér zi
我儿子
my son

wǒ nǚ ér
我女儿
my daughter

If you want to use a string of possessive forms, all except the final **的** de are usually omitted.

wǒ de lǎo shī de mā ma
我的老师的妈妈 →

wǒ lǎo shī de mā ma
我老师的妈妈
my teacher's mother

wǒ de bà ba de gōng zuò
我的爸爸的工作 →

wǒ bà ba de gōng zuò
我爸爸的工作
my father's job

1.2 *Use of the negating words* 不 bù *and* 没 méi

不 **Bù** is used to negate all adjectives and most verbs, except 'has/have', which is negated by 没 **méi**. To negate an adjective or verb, simply add 不 **bù** before it.

adjectives:

hǎo 好	bù hǎo 不好 not good		
dà 大	bú dà 不大 not big		
máng 忙	bù máng 不忙 not busy		
lèi 累	bú lèi 不累 not tired		
cuò 错	bú cuò 不错 not bad		

verbs:

shì 是	bú shì 不是 am/is/are not
jiào 叫	bú jiào 不叫 is not called
zhù 住	bú zhù 不住 does not live
gōng zuò 工作	bù gōng zuò 不工作 does not work
jiàn 见	bú jiàn 不见 does not see

As mentioned in the Introduction, you might remember that the tone of 不 **bù** actually changes. It is pronounced as a fourth tone (**bù**) except when it is followed by another fourth tone, in which case it changes into a second tone (**bú**). To negate the verb 'has' or 'have', just add 没 **méi** before it: 没有 **méiyǒu** (don't/doesn't have).

1.3 *Use of the location indicator* 在 zài

Unlike English, there aren't any prepositions in Chinese (words such as 'in', 'at', 'under'). Instead, the verb 在 **zài** is used to indicate location in, on or at a place. 在 **Zài** could be translated as 'to be in/on/at', 'to be located in/on/at', or just 'in/on/at'. It is always used before a place or location word.

Wǒ men zài Zhōng guó
我们在中国。   We *are in* China. (to be in)

Wǒ de jiā zài Yīng guó
我的家在英国。   My home *is in* Britain. (to be in)

Nǐ men de lǎo shī zài nǎ li
你们的老师在哪里?   Where *is* your teacher? (to be)

Tā zhù zài Běi jīng
他住在北京。   He lives *in* Beijing. (in)

NB: 是 Shì (is/are) is not used in these sentences because the word 在 zài already includes the meaning 'to be'.

Practice

8 Now check your understanding of the text in Exercise 7 by completing the family tree using each person's name:

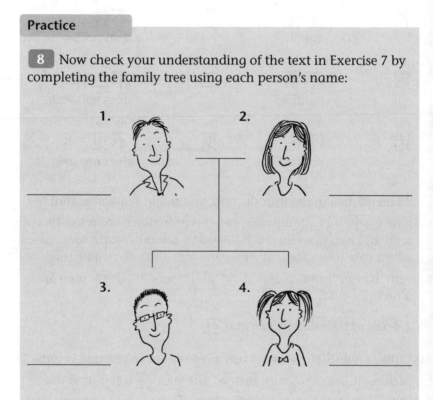

9 Complete the following sentences according to the text in Exercise 7. Use either Pinyin or Chinese characters. You can use Pinyin first and then try writing the characters if you want.

Liú Hóng shì   Lǐ Míng de
1. 刘红是李明的 _____。

Lì   li   shì Liú Hóng de
2. 力力是刘红的 _____。

Tā men zhù zài
3. 他们住在 _____。

Liú Hóng hé   Lǐ Míng yǒu   yí   ge   hé   yí   ge
4. 刘红和李明有一个 _____ 和一个

_____。

Lì   li   shì Yún yun de
5. 力力是云云的 _____。

Yún yun shì Lì   li   de
6. 云云是力力的 _____。

10 Listen to the questions and choose the correct answer based on the text in Exercise 7.

	a.	b.	c.
1.	Shàng hǎi 上海	Běi jīng 北京	Nán jīng 南京
2.	lǎo shī 老师	xué sheng 学生	gōng chéng shī 工程师
3.	bà ba 爸爸	gē ge 哥哥	yé ye 爷爷
4.	hěn dà 很大	bú dà 不大	hěn xiǎo 很小
5.	Yún yun 云云	Liú Hóng 刘红	Lì li 力力

11 Now say something about your own family. Say their names, jobs, nationalities, etc. If you are in a class, bring in some family photos and tell your classmates about your family.

12 Change the following sentences into negatives using
不 **bù** or 没 **méi**. The first one has been done for you.
Take care with the change of tone of 不 **bù**.

Wǒ shì Zhōng guó rén   Wǒ bú shì Zhōng guó rén
1. 我是中国人。   我不是中国人。

Tā shì wǒ de ér zi   Tā   shì wǒ de ér zi
2. 他是我的儿子。   他 ＿＿ 是我的儿子。

Tā men zhù zài Běi jīng   Tā men   zhù zài Běi jīng
3. 他们住在北京。   他们 ＿＿ 住在北京。

Wǒ de bà ba zài Shàng hǎi gōng zuò
4. 我的爸爸在上海工作。

Wǒ de bà ba   zài Shàng hǎi gōng zuò
我的爸爸 ＿＿ 在上海工作。

Tā jiào Mǎ lì   Tā   jiào Mǎ lì
5. 她叫玛丽。   她 ＿＿ 叫玛丽。

Wǒ yǒu gē ge   Wǒ   yǒu gē ge
6. 我有哥哥。   我 ＿＿ 有哥哥。

Jiè shào péng you
2 Introducing a friend
介绍朋友

> **Key expressions: More on introductions**
>
> *To start your introduction:*
> Ràng wǒ lái jiè shào yí xià
> 让我来介绍一下。
> Let me make an introduction. / Let me introduce … .
>
> *To greet someone when meeting for the first time:*
> Rèn shi nín hěn gāo xìng
> 认识您很高兴!
> Very pleased to meet you!

To find out who someone is:

Zhè shì shuí	Nà shì shuí	Tā　Tā shì shuí
这是谁?	那是谁?	他 / 她是谁?
Who is this?	Who is that?	Who is he/she?

13 Li Ming is doing some shopping with his wife Liu Hong and daughter Yunyun. They meet his colleague Manager Zhang on the street. Listen to their conversation and focus on how Li Ming introduces his family:

Li:
Nǐ hǎo　　Zhāng jīng lǐ　　zhēn qiǎo　　Nǐ hǎo ma
你好，张经理，真巧！你好吗?

Zhang:
Wǒ hěn hǎo　　nǐ ne
我很好，你呢?

Li:
Wǒ yě bú cuò　　Lái　　ràng wǒ lái jiè shào yí xià
我也不错。来，让我来介绍一下。

Zhè shì wǒ tài tai　　Liú Hóng　　Liú Hóng　　zhè shì
这是我太太，刘红。刘红，这是

wǒ men gōng sī de Zhāng jīng lǐ
我们公司的张经理。

Liu:
Zhāng jīng lǐ　　rèn shi nín hěn gāo xìng
张经理，认识您很高兴!

Zhang:
Wǒ yě hěn gāo xìng rèn shi nín　　Zhè shì shuí
我也很高兴认识您。这是谁?

Liu:
Zhè shì Yún yun　　wǒ men de nǚ ér　　Yún yun
这是云云，我们的女儿。云云，

jiào Zhāng shū shu
叫张叔叔!

Yunyun:
Zhāng shū shu hǎo
张叔叔好!

Zhang:
Nǐ hǎo
你好!

New words and phrases: Introducing a friend

真巧!	Zhēnqiǎo!	What a coincidence!
来	lái	to come, come
让	ràng	to let
介绍	jièshào	to introduce
一下	yíxià	(grammar word – refers to a brief action – see Language note 2.2)
公司	gōngsī	company
谁	shúi *or* shéi	who, whom
叔叔	shūshu	uncle (father's younger brother)
那	nà	that

Language notes

2.1 *Questions with a question word (what? where? who? how?)*

So far you have met four question words in Chinese:

shén me	nǎ li	shuí	zěn me yàng
什么	哪里	谁	怎么样
what	where	who	how

These question words tend to appear at the end of sentences. The answer to the question will simply replace the question word (in the same position). It is important to remember that the word order of a sentence does not change when it transforms from a statement to a question. Look at the following sentences and pay attention to the words that are underlined. Each question should contain only one question word, thus question particles such as **ma** and **ne** should not be used.

Nǐ jiào shén me
你叫什么?
What's your name?

Wǒ jiào Lǐ Míng
我叫李明。
I am called Li Ming.

Tā xìng shén me
他姓什么?
What's his surname?

Tā xìng Wáng
他姓王。
His surname is Wang.

Tā shì nǎ li rén
她是哪里人?
Where is she from?

Tā shì Zhōng guó rén
她是中国人。
She's Chinese.

Tā men shì shuí
他们是谁?
Who are they?

Tā men shì wǒ de lǎo shī
他们是我的老师。
They are my teachers.

Nǐ de bà ba mā ma zěn me yàng
你的爸爸妈妈怎么样?
How are your parents?

Tā men hěn hǎo
他们很好。
They are very well.

yí xià
2.2 *Use of* 一下

The structure **verb + yí xià** refers to a brief action. It is most commonly used as a 'softener' while giving instructions or orders so that they sound more polite.

lái yí xià
来一下
to come
(for a short time)

kàn yí xià
看一下
to have a (quick) look

shuō yí xià
说一下
to talk (briefly)

tīng yí xià
听一下
to have a listen

shì yí xià
试一下
to have a try

chá yí xià
查一下
to check briefly

Practice

14 How do you say the following in Chinese?

1. What a coincidence!   4. This is my wife.
2. Let me introduce ....   5. Who is that?
3. Pleased to meet you!

15 Now it is your turn to speak. Imagine you have been introduced to someone new by a friend at a party. Greet them and tell them your name. And then turn on the recording and answer the questions they ask you. There are some sample answers at the back of the book.

16 a. For each short exchange, look at the picture and the response given. Write down what question you think is being asked. The first one has been completed for you. You can write in either Pinyin or Chinese characters, or both.

1.
Tā shì shéi
他是谁?
Tā shì wǒ de bà ba
他是我的爸爸。

2. _____?
Tā jiào Hǎi lún
她叫海伦。(Helen)

3. _____?
Wǒ men de lǎo shī shì Zhōng guó rén
我们的老师是中国人。

4. _____?
Wǒ zhù zài Yīng guó
我住在英国。

5. _____?
Wǒ shì gōng chéng shī
我是工程师。

b. Now you ask the questions and listen to the correct version and the replies on the audio.

17 Match the sentences with their English translation. The first one has been done for you.

Wǒ shì Měi guó rén
1. 我是美国人。

     a. My son lives in Beijing.

Tā de mā ma shì jīng lǐ
2. 他的妈妈是经理。

     b. This is my wife.

Wǒ jiào Liú Hóng
3. 我叫刘红。

     c. I am American.

Wǒ de ér zi zhù zài Běi jīng
4. 我的儿子住在北京。

     d. She's our teacher.

Wǒ bà ba de gōng zuò hěn máng
5. 我爸爸的工作很忙。

     e. Her daughter works in France.

Zhè shì wǒ tài tai
6. 这是我太太。

     f. My name is Liu Hong.

Tā shì wǒ men de lǎo shī
7. 她是我们的老师。

     g. My father's job is very busy.

Tā de nǚ ér zài Fǎ guó gōng zuò
8. 她的女儿在法国工作。

     h. His mother is a manager.

Qianmen Gate, Beijing

Learning Chinese characters

Basic structures of Chinese characters

1. Left and right structure

e.g. 你　亻＋尔　　好　女＋子

妈　女＋马　　对　又＋寸

2. Top and bottom structure

e.g. 早　日　　室　宀　　爸　父　　学　⺌
＋　　　＋　　　＋　　　＋

十　　　至　　　巴　　　子

3. Inside and outside structure

e.g.

国　囗＋玉　　四　囗＋儿

囚　囗＋人　　闷　门＋心

18 Categorize the following characters according to their structure. The first one has been done for you.

1. 外　2. 婆　3. 爸　4. 妈　5. 国　6. 宝
7. 围　8. 你　9. 的　10. 爷　11. 果　12. 问
13. 英　14. 妹　15. 早

a. Left and right structure: ＿＿*1*＿＿＿＿＿＿＿

b. Top and bottom structure: ＿＿＿＿＿＿＿＿＿

c. Inside and outside structure: ＿＿＿＿＿＿＿＿

Recognize the characters in the text

19 Read the following sentences and see how much you have understood by answering the questions in English. A translation of the text and the answers to the questions are in the Answers section.

你好。我叫<u>刘红</u>。我是老师。我的爸爸是
医生。他是中国人。我的妈妈是英国人。
她是公司经理。我有一个哥哥和一个妹妹。
我爱我的家。

1. What's her name?

2. What's her job?

3. Where is her father from?

4. Is her mother a teacher?

5. Does she have any older brothers?

Write the characters in the text

20 Try writing the following characters using the stroke order indicated.

这 zhè this	丶	二	亠	文	文	讠文	这		
有 yǒu to have	一	丆	𠂇	右	有	有			
爸 bà father	丿	八	𡗗	父	𤕄	爷	爸	爸	
妈 mā mother	𡿨	𡿨	女	𡚼	妈	妈			

住 zhù to live	丿	亻	彳	仁	仨	住	住		
在 zài to be at, in...	一	广	才	右	存	在			
大 dà big	一	大	大						
叫 jiào to be called	丶	冂	口	叮	叫				
儿 ér son, child	丿	儿							
子 zǐ child	乛	了	子						
女 nǚ female	乚	女	女						
个 gè measure word	丿	人	个						

21 Use Chinese characters to write a few sentences introducing yourself and your family. Use Pinyin where you don't know how to write the characters. There are some sample sentences in the Answers section at the back of the book.

Family values in China

Family means a lot to Chinese people. It is considered to be the most important aspect of interpersonal relationships and social communication in China. Chinese people often refer to family relationships

as 骨肉之情 **gǔ ròu zhī qíng**, 手足之情 **shǒu zú zhī qíng** (as inseparable as flesh and bone, as inseparable as hands and feet). Because of the traditional hierarchy values, it is essential to address each family member, especially those older than you, with the terms you've learnt in this unit. It is not acceptable for the younger generation to address the older generation using just their names. This indicates a lack of respect.

Parents usually provide financial support for their children's food, clothes and education. Children thus have an obligation to support and take care of their parents when they grow older to repay the 'debt for giving birth and raising

them' 养育之恩 **yǎng yù zhī ēn**. It is taken for granted that a family needs to support each other in all aspects of life. So, it is not common to say 'thank you', 'sorry' or 'please' within the family as this is seen as placing distance between family members.

unit

4 Numbers

Dì sì kè   Shù zì
第四课   数字

In this unit, you will learn:
- How to pronounce Pinyin combinations containing: y, w, ai, ui, ei, iu, ie, ou, an, in and en
- How to count in Chinese and how to use numbers for personal information such as ages, telephone numbers and addresses
- About the rules of writing Chinese characters
- About lucky and unlucky numbers in China

Getting the pronunciation right

Pīn yīn liàn xí
拼音练习

In this unit, you will continue to hear and say some basic sound combinations. First, can you recall how the following sounds are pronounced? Check your pronunciation with the audio.

y   w   ai   ui   ei   iu   ie   ou   an   in   en

1 Listen to the four tones with the following sounds and repeat them out loud after each set:

dāi dái dǎi dài	bān bán bǎn bàn	nāi nái nǎi nài
jiē jié jiě jiè	qiē qié qiě qiè	xiū xiú xiǔ xiù
yīn yín yǐn yìn	tuī tuí tuǐ tuì	huī huí huǐ huì
liū liú liǔ liù	wū wú wǔ wù	gēn gén gěn gèn
fēi féi fěi fèi	yū yú yǔ yù	rōu róu rǒu ròu

2 Listen and circle the syllables you hear:

1. dai tai hai nai
2. xiu qiu jiu liu
3. lie jie ri qin

4. hen wen gen ren
5. nei hui gai wei

3 Listen and circle the tones based on what you hear:

1. wā wá wǎ wà
2. ruī ruí ruǐ ruì
3. bāi bái bǎi bài

4. qīn qín qǐn qìn
5. gēi géi gěi gèi

4 You met these words in the previous unit. See if you can remember the meaning of the words and mark up their correct tones. Then check them against the word lists in Unit 3 on pages 46 and 54.

1. baba   2. mama   3. gege   4. jiejie

5. didi   6. meimei   7. jia   8. you

9. erzi   10. nü'er   11. zai   12. lai

13. rang   14. jieshao   15. gongsi   16. shui

Communicating in Chinese

Hàn yǔ jiāo liú
汉语交流

1 Numbers

Shù zì
数字

5 The key to saying numbers in Chinese is remembering how to count from 1 to 10. The rest is just a matter of saying the numbers in a particular order. Listen to the audio and repeat after each number. See if you can identify any patterns once you get past 10.

0	líng 零	11	shí yī 十一	22	èr shí èr 二十二
1	yī 一	12	shí èr 十二	23	èr shí sān 二十三
2	èr liǎng 二 / 两	13	shí sān 十三		...
3	sān 三	14	shí sì 十四	30	sān shí 三十
4	sì 四	15	shí wǔ 十五	40	sì shí 四十
5	wǔ 五	16	shí liù 十六	50	wǔ shí 五十
6	liù 六	17	shí qī 十七	60	liù shí 六十
7	qī 七	18	shí bā 十八	70	qī shí 七十
8	bā 八	19	shí jiǔ 十九	80	bā shí 八十
9	jiǔ 九	20	èr shí 二十	90	jiǔ shí 九十
10	shí 十	21	èr shí yī 二十一	100	yì bǎi 一百

1,000 一千 yì qiān	10,000 一万 (1,0000) yí wàn	100,000 十万 (10,0000) shí wàn
2,000 两千 liǎng qiān	20,000 两万 (2,0000) liǎng wàn	200,000 二十万 (20,0000) èr shí wàn
3,000 三千 sān qiān	30,000 三万 (3,0000) sān wàn	300,000 三十万 (30,0000) sān shí wàn
4,000 四千 sì qiān	40,000 四万 (4,0000) sì wàn	1,000,000 一百万 (100,0000) yì bǎi wàn

The numbers are the **New words and phrases** for this section.

Language note

1.1 *Use of numbers*

There are two words for the number 2. When counting numbers, 二 **èr** is used. When measuring an amount, in other words, counting any objects, 两 **liǎng** is used. So, if you want to say two cups (两个杯子 **liǎng ge bēizi**) or two cats (两只猫 **liǎng zhī māo**), then you need to say 两 **liǎng** instead of 二 **èr**.

In Chinese, there is also a slightly different counting system. Numbers are clustered together with four digits rather than three. So, 10,000 is thought of as 1,0000 in Chinese, and it is called **yí wàn** instead of **shí qiān**.

i

Do you know how Chinese people count with their fingers? Look at the following hand gestures for numbers in China. Some of them actually represent the shape of the corresponding characters, such as 6, 8 and 10.

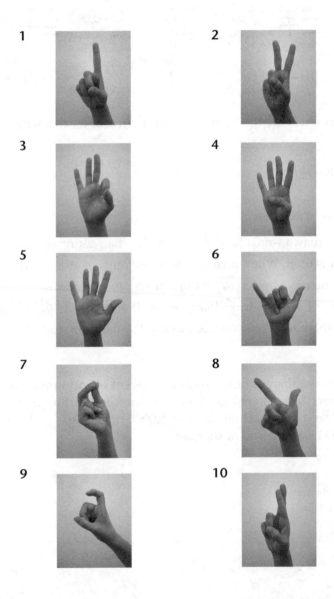

1

2

3

4

5

6

7

8

9

10

Practice

6 **a.** You will hear a range of numbers in English. Say the Chinese equivalent out loud in the pause that follows each one and then wait to check your answer with the Chinese speaker. **b.** This time the numbers are in Chinese. Try to say the English quickly after each one and then check your answers at the back of the book.

7 Now listen to some numbers in Chinese. Write down the numbers you hear:

_____   _____   _____   _____   _____

8 Now try saying some big numbers out loud in Chinese. You can check whether you are saying them correctly with the answers at the back of the book.

a. 482 **b.** 1990 **c.** 4762 **d.** 27967 **e.** 533612 **f.** 8376214

2 Measure words

Liàng cí
量词

The concept of measure words exists in the English language too. Think of expressions such as three *cups* of coffee, a *piece* of paper, a *bottle* of wine. You don't say 'a milk' or 'a wine'. And 'three coffees' implies 'three *cups* of coffee'. This applies to most nouns in Chinese. Whenever you talk about a specific amount of something in Chinese, including 'a' indicating 'one', 'every', 'this', 'that' and 'which', you need to use a measure word. Measure words are not required, however, when you express an unspecific quantity, such as 'a lot', 'some', 'a few', 'there isn't a' or 'there aren't any'.

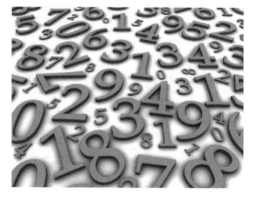

9 In this section, you will learn some of the most commonly used measure words. Listen to the following phrases and repeat them.

  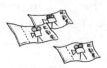

yì bēi kā fēi
一杯咖啡
a cup of coffee

liǎng běn shū
两本书
two books

sān zhāng diàn yǐng piào
三张电影票
three film tickets

sì píng pí jiǔ
四瓶啤酒
four bottles of beer

wǔ ge péng you
五个朋友
five friends

liù fú huà
六幅画
six paintings

qī jiàn máo yī
七件毛衣
seven sweaters

bā tiáo qún zi
八条裙子
eight skirts

jiǔ shuāng xié
九双鞋
nine pairs of shoes

The measure words are the **New words and phrases** for this section.

Language notes

2.1 *More on measure words*

The most common measure word in Chinese is 个 **gè**. It is used for most objects and people, for example, 一个弟弟 **yí ge dìdi**. The other measure words given here follow some general rules:

杯 **bēi**: means 'cup or glass', used in the same way as in English, so mainly for drinks

本 **běn**: used for books, magazines, notebooks and dictionaries

张 **zhāng**: used for flat objects, such as paper, tickets, newspapers, beds, desks and stamps

瓶 **píng**: used in the same way as in English, for bottles of drink or other liquids

幅 **fú**: used for paintings, art work; also used for indicating a pair of ear-rings or gloves

件 **jiàn**: used for all clothes that go on the top half of the body, such as shirts, t-shirts and blouses

条 **tiáo**: used for all clothes that go on the lower half of the body, such as trousers, skirts, jeans and dresses; also used for long and thin objects such as ties, ropes, fish, rivers and streets

双 **shuāng**: used for pairs, such as shoes, socks and chopsticks.

It is not possible to introduce all the measure words in this unit and there are no absolute rules to follow. It is the awareness of this concept that is important. You can learn the vocabulary and different combinations more naturally with time.

2.2 *Plural nouns*

As you may have already noticed, the form of a noun does not change in the plural as it does in English, where 's' or 'es' is added. However, in the case of personal pronouns, such as 'we', 'you' and 'they', **men** is added to indicate the plural – see Unit 1, Language note 1.2.

Practice

10 Choose the appropriate measure word to complete the sentences. Write the corresponding number in the spaces below:

gè		bēi		běn		zhāng	
1. 个		2. 杯		3. 本		4. 张	
píng		jiàn		shuāng		fú	
5. 瓶		6. 件		7. 双		8. 幅	

Wǒ yǒu sān　　shū
a. 我有三___书。

Wǒ bà ba yǒu liǎng　　máo yī
b. 我爸爸有两___毛衣。

Tā yǒu yì　　kā fēi
c. 她有一___咖啡。

Wǒ de mèi mei yǒu shí　　xié
d. 我的妹妹有十___鞋。

Tā yǒu sì　　kě lè
e. 他有四___可乐
(Coke)。

Lǎo shī yǒu qī　　yóu piào
f. 老师有七___邮票
(stamps)。

Wǒ jiā yǒu liǎng　　huà
g. 我家有两___画。

Mā ma yǒu wǔ　　píng guǒ
h. 妈妈有五___苹果。

11 Now it's time for you to talk. How would you say the following in Chinese? Say them out loud and then check your answers at the back of the book.

1. I have two older brothers.
2. He has five paintings.
3. There are seven people in her family. (lit. Her family has seven people.)
4. I have two bottles of beer.
5. She has six pairs of shoes.
6. My mother has one younger sister.

3 Numbers in use

Shǐ yòng shù zì
使用数字

Key expressions: More personal information

To ask where someone lives:

Nǐ zhù zài nǎ li
你住在哪里？
Where do you live?

Wǒ zhù zài Běi jīng
我住在北京。
I live in Beijing.

To ask someone's nationality:

Nǐ shì nǎ guó rén
你是哪国人？
What nationality are you?

Wǒ shì Yīng guó rén
我是英国人。
I am British.

To ask how many people are in someone's family:

Nǐ jiā yǒu jǐ ge rén
你家有几个人？
How many people are there in your family?

Wǒ jiā yǒu sì ge rén
我家有四个人。
There are four people in my family.

To ask someone's age:

Nǐ jǐ suì
你几岁?
How old are you?
(only to someone young (under 15))

Wǒ liù suì
我六岁。
I am 6 years old.

Nǐ duō dà
你多大?
How old are you?

Wǒ sān shí suì
我三十岁。
I am 30 years old.

To ask for someone's telephone number:

Nǐ de diàn huà hào mǎ shì duō shǎo
你的电话号码是多少?
What's your phone number?

Wǒ de diàn huà hào mǎ shì wǔ liù liù bā jiǔ sān qī wǔ
我的电话号码是五六六八九三七五。
My phone number is 56689375.

 12 Listen to the following dialogue between two university students. Pay attention to how they give more information about their families, and how they give their ages, telephone numbers and addresses.

Nǐ hǎo   wǒ jiào Tāng mǔ   Wǒ xué xí Zhōng wén
Tom: 你好，我叫汤姆。我学习中文，
nǐ ne
你呢?

Nǐ hǎo   wǒ shì Zhāng Mǐn   Wǒ xué xí jīn róng
Min: 你好，我是张敏。我学习金融。

Nǐ yě zhù zài zhè lǐ ma
Tom: 你也住在这里吗?

Min: Duì wǒ zhù zài wǔ lóu èr líng bā shì Nǐ ne
对，我住在五楼二零八室。你呢？

Tom: Wǒ zhù zài sān lóu sì líng liù shì Nǐ men xué yuàn dà
我住在三楼四零六室。你们学院大
bú dà
不大？

Min: Hěn dà yǒu sì shí wǔ ge lǎo shī liù bǎi ge xué
很大，有四十五个老师，六百个学
sheng Nǐ shì nǎ guó rén
生。你是哪国人？

Tom: Wǒ shì Yīng guó rén Wǒ yǒu yí ge jiě jie hé liǎng ge
我是英国人。我有一个姐姐和两个
dì di Nǐ jiā yǒu jǐ ge rén
弟弟。你家有几个人？

Min: Sì ge Wǒ yǒu yí ge mèi mei
四个。我有一个妹妹。

Tom: Tā jīn nián jǐ suì
她今年几岁？

Min: Jiǔ suì Nǐ de diàn huà hào mǎ shì duō shǎo Wǒ men yǒu
九岁。你的电话号码是多少？我们有
kòng yì qǐ qù hē kā fēi hǎo ma
空一起去喝咖啡，好吗？

Tom: Tài hǎo le Wǒ de diàn huà hào mǎ shì
太好了！我的电话号码是
wǔ liù liù bā jiǔ sān qī wǔ
五六六八九三七五。

Min: Hǎo huí tóu jiàn
好，回头见！

How much have you understood? Can you answer the following questions in English?

1. What does Tom study?
2. What is Min's room number?
3. How many brothers and sisters does Tom have?
4. How old is Min's younger sister?
5. What is Tom's telephone number?

New words and phrases: Numbers in use

学习	xuéxí	to study/study
中文	Zhōngwén	Chinese language
金融	jīnróng	finance
这里	zhèlǐ	here
学院	xuéyuàn	college; school
对	duì	correct; yes
楼	lóu	building
室	shì	room
哪	nǎ or něi	which
几	jǐ	how many
多	duō	how (question word, refers to degree, e.g. how old, how fast, how deep)
今年	jīnnián	this year
岁	suì	years old
电话	diànhuà	telephone (lit. electricity conversation)
电话号码	diànhuàhàomǎ	telephone number

多少	duōshǎo	how much/how many
有空	yǒukòng	to be free/have time (lit. to have emptiness/space)
一起	yìqǐ	together
去	qù	to go
喝	hē	to drink
咖啡	kāfēi	coffee

Language note

3.1 *Use of numbers for reference*

When you are giving your house number, a bus number, a building number or the size of clothes or shoes, in Chinese you say the whole number rather than the individual digits.

e.g. No. 534 Huaihai Road is: Huǎihǎi Lù wǔbǎisānshísì hào

When you are giving a room number, a telephone number, or any reference numbers, however, you say the individual digits of the number. 'One' is usually pronounced as **yāo** instead of **yī** in order to avoid confusion with the similar-sounding number seven (**qī**).

e.g. Room 301 is: sān líng **yāo** shì

Practice

13 Now play the role of Tom. First introduce yourself, then ask Wei, a Chinese friend, for her name, nationality, age, telephone number and how many people are in her family. You will be prompted on the audio and will hear the correct question after each of your attempts, before Wei answers your questions.

14 Listen to three people talking about themselves, and fill in all the information you find out about them in English in the table below.

	a.	b.	c.
Name			
Nationality			
Age			
Telephone number			
No. of family members			

15 Read the following text and then answer the questions about it in Chinese.

Wǒ jiào Tāng mǔ　　Wǒ xué xí Zhōng wén　　Wǒ shì Yīng guó rén　　Wǒ
我叫汤姆。我学习中文。我是英国人。我

de jiā zài Yīng guó　　wǒ men shì liù ge rén　　wǒ bà ba mā ma
的家在英国，我们是六个人，我爸爸妈妈，

yī ge jiě jie　　liǎng ge dì di hé wǒ　　Wǒ de diàn huà hào mǎ
一个姐姐，两个弟弟和我。我的电话号码

shì wǔ liù liù bā jiǔ sān qī wǔ　　Wǒ jīn tiān　　rèn shi
是五六六八九三七五。我今天 (today) 认识

le Zhāng Mǐn　　Tā xué xí jīn róng　　Rèn shi tā wǒ hěn gāo xìng
了张敏。她学习金融。认识她我很高兴!

Wǒ zhù zài sān lóu sì líng liù shì　　tā zhù zài wǔ lóu èr líng
我住在三楼四零六室，她住在五楼二零

bā shì　　Wǒ de xué yuàn bú dà　　yǒu èr shí ge lǎo shī hé
八室。我的学院不大，有二十个老师和

yì bǎi sān shí ge xué sheng　　Zhāng Mǐn de xué yuàn hěn dà　　yǒu
一百三十个学生。张敏的学院很大，有

sì shí wǔ ge lǎo shī　　liù bǎi ge xué sheng　　Zhāng Mǐn de mèi mei
四十五个老师，六百个学生。张敏的妹妹

jīn nián jiǔ suì　　Tā hé wǒ yǒu kòng yì qǐ qù hē kā fēi　　wǒ
今年九岁。她和我有空一起去喝咖啡，我

hěn gāo xìng
很高兴。

Tāng mǔ xué xí shén me
1. 汤姆学习什么？

Tā de jiā yǒu jǐ ge rén
2. 他的家有几个人？

Tā de jiā zài nǎ li
3. 他的家在哪里？

Tā de diàn huà hào mǎ shì duō shǎo
4. 他的电话号码是多少？

Zhāng Mǐn yǒu jǐ ge mèi mei
5. 张敏有几个妹妹？

Zhāng Mǐn de mèi mei jīn nián jǐ suì
6. 张敏的妹妹今年几岁？

Shuí de xué yuàn hěn dà　　Yǒu duō shǎo lǎo shī hé xué sheng
7. 谁的学院很大？ 有多少老师和学生？

16 Using the text in Exercise 15 as a guide, say something about Min. Include the words listed below. Start with 这叫张敏。她学习金融··· **Zhè jiào Zhāng Mǐn. Tā xuéxí jīnróng.**

xué yuàn　　lóu　　shì　　yǒu　　jīn nián　　suì　　yì qǐ
学院　楼　室　有　今年　岁　一起

hē kā fēi　　diàn huà hào mǎ
喝咖啡　电话号码

Learning Chinese characters

Xué hàn zì
学汉字

Summary of the general rules of stroke order

1. Top to bottom, left to right

As a general rule, strokes are written from top to bottom and from left to right.

èr
二   two   一 二

sān
三   three   一 二 三

When a character has a left and right structure, the left part is usually written before the right part.

hǎo
好   good, well   く く 女 女⁷ 好 好

duì
对   correct   フ ヌ ヌ一 对 对

When a character has a top and bottom structure, the top part is usually written first and then the bottom part.

zhī
只   (measure word   ヽ 冂 口 尸 只
          for animals)

zǎo
早   morning; early   ヽ 冂 冃 日 旦 早

2. Horizontal before vertical

When horizontal and vertical strokes cross, horizontal strokes are usually written before vertical strokes.

shí
十   ten   一 十

kāi
开   to open   一 二 开 开

3. Character-spanning strokes last
Vertical strokes that pass through many other strokes are written after the strokes through which they pass.

zhōng
中 middle, centre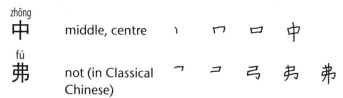

fú
弗 not (in Classical Chinese)

4. Downward-left before downward-right
Right-to-left down strokes are written before left-to-right down strokes.

rén
人 person

wén
文 language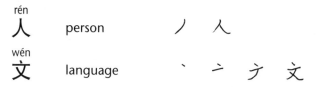

5. Centre before outside in vertically symmetrical characters
In vertically symmetrical characters, the centre component is written before the components on the left and right.

xiǎo
小 small

shuǐ
水 water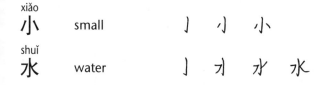

6. Outside before inside before closing
Outside enclosing components are written before inside components; although the bottom 'closing' stroke in the enclosure is written last if present.

guó
国 country

yuè
月 moon

7. Bottom enclosures last
Bottom enclosing components are usually written last.

zhè
这   this   丶   亠   文   文   文   讠文   这

xiōng
凶   fierce   丿   ㄨ   凶   凶

8. Dots and minor strokes last
Minor strokes, like 'dots', are usually written last.

shū
书   book   ㄱ   乛   书   书

wǒ
我   I, me   丿   二   手   扌   我   我   我

Write the characters in the text

17 Try writing the following characters using the stroke order indicated.

一 yī one	一							
二 èr two	一	二						
三 sān three	一	二	三					
四 sì four	丨	冂	冂	四	四			

五 wǔ five	一	丁	五	五					
六 liù six	丶	亠	宀	六					
七 qī seven	一	七							
八 bā eight	丿	八							
九 jiǔ nine	丿	九							
十 shí ten	一	十							
百 bǎi hundred	一	丆	丆	历	百	百			
千 qiān thousand	丿	二	千						
万 wàn 10,000	一	丅	万						

几	丿	几						
jǐ how many								

 Lucky and unlucky numbers in China

As in many countries, some numbers are considered to be lucky in China while others are not. The numbers 6, 8 and 9 are all thought to be lucky. The most popular number in China is 8 because its pronunciation 八 **bā** sounds very similar to 发 **fā**, which means 'growth of wealth' or 'prosperity'. Thus, many Chinese people like to buy a car with a registration plate ending with an 8, or have a mobile phone number which ends with the number 8. Despite the fact that people may have to pay extra to do this, they will still do it. People tend to get married on the 8th, 18th and 28th of the month. Flats on the 8th floor can be more expensive than other floors. The Beijing Olympics started on 08/08/2008 and the opening ceremony began at 8:08pm Beijing time. The number 6 is lucky because it is used in the Chinese idiom 六六大顺 **liù liù dà shùn**, which means 'Everything will go smoothly'. And the number 9 is considered to be lucky by some people because its sound is the same as the word for 'eternity', as in the Chinese idiom 天长地久 **tiān cháng dì jiǔ**, which refers to the ever-lasting nature of love and happiness.

The number that is considered unlucky in China is 4. The pronunciation of 4 is similar to the word for 'death' 死 **sǐ**, thus it is considered bad luck. In some areas of China, buildings do not even have a 4th floor – you go straight from the 3rd to the 5th!

Greetings, families, personal details and numbers

Communicating in Chinese

Hàn yǔ jiāo liú
汉语交流

1 Look at the following pictures and fill in the appropriate responses in Pinyin. The first one has been done for you.

1.

Zǎoshang hǎo! — *Zǎoshang hǎo*

2.

Nǐhǎo. Nǐ jiào shénme?

3.

Xièxie

4.

Zài jiàn!

5.

Nǐ shì nǎli rén?

6.

Wǒ hěn hǎo.

2 Listen to a few short dialogues and choose the right answers to the questions.

1. What time of day is it?
   a. morning **b.** afternoon **c.** evening

2. How is the girl?
   a. well **b.** busy **c.** tired

3. Where is the man from?
   a. USA **b.** Canada **c.** France

4. How old is Mr Cheng?
   a. 35 **b.** 30 **c.** 42

5. How many people are there in Xiaomin's family?
   a. 4 **b.** 5 **c.** 6

6. Which of the following statements is not true based on the dialogue?
   a. He has one son and one daughter.
   b. His wife is a doctor.
   c. His daughter is a student.

3 You will be asked a few questions about yourself on the audio. Respond to each of them accordingly. You will find model responses in the Answers section.

4 Complete the gaps in English about each speaker. You'll hear: 伦敦 **Lúndūn** (London).

	Speaker 1	Speaker 2	Speaker 3
Name			
Nationality			
City			
Age			
Job			
Telephone no.			
No. of family members			

5 Relationship mystery: Who is who? Read the following clues and then complete the family tree. The names are underlined for you.

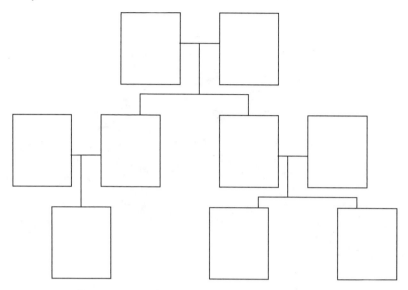

Zhāng Míng shì Zhāng Lì de bà ba
张明是张丽的爸爸。

Wáng Líng yǒu yí ge ér zi hé yí ge nǚ ér
王灵有一个儿子和一个女儿。

Zhāng Wén hé   Lǐ Yún yǒu yí ge nǚ ér
张文和李云有一个女儿。

Zhāng Wén yǒu yí ge jiě jie   jiào Zhāng Lì
张文有一个姐姐，叫张丽。

Chén Jùn de bà ba jiào Chén Qiáng
陈俊的爸爸叫陈强。

Chén Jùn de gē ge shì Chén Huá
陈俊的哥哥是陈华。

Wáng Líng shì Zhāng Měi de nǎi nai   Chén Huá de lǎo lao
王灵是张美的奶奶，陈华的姥姥。

6 The following is a picture of Xiaoli's room. Her room is full of things: books, skirts, shoes, sweaters, pictures, etc. Have a count and describe her room using the correct measure words for the things you know.

7 What would you say in the following situations?

1. You meet a few Chinese people at a party. You would like to get to know them.
2. You bump into an old friend whom you haven't seen for a long time.
3. You've been introduced to a Chinese manager in a business meeting.
4. You would like to ask a Chinese friend to go for a coffee.

Check your answers in the Answers section.

8 Rearrange the following words to form sentences.

1. 这　妈妈　是　的　我
   zhè　mā ma　shì　de　wǒ

2. 忙　他　不
   máng　tā　bù

3. 我　让　一下　介绍　来
   wǒ　ràng　yí xià　jiè shào　lái

4. 他 经理 是 我们 的 公司
    tā jīng lǐ shì wǒ men de gōng sī

5. 我 家 在 的 中国
    wǒ jiā zài de Zhōng guó

6. 有 中文 个 学院 三十 老师
    yǒu Zhōng wén ge xué yuàn sān shí lǎo shī

Getting the pronunciation right
Pīn yīn liàn xí
拼音练习

9 Listen and write the correct initials.

____a ____o ____e ____i ____u ____ü ____ai ____ui

____en ____i ____u ____ü ____ie ____ou ____an ____in

____ei ____a ____u ____o ____u ____iu ____i ____e

10 Listen and write the correct finals.

b____ p____ m____ f____ d____ t____ n____ l____

g____ k____ h____ j____ q____ x____ p____ r____

y____ w____ t____ q____ j____ k____ q____ f____

11 Listen and circle the correct tones.

1. pān pán pǎn pàn
2. jīn jín jǐn jìn
3. kōu kóu kǒu kòu
4. dū dú dǔ dù
5. qiū qiú qiǔ qiù
6. rī-jì rí-jǐ rǐ-jī rì-jì
7. guā-guǒ guá-guǒ guǎ-guǒ guà-guǒ
8. hū-tu hú-tu hǔ-tu hù-tu
9. xīn-qí xín-qī xǐn-qì xìn-qǐ
10. nū-hái nú-hái nǔ-hái nù-hái

12 Listen and mark the correct tones.

1. dun
2. nie
3. lou
4. xiu
5. bi
6. kexi
7. yurou
8. jiqi
9. tebie
10. wuye

Learning Chinese characters

13 How do you write the following characters and how many strokes does each character have?

你 _____

好 _____

我 _____

五 _____

不 _____

很 _____

四 _____

国 _____

是 _____

有 _____

中 _____

人 _____

14 Translate the following sentences into English.

1. 我的爸爸很好。

2. 你是中国人吗？

3. 我叫 Peter。

4. 这不是我的女儿。

5. 我住在北京。

6. 我有一个妹妹，没有弟弟。

5 Dates and plans

Dì wǔ kè　　Rì qī hé jì huà
第五课　日期和计划

In this unit, you will learn:
- How to pronounce Pinyin combinations containing:
  ao, er, un, ün, ang, eng, ing, ong, zh, ch and sh
- How to express days and dates
- How to make plans and talk about birthdays and holidays
- How Chinese characters are formed (1)
- About Chinese horoscopes

Getting the pronunciation right

Pīn yīn liàn xí
拼音练习

In this unit, you will continue to go over some basic sound combinations. First, can you recall how these initials and finals are pronounced? Check your pronunciation with the audio.

ao　er　un　ün　ang　eng　ing　ong　zh　ch　sh

1 Listen to the four tones with the following sounds and repeat them out loud after each set:

zhāi zhái zhǎi zhài　　　bāo báo bǎo bào
lāng láng lǎng làng　　　chāo cháo chǎo chào
qīng qíng qǐng qìng　　　zhī zhí zhǐ zhì
yīng yíng yǐng yìng　　　shuī shuí shuǐ shuì
hōng hóng hǒng hòng　　　wēn wén wěn wèn
chēng chéng chěng chèng　　ēr ér ěr èr
yūn yún yǔn yùn　　　　shōu shóu shǒu shòu

2 Listen and circle the tones based on what you hear:

1. chāi chái chǎi chài
2. zhuī zhuí zhuǐ zhuì
3. bāng báng bǎng bàng
4. qīng qíng qǐng qìng
5. kēng kéng kěng kèng

3 Listen and write down the words you hear in Pinyin with tones:

1. _____   2. _____   3. _____

4. _____   5. _____

4 You met these words in the previous unit. See if you can remember their meanings and mark up their tones. Then check them against the numbers and word list on pages 64 and 74.

1. ling   2. er   3. si   4. qi   5. shiwu   6. sanshijiu
7. xuexi   8. zhongwen   9. dui   10. jinnian   11. ji
12. dianhua   13. qu   14. he   15. sui   16. yiqi

Communicating in Chinese

Hàn yǔ jiāo liú
汉语交流

1 When is your birthday?

Nǐ de shēng rì shì jǐ yuè jǐ hào
你的生日是几月几号?

In Chinese, the days of the week are wonderfully simple. Just say the word for 'week' and add a number, starting with 'one' for Monday. The only exception is Sunday, 'week' + 'day'.

Key expressions: **Days of the week**

1. xīng qī yī
星期一
Monday

2. xīng qī èr
星期二
Tuesday

3. xīng qī sān
星期三
Wednesday

4. xīng qī sì
星期四
Thursday

5. xīng qī wǔ
星期五
Friday

6. xīng qī liù
星期六
Saturday

7. xīng qī rì / xīng qī tiān
星期日 / 星期天   Sunday

In Chinese, you also use numbers to say the months. Just say the number and add the word for 'month'.

Key expressions: Months of the year

yī yuè 一月 January	èr yuè 二月 February	sān yuè 三月 March	sì yuè 四月 April
wǔ yuè 五月 May	liù yuè 六月 June	qī yuè 七月 July	bā yuè 八月 August
jiǔ yuè 九月 September	shí yuè 十月 October	shí yī yuè 十一月 November	shí èr yuè 十二月 December

Spring Festival/Chinese New Year (Jan/Feb)

Mooncakes for the Moon Festival (Sept/Oct)

Dragon Boat Festival (May/June)

Lantern Festival (Jan/Feb)

Key expressions: **Talking about birthdays and dates**

To ask when someone's birthday is:

Nǐ de shēng rì shì
你的生日是
jǐ yuè jǐ hào
几月几号？

When is your birthday?

Wǒ de shēng rì shì
我的生日是
sān yuè shí liù hào
三月十六号。

My birthday is the 16th of March.

To wish someone 'Happy Birthday!':

Zhù nǐ shēng rì kuài lè
祝你生日快乐!

Happy Birthday!

To ask about someone's Chinese horoscope:

Nǐ shǔ shén me
你属什么？

Which year were you
born in? (lit. What do
you belong to?)

Wǒ shǔ mǎ
我属马。

I was born in the year of the
horse. (lit. I belong to the
horse.)

To ask about and give dates:

Jīn tiān jǐ yuè jǐ hào
今天几月几号？

What is the date today?

Jīn tiān sān yuè shí liù hào
今天三月十六号。

Today is 16th March.

To ask about and give the days of the week:

Míng tiān xīng qī jǐ
明天星期几？

What day is it tomorrow?

Zuó tiān xīng qī èr
昨天星期二。

Yesterday was Tuesday.

To ask about and give the year:

Míng nián jǐ   jǐ nián
明年几几年?
What year is it next year?

Qù nián èr líng líng jiǔ nián
去年二零零九年。
Last year was 2009.

When expressing days and dates 是 **shì**, the verb 'to be', is usually omitted in colloquial Chinese.

5 Chen Hui's birthday is coming up soon. Listen to his conversation with his friends Xiaoyan and David.

Chen Hui:
Sì yuè shí wǔ hào shì wǒ de shēng rì   nǐ men lái
四月十五号是我的生日，你们来
wǒ jiā chī dàn gāo ba
我家吃蛋糕吧！

Xiaoyan:
Tài hǎo le   Sì yuè shí wǔ hào shì xīng qī jǐ
太好了！四月十五号是星期几？

Chen Hui:
Shì xīng qī liù   xià ge zhōu mò
是星期六，下个周末。

David:
Chén Huī   nǐ shǔ shén me
陈辉，你属什么？

Chen Hui:
Wǒ shì yī jiǔ qī bā nián chū shēng de   shǔ mǎ
我是一九七八年出生的，属马。
Nǐ ne   Nǐ de shēng rì shì jǐ yuè jǐ hào
你呢？你的生日是几月几号？

David:
Wǒ de shēng rì shì shí yuè yī hào   Wǒ shǔ jī
我的生日是十月一号。我属鸡。

Xiaoyan:
À   Dà wèi   nǐ de shēng rì yě shì Zhōng guó de
啊，大卫，你的生日也是中国的
guó qìng jié
国庆节！

David:
Shì ma   Wǒ jīn nián zài Zhōng guó guò shēng rì
是吗？我今年在中国过生日
yí dìng hěn yǒu yì si
一定很有意思！

Xiaoyan:
Duì   zhù nǐ shēng rì kuài lè
对，祝你生日快乐！

New words and phrases: Talking about birthdays and dates

年	nián	year
月	yuè	month
号	hào	day (used in dates)
生日	shēngrì	birthday
吃	chī	to eat
蛋糕	dàngāo	cake
星期	xīngqī	week
下个	xiàge	next
周末	zhōumò	weekend
出生	chūshēng	to be born
属	shǔ	to be born in the year of (Chinese horoscope)
马	mǎ	horse
鸡	jī	rooster, chicken
啊	à	(an exclamation: sudden realization)
国庆节	guóqìngjié	National Day
过	guò	to spend, to celebrate
一定	yídìng	definitely
有意思	yǒuyìsi	interesting (lit. has meaning)
祝	zhù	to wish
快乐	kuàilè	happy; happiness

NB: The days of the week and months of the year are also key new words for this section.

Language notes

1.1 *Expressions for years, months, dates and days*

You already know that when giving locations in Chinese, you
start with the more general and work down to the specific. Dates
in Chinese are also expressed in this order: year, month, date,
day. Therefore, 23 March 2008 would be 2008/03/23. To say
the year, you read out each individual number, so 2008 would
be 二零零八年 **èr líng líng bā nián**. The twelve months
are expressed with the numbers 1 to 12 and then 月 **yuè** (lit.
'moon'), and dates are expressed with the numbers 1 to 31 and
then 号 **hào** or 日 **rì**. 号 **Hào** is more commonly used in
speaking, whereas 日 **rì** is more commonly used in writing.

Here are some examples:

23 June
1968

yī jiǔ liù bā nián liù yuè èr shí sān hào   rì
一九六八年六月二十三号 / 日

07 September
1765

yī qī liù wǔ nián jiǔ yuè qī hào   rì
一七六五年九月七号 / 日

13 December
2002

èr líng líng èr nián shí èr yuè shí sān hào   rì
二零零二年十二月十三号 / 日

As you have seen, the days of the week all start with the word
星期 **xīngqī** (week), followed by numbers. The only exception
is Sunday, which is expressed as 'the week day': 星期日 /
星期天 **xīngqīrì / xīngqītiān**. An interesting point is that
when asking about dates in Chinese, the question marker is
几 **jǐ**, which means 'how many' rather than 'which'. This is
because all the dates are expressed with numbers. Therefore
the question marker is the one used for asking about specific
numbers.

1.2 The 是⋯的 *shì* ... *de* construction

The 是⋯的 **shì** ... **de** construction is used for emphasis. When you want to emphasize the time, the place, the person, the means of conveyance or the purpose of an action that has already happened, etc., you place the information you want to stress right after 是 **shì**, and end the sentence with 的 **de**. It can be roughly translated as the structure 'It was ... that ...' in English.

Read the following examples. The parts that are stressed are underlined.

Wǒ shì liù yuè èr hào chū shēng de
我是六月二号出生的。

I was born on the 2nd of June. (lit. It was on the 2nd of June that I was born.)

Wǒ shì zài Shàng hǎi chū shēng de
我是在上海出生的。

I was born in Shanghai. (lit. It was in Shanghai that I was born.)

Tā shì zuó tiān lái de
他是昨天来的。

He came yesterday. (lit. It was yesterday that he came.)

Tā shì hé péng you lái de
他是和朋友来的。

He came with friends. (lit. It was with friends that he came.)

The 是⋯的 **shì** ... **de** construction can also be used to emphasize the condition of a present situation.

Tā shì bú duì de
他是不对的。　　　　He is wrong.

Zhè jiàn máo yī shì xīn de
这件毛衣是新的。　　This sweater is new.

Practice

6 Try asking and then giving your date of birth in Chinese, either with a partner or by yourself. Gather the dates of your family or friends' birthdays and create a birthday reminder book in Chinese.

7 You will hear the following dates on the audio. Mark the order (1–4) in which you hear them.

___. 1978 年 09 月 24 号   ___. 1999 年 01 月 31 号

___. 2004 年 11 月 17 号   ___. 2020 年 07 月 29 号

Now how would you say each of the above? Read out each date in the order you have just established, and check with the audio again to make sure you are right.

8 Do you know any festivals and holidays in China? Read the following text and then match the names of the festivals on the next page with their date on the right. The first one has been done for you. Notice the difference when expressing the dates of traditional Chinese festivals based on the lunar calendar.

Yuán dàn shì yī yuè yī rì
元旦是一月一日。

Chūn jié shì zhēng yuè chū yī
春节是正月初一。

Yuán xiāo jié shì zhēng yuè shí wǔ
元宵节是正月十五。

Duān wǔ jié shì wǔ yuè chū wǔ
端午节是五月初五。

Zhōng qiū jié shì bā yuè shí wǔ
中秋节是八月十五。

Láo dòng jié shì wǔ yuè yī rì
劳动节是五月一日。

Guó qìng jié shì shí yuè yī rì
国庆节是十月一日。

Ér tóng jié shì liù yuè yī rì
儿童节是六月一日。

Jiào shī jié shì jiǔ yuè shí rì
教师节是九月十日。

Zhí shù jié shì sān yuè shí èr rì
植树节是三月十二日。

yuán dàn
1. 元旦
New Year

a. shí yuè yī rì
十月一日

chūn jié
2. 春节
Spring Festival (Chinese New Year)

b. yī yuè yī rì
一月一日

yuán xiāo jié
3. 元宵节
Lantern Festival

c. liù yuè yī rì
六月一日

duān wǔ jié
4. 端午节
Dragon Boat Festival

d. zhēng yuè chū yī
正月初一

zhōng qiū jié
5. 中秋节
Moon Festival

e. bā yuè shí wǔ
八月十五

láo dòng jié
6. 劳动节
Labour Day

f. zhēng yuè shí wǔ
正月十五

guó qìng jié
7. 国庆节
National Day

g. sān yuè shí èr rì
三月十二日

ér tóng jié
8. 儿童节
Children's Day

h. jiǔ yuè shí rì
九月十日

jiào shī jié
9. 教师节
Teachers' Day

i. wǔ yuè chū wǔ
五月初五

zhí shù jié
10. 植树节
Arbour Day

j. wǔ yuè yī rì
五月一日

9 Role play: You are going to celebrate your birthday in China this year. Tell your Chinese friend when your birthday is and invite him or her to your home.

2 Talking about travel plans

Key expressions: **Talking about travel plans**

To ask for and give information about travel plans:

Nǐ dǎ suan shén me shí hou zǒu
你打算什么时候走?
When do you plan to leave?

Wǒ dǎ suan wǔ yuè jiǔ hào zǒu
我打算五月九号走。
I plan to leave on the 9th of May.

Nǐ huì qù nǎ li
你会去哪里?
Where will you go?

Wǒ huì qù Xiāng gǎng   Ào mén hé Guǎng zhōu
我会去香港，澳门和广州。
I will go to Hong Kong, Macau and Guangzhou.

Nǐ zhù jǐ tiān
你住几天?
How many days will you stay?

Wǒ zhù sì tiān
我住四天。
I will stay for 4 days.

Nǐ shén me shí hou huí lai
你什么时候回来?
When will you be back?

Wǒ xīng qī liù huí lai
我星期六回来。
I will be back on Saturday.

To wish someone a good journey:

Zhù nǐ yí lù shùn fēng
祝你一路顺风!
Bon voyage! (lit. Wishing you a downwind journey!)

10 Listen to David talking about his travel plans to China with a Chinese friend, Xiaoli.

Xiaoli:
Dà wèi   tīng shuō nǐ liù yuè qù Zhōng guó lǚ xíng   nǐ
大卫，听说你六月去中国旅行，你

dǎ suan shén me shí hou zǒu
打算什么时候走？

David:
Liù yuè shí hào   yí gòng qù sān ge xīng qī
六月十号，一共去三个星期。

Xiaoli:
Nǐ huì qù Zhōng guó nǎ li
你会去中国哪里？

David:
Běi jīng   Shàng hǎi   Xī ān hé Guì lín
北京，上海，西安和桂林。

Xiaoli:
Sān ge xīng qī gòu ma
三个星期够吗？

David:
Gòu le   Wǒ xiān dào Běi jīng   shí wǔ hào zài qù
够了。我先到北京，十五号再去

Xī ān
西安。

Xiaoli:
Nǐ huì zài Xī ān zhù jǐ tiān
你会在西安住几天？

David:
Sān tiān   rán hòu qù Shàng hǎi   Wǒ dǎ suan zài Shàng hǎi
三天，然后去上海。我打算在上海

zhù sì tiān   zuì hòu cóng Shàng hǎi qù Guì lín
住四天，最后从上海去桂林。

Xiaoli:
Shén me shí hou huí Yīng guó
什么时候回英国？

David:
Qī yuè sān hào
七月三号。

Xiaoli:
Tài hǎo le   Zhù nǐ yí lù shùn fēng
太好了！祝你一路顺风！

David:
Xiè xie
谢谢！

Guilin

The Bund, Shanghai

New words and phrases: Talking about travel plans

听说	tīngshuō	to have heard that
旅行	lǚxíng	to travel
打算	dǎsuan	to plan
什么时候	shénmeshíhou	what time, when
走	zǒu	to leave
一共	yígòng	altogether
够	gòu	enough
先…再…	xiān … zài …	first … then …
到	dào	to arrive
从	cóng	from
然后	ránhòu	then, afterwards
最后	zùihòu	finally, at the end
回	húi	to return
回来	huílai	to return, to come back
一路顺风	yílùshùnfēng	to have a good journey

Language notes

2.1 *More questions with question words (when? how many? how much? which?)*

In Unit 3 (page 54), you saw how to ask questions with the question words: 什么 shénme (what), 哪里 nǎli (where), 谁 shuí (who) and 怎么样 zěnmeyàng (how).

Now let's look at some more question words:

shén me shí hou
什么时候
when

jǐ
几
how many

duō shǎo
多少
how many/how much

nǎ xiē
哪（些）
which (plural)

As explained in Unit 3, these question words are not used at the beginning of sentences as in English. Their position in a sentence is just the same as it would be in a statement. Look at the following examples and pay attention to the words that are underlined.

Nǐ shén me shí hou qù Zhōng guó
你<u>什么时候</u>去中国?
When will you go to China?

Wǒ míng tiān qù Zhōng guó
我<u>明天</u>去中国。
I will go to China tomorrow.

Tā shén me shí hou huí jiā
她<u>什么时候</u>回家?
When will she go home?

Tā xià ge yuè huí jiā
她<u>下个月</u>回家。
She will go home next month.

Nǐ de shēng rì shì jǐ yuè
你的生日是<u>几月</u>
jǐ hào
<u>几号</u>?
When is your birthday?

Wǒ de shēng rì shì bā yuè
我的生日是<u>八月</u>
wǔ hào
<u>五号</u>。
My birthday is the 5th of August.

Tā yǒu jǐ ge mèi mei
他有几个妹妹?
How many younger sisters
does he have?

Tā yǒu sān ge mèi mei
他有三个妹妹。
He has three younger sisters.

Nǐ de diàn huà hào mǎ shì
你的电话号码是
duō shǎo
多少?
What's your telephone
number?

Wǒ de diàn huà hào mǎ shì
我的电话号码是
53837126。
My telephone number is
53837126.

Nǐ de xué yuàn yǒu duō shǎo
你的学院有多少
lǎo shī
老师?
How many teachers are there
at your college?

Wǒ de xué yuàn yǒu liù shí ge
我的学院有六十个
lǎo shī
老师。
There are 60 teachers at my
college.

Nǐ shì nǎ guó rén
你是哪国人?
What nationality are you?

Wǒ shì Yīng guó rén
我是英国人。
I am British.

Nǐ men xué yuàn yǒu nǎ xiē
你们学院有哪些
zhuān yè
专业?
Which majors does your
college offer?

Wǒ men xué yuàn yǒu Zhōng wén
我们学院有中文,
Yīng wén hé měi shù zhuān yè
英文和美术专业。
Our college offers Chinese,
English and Art majors.

yào   huì   dǎ suan
2.2 *The simple future with* 要 *,* 会 *and* 打算

You can use 要 **yào** (want to), 会 **huì** (will) and 打算 **dǎsuan**
(plan to) to indicate simple future events. The structure of the
simple future tense in Chinese is the same as in English – you just
put 要 **yào** (want to), 会 **huì** (will) or 打算 **dǎsuan** (plan to)
in front of the main verb. For example:

Zhè ge xīng qī liù wǒ yào qù Běi jīng
这个星期六我要去北京。
I am going to Beijing this Saturday.

Zhōu mò tā yào qù kàn tā de péng you
周末他要去看他的朋友。
He's going to see his friend at the weekend.

Míng tiān wǒ huì qù xué yuàn
明天我会去学院。
I will go to college tomorrow.

Beijing

Xià ge xīng qī wǒ bà ba huì zài Shàng hǎi gōng zuò
下个星期我爸爸会在上海工作。
My father will work in Shanghai next week.

Wǒ dǎ suan xià ge yuè huí Měi guó
我打算下个月回美国。
I plan to return to the USA next month.

Wǒ dǎ suan jīn nián zài Zhōng guó guò chūn jié
我打算今年在中国过春节。
I plan to spend Spring Festival in China this year.

Practice

11 Listen to Liu Hong talking about her holiday plans to Europe (欧洲 **Ōuzhōu**). Based on the information you hear, complete her schedule in English:

Departure time	Country to visit	Arrival time
8 March	_____	_____
_____	Italy	Tuesday
20 March	_____	_____
_____	_____	

12 Two Chinese friends are discussing their holiday plans to Europe (欧洲 Ōuzhōu). Fill in the blanks, choosing from the words given. The first one has been done for you. Then listen to the audio to check if you were right.

yí gòng	cóng	lǚ xíng	yí lù shùn fēng	huí
一共	从	旅行	一路顺风	回

xīng qī	zài	dǎ suan	rán hòu	qù
星期	在	打算	然后	去

Wǒ míng nián huì qù Ōu zhōu   lǚ xíng
A: 我明年会去欧洲 (1)____旅行____。

Tài hǎo le   Nǐ   shén me shí hou zǒu
B: 太好了！你 (2) _____ 什么时候走?

Míng nián wǔ yuè   (3)   qù liǎng ge
A: 明年五月，(3) _____ 去两个

(4) _____ 。

Nǐ huì qù Ōu zhōu nǎ li
B: 你会去欧洲哪里?

Wǒ huì zài Yīng guó zhù wǔ tiān   shí hào cóng Yīng guó
A: 我会在英国住五天，十号从英国

Fǎ guó
(5) _____ 法国。

Rán hòu ne
B: 然后呢?

Rán hòu wǒ huì   Fǎ guó zhù sān tiān
A: 然后我会 (6) _____ 法国住三天，

qù Yì dà lì   Zuì hòu
(7) _____ 去意大利。最后 (8) _____

Yì dà lì qù Xī bān yá   Wǒ wǔ yuè èr shí liù hào
意大利去西班牙。我五月二十六号

Shàng hǎi
(9) _____ 上海。

Zhù nǐ
B: 祝你 (10) _____ !

13 **a.** Imagine that you are going to travel to China. You can see some famous tourist spots on the map below. Decide the dates that you would like to leave and return, what you would like to see in each location and the number of days you will spend there. Discuss your plans with a Chinese friend. Create a short dialogue by yourself or work with a partner.

Great Wall

Forbidden City

Terracotta Warriors

Běijīng
北京

Xī'ān
西安

Sūzhōu
苏州

Shànghǎi
上海

ancient gardens

Hángzhōu
杭州

Guìlín
桂林

Hǎinándǎo
海南岛

City God Temple

beach resorts

West Lake

b. Now you are at a travel agent's. A Chinese person will ask you a few questions. Listen and respond accordingly. There are some sample answers in the Answers section.

14 Read the following and decide which Chinese translation is correct:

1. This Friday is my birthday.

Zhè ge xīng qī sān shì wǒ de shēng rì
a. 这个星期三是我的生日。

Zhè ge xīng qī wǔ shì wǒ de shēng rì
b. 这个星期五是我的生日。

2. I plan to go for a coffee with a friend tomorrow.

Wǒ dǎ suan míng tiān hé wǒ de yí ge péng you qù hē kā fēi
a. 我打算明天和我的一个朋友去喝咖啡。

Wǒ dǎ suan míng tiān qù hē kā fēi hé wǒ de yí ge péng you
b. 我打算明天去喝咖啡和我的一个朋友。

3. David will stay two days in France first.

Dà wéi huì zài Fǎ guó zhù liǎng tiān xiān
a. 大为会在法国住两天先。

Dà wéi huì xiān zài Fǎ guó zhù liǎng tiān
b. 大为会先在法国住两天。

4. When will you go home today?

Nǐ jīn tiān shén me shí hou huí jiā
a. 你今天什么时候回家？

Nǐ jīn tiān shén me shí hou dào jiā
b. 你今天什么时候到家？

5. Where will you go to in China?

Nǐ huì qù Zhōng guó nǎ li
a. 你会去中国哪里？

Nǐ huì qù Zhōng guó ma
b. 你会去中国吗？

6. How many days will you stay in Spain for?

Nǐ huì zài Xī bān yá zhù jǐ ge xīng qī
a. 你会在西班牙住几个星期？

Nǐ huì zài Xī bān yá zhù jǐ tiān
b. 你会在西班牙住几天？

Learning Chinese characters

How Chinese characters are formed (1)

There are a number of ways in which Chinese characters are formed. This will help you to understand the creation and logic behind characters. In this unit, you will learn about 'meaning plus meaning' characters.

These characters are formed with two different components ('radicals' or characters). The meaning of the new character is based on a combination of the two components. Let's take a look at some examples with interesting interpretations:

nán
男 male, man

tián　　　　lì
田 (field) + 力 (strength)

The strength in the field is men.

hǎo
好 good

nǚ　　　　zǐ
女 (female) + 子 (child)

A mother with her child is considered to be a good thing.

ān
安 peace

　　　　　　nǚ
宀 (roof radical) + 女 (female)

In olden times, men could marry as many women as they wanted. But they only found peace if there was one lady in the house.

míng
明 bright

rì　　　yuè
日 (sun) + 月 (moon)

If the sun and the moon were both shining, it would be really bright.

xiū
休 to rest

rén　　　　mù
人 (person) + 木 (tree)

A person leaning against a tree is resting.

Write the characters in the text

15 Try writing the following characters using the stroke order indicated.

年 **nián** year	ノ	┌	仁	┌	丘	年		
月 **yuè** moon, month	)	刀	月	月				
日 **rì** sun, day	l	冂	月	日				
星 **xīng** star	丶	冖	冂	日	尸	尸	星	星	星
期 **qī** period	一	十	廿	廿	甘	其	其	其	期
	期	期	期					
天 **tiān** sky, day	一	二	于	天				
号 **hào** no., date	丶	冖	口	吕	号			
祝 **zhù** to wish	丶	⼀	礻	礻	礻	初	初	祀	祝

今 jīn present	丿	人	仒	今				
明 míng bright	丨	刀	月	日	旳	明	明	明
生 shēng to be born	丿	丶	仁	牛	生			
快 kuài fast, happy	丶	丿	忄	忄	忆	快	快	
乐 lè happy	一	匚	乎	乐	乐			
走 zǒu to walk	一	十	土	卡	走	走	走	
回 huí to return	丨	冂	冋	囘	回	回		
从 cóng from	丿	人	从	从				
到 dào to, arrive	一	工	五	丟	至	至	到	到

Write a birthday card in Chinese

16 Can you read the birthday card 小明 wrote to his mother?

亲爱的妈妈，
祝你
生日快乐!

儿子：小明
2008 年 4 月 24 日
星期四

Now, using the card above as a guide, write your own card in the following space. You may have already figured out that 亲爱的 … **qīn'ài de** … means 'Dear …'. Don't forget to sign your name and write the date at the bottom right of your card.

亲爱的＿＿＿＿＿，

The Chinese horoscope

There are 12 animal signs in the Chinese horoscope: Rat, Ox, Tiger, Rabbit, Dragon, Snake, Horse, Sheep, Monkey, Rooster, Dog and Pig. The year you were born does not necessarily tell you your sign or age in China, because each year the date of the Chinese New Year varies according to the lunar calendar. There are also  five elements attached to each animal sign: wood, water, fire, earth and metal. Therefore, according to the Chinese horoscope, the year of your birth indicates a certain phase of a 60-year period of  time (i.e. 12 signs × 5 elements). There are many different stories relating to the origin of the Chinese horoscope, however, no one really knows the truth. There are many websites nowadays where you can find out your Chinese sign and your Chinese profile. Each sign embodies the characteristics of the animal associated with it from a Chinese perspective. For  example, people born in the year of the horse are outgoing and independent; people born in the year of the monkey are fun and active; and people born in the year of  the dragon are lucky and successful. It is very interesting to learn about Chinese astrology and you will discover that many Chinese people do believe in it.

unit 6
Time

Dì liù kè　　Shí jiān
第六课　时间

In this unit, you will learn:
- How to pronounce Pinyin combinations containing: z, c, s, ua, uo, ia, iao, iang, iong and uan
- How to tell the time and describe your daily routine
- How to make arrangements to go out
- How the Chinese characters are formed (2)
- About traditional festivals in China

Getting the pronunciation right

Pīn yīn liàn xí
拼音练习

In this unit, you will continue to do some basic sound combination practice. First, can you recall how these initials and finals are pronounced? Check your pronunciation with the audio.

z　c　s　ua　uo　ia　iao　iang　iong　uan

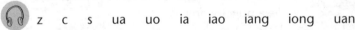

1 Listen to the four tones with the following sounds and repeat them out loud after each set:

zāi zái zǎi zài	suān suán suǎn suàn
jiā jiá jiǎ jià	cāo cáo cǎo cào
xiōng xióng xiǒng xiòng	zuī zuí zuǐ zuì
huā huá huǎ huà	kuō kuó kuǒ kuò
yuān yuán yuǎn yuàn	qiāng qiáng qiǎng qiàng
cē cé cě cè	liāo liáo liǎo liào

2 Listen and circle the tones based on what you hear:

1. cān cán cǎn càn **4.** sī sí sǐ sì
2. zū zú zǔ zù **5.** cēng céng cěng cèng
3. piāo piáo piǎo piào

3 Listen and write down the words you hear in Pinyin with tones:

1. _____ **2.** _____ **3.** _____

4. _____ **5.** _____

4 You met these words in the previous unit. See if you can remember the meaning of the words and mark up their correct tones. Check them against the word lists in Unit 5 on pages 90, 95 and 102.

1. nian **2.** xingqi **3.** wuyue **4.** shengri **5.** zhoumo
6. shu **7.** guo **8.** yiding **9.** youyisi **10.** tingshuo
11. dasuan **12.** shenmeshihou **13.** zou **14.** yigong
15. ranhou **16.** zuihou

Now you have met *all* the sounds in Mandarin Chinese and a lot of the possible combinations. Congratulations! From the next unit on, you will be introduced to all the possible combinations, which means that by the end of the book you should be able to pronounce anything in Mandarin Chinese!

Communicating in Chinese

Hàn yǔ jiāo liú
汉语交流

1 What time is it?

Jǐ diǎn le
几点了?

Key expressions: **Telling the time**

To ask what the time is:

Jǐ diǎn le
几点了?
What time is it?

To say what time it is:

yī diǎn	liǎng diǎn shí fēn	sān diǎn bàn
一点	两点十分	三点半
1 o'clock	10 minutes past 2	half past 3

sì diǎn yí kè	wǔ diǎn sān kè
四点一刻	五点三刻
quarter past 4	quarter to 6 (lit. 3 quarters past 5)

liù diǎn chà wǔ fēn　　chà wǔ fēn liù diǎn
六点差五分 / 差五分六点
5 minutes to 6

5 Listen to three different people asking what the time is.

a. On the street

Qǐngwèn　　jǐ diǎn le
A: 请问, 几点了?

Sān diǎn
B: 三点。

Xiè xie
A: 谢谢!

b. At home

Mā ma   jǐ diǎn le
A: 妈妈，几点了？

Sì diǎn bàn
B: 四点半。

c. In an office

XiǎoWáng   xiàn zài jǐ diǎn le
A: 小王，现在几点了？

Shí yī diǎn sān kè
B: 十一点三刻。

The Bund, Shanghai

6 **a.** Have a look at the following time expressions, and then listen to the recording and repeat each one:

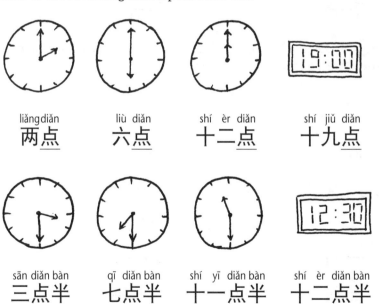

liǎngdiǎn   liù diǎn   shí èr diǎn   shí jiǔ diǎn
两点   六点   十二点   十九点

sān diǎn bàn   qī diǎn bàn   shí yī diǎn bàn   shí èr diǎn bàn
三点半   七点半   十一点半   十二点半

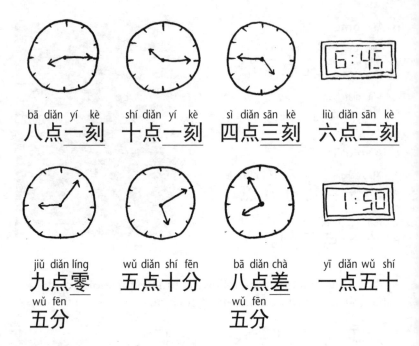

bā diǎn yí kè
八点一刻

shí diǎn yí kè
十点一刻

sì diǎn sān kè
四点三刻

liù diǎn sān kè
六点三刻

jiǔ diǎn líng
九点零
wǔ fēn
五分

wǔ diǎn shí fēn
五点十分

bā diǎn chà
八点差
wǔ fēn
五分

yī diǎn wǔ shí
一点五十

b. Now say the time on each clock in **a** above *before* you hear the correct version on the audio.

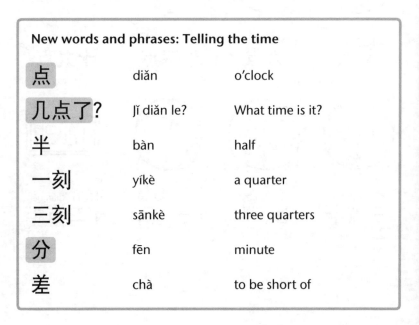

New words and phrases: Telling the time

点	diǎn	o'clock
几点了?	Jǐ diǎn le?	What time is it?
半	bàn	half
一刻	yíkè	a quarter
三刻	sānkè	three quarters
分	fēn	minute
差	chà	to be short of

| 请问 | qǐngwèn | excuse me (lit. please ask) |
| 现在 | xiànzài | now |

了 **Le** is used to indicate that an action or an event has already happened or has been completed. When asking for the time in Chinese, it is usually added to the end of the question as it is assumed that when you give the time, that time has already passed. You will learn more about how it is used to indicate past events in the Chinese language in the later units.

Practice

7 Some people are asking for the time. Write down the answers they are given. Remember the question for asking the time is simply: 几点了? **Jǐ diǎn le?**

1. _____ 2. _____ 3. _____

4. _____ 5. _____ 6. _____

8 Listen to the audio and number the clocks below in the order that you hear them.

9 Looking at the clocks above, ask what the time is and then answer, either with a partner or just by yourself – but out loud!

Rì chéng ān pái
日程安排

2 Talking about daily routines

Key expressions: **Time expressions**

Some time expressions:

měi tiān	měi ge xīng qī	měi ge yuè	měi nián
每天	每个星期	每个月	每年
every day	every week	every month	every year

jīn tiān zǎo shang
今天早上
this morning

jīn tiān xià wǔ
今天下午
this afternoon

jīn tiān wǎn shang
今天晚上
tonight

míng tiān zǎo shang
明天早上
tomorrow morning

míng tiān xià wǔ
明天下午
tomorrow afternoon

míng tiān wǎn shang
明天晚上
tomorrow night

xīng qī yī zǎo shang
星期一早上
Monday morning

xīng qī liù xià wǔ
星期六下午
Saturday afternoon

xīng qī sān wǎn shang
星期三晚上
Wednesday evening

cóng xīng qī èr dào xīng qī tiān
从星期二到星期天
from Tuesday to Sunday

cóng zǎo shang shí diǎn dào xià wǔ sān diǎn
从早上十点到下午三点
from 10am to 3pm

---

10 Look at the cartoon strip on the facing page while listening to 刘红 **Liú Hóng** talking about her daily routine. Listen out for the time expressions used with each activity before you check the text. Listen as many times as you like.

我每天早上八点起床，八点半吃早饭，
Wǒ měi tiān zǎo shang bā diǎn qǐ chuáng   bā diǎn bàn chī zǎo fàn

九点去上班。中午十二点一刻，我在
jiǔ diǎn qù shàng bān   Zhōng wǔ shí èr diǎn yí kè   wǒ zài

公司吃午饭。下午五点下班，我一般六点
gōng sī chī wǔ fàn   Xià wǔ wǔ diǎn xià bān   wǒ yì bān liù diǎn

到家。晚上我七点做饭，孩子们做作业。
dào jiā   Wǎn shang wǒ qī diǎn zuò fàn   hái zi men zuò zuò yè

八点我们吃晚饭。晚饭后，我们有时去
Bā diǎn wǒ men chī wǎn fàn   Wǎn fàn hòu   wǒ men yǒu shí qù

散步，有时看电视，一般十一点睡觉。
sàn bù   yǒu shí kàn diàn shì   yì bān shí yī diǎn shuì jiào

周末的时候，我们常去公园玩儿，也常去
Zhōu mò de shí hou   wǒ men cháng qù gōng yuán wán 'r   yě cháng qù

看电影和买东西。
kàn diàn yǐng hé mǎi dōng xi

New words and phrases: Time expressions and daily routines

每天	měitiān	every day
起床	qǐchuáng	to get up (lit. raise from the bed)
早饭	zǎofàn	breakfast
上班	shàngbān	to (start) work
上午	shàngwǔ	morning
中午	zhōngwǔ	noon
午饭	wǔfàn	lunch
下班	xiàbān	to finish work
一般	yìbān	usually; in general
做	zuò	to make; to do
做饭	zuòfàn	to cook (lit. to make rice)
作业	zuòyè	homework
晚饭	wǎnfàn	dinner
后	hòu	after; afterwards
有时	yǒushí	sometimes
散步	sànbù	to go for a walk
看	kàn	to watch; to see
电视	diànshì	TV (lit. electric vision)
睡觉	shuìjiào	to sleep

···的时候	... de shíhou	When ...
常	cháng	often
公园	gōngyuán	park (lit. public garden)
玩（儿）	wán('r)	to play; have a good time
电影	diànyǐng	film/movie (lit. electric shadow)
买东西	mǎidōngxi	to shop (lit. buy things)

Language note

2.1 *Position of time expressions in a sentence*

The way to express time in Chinese is very similar to English. However, one thing that you need to be careful with is the position of time expressions within a sentence, as this is very different from English. In Chinese, time expressions are used before the events/actions/verbs rather than at the end of sentences, as happens most of the time in English. Take a look at the following sentences expressed in both English and Chinese with the time expressions underlined:

Wǒ zǎo shang qī diǎn qǐ chuáng
我早上七点起床。　　I get up <u>at 7 in the morning</u>.

Tā jiǔ diǎn qù shàng bān
他九点去上班。　　He goes to work <u>at 9 o'clock</u>.

Tā men xīng qī èr shàng wǔ qù mǎi dōng xi
他们星期二上午去买东西。　They go shopping <u>on Tuesday mornings</u>.

To change these sentences into questions, you can use 几点 **jǐ diǎn** for specific times or 什么时候 **shénme shíhou** for more general time spans in place of the time expressions.

Nǐ měi tiān jǐ diǎn qǐ chuáng
你每天几点起床？

What time do you get up every day?

Tā jǐ diǎn qù shàng bān
他几点去上班？

What time does he go to work?

Tā menshén me shí hou qù mǎi dōng xi
他们什么时候去买东西？

When do they go shopping?

Practice

11 Match the time expressions with Liu Hong's activities according to the text in Exercise 10. The first one has been done for you.

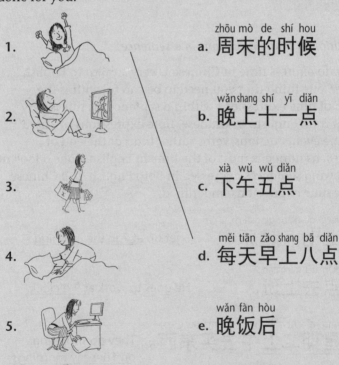

1.

zhōu mò de shí hou
a. 周末的时候

2.

wǎnshang shí yī diǎn
b. 晚上十一点

3.

xià wǔ wǔ diǎn
c. 下午五点

4.

měi tiān zǎo shang bā diǎn
d. 每天早上八点

5.

wǎn fàn hòu
e. 晚饭后

6.

wǎnshang qī diǎn
f. 晚上七点

12 **a.** Now imagine you are Liu Hong. Based on the text, answer the following questions about her routine out loud. Check your answers with the sample answers on the audio.

Nǐ měi tiān jǐ diǎn qǐ chuáng
1. 你每天几点起床？

Nǐ jǐ diǎn qù shàng bān
2. 你几点去上班？

Nǐ zhōng wǔ zài nǎ 'r chī wǔ fàn
3. 你中午在哪儿吃午饭？

Nǐ jǐ diǎn xià bān
4. 你几点下班？

Nǐ jǐ diǎn dào jiā
5. 你几点到家？

Wǎnshang shuí zuò fàn
6. 晚上谁做饭？

Wǎn fàn hòu nǐ zuò shén me
7. 晚饭后，你做什么？

Nǐ jǐ diǎn shuì jiào
8. 你几点睡觉？

Zhōu mò de shí hou nǐ zuò shén me
9. 周末的时候，你做什么？

b. Can you answer the same questions about your own routine? Try it out! Interview a partner in class or a Chinese friend if you can.

13 Look at this page from 李风 **Lǐ Fēng**'s schedule for the week, and answer the questions that follow.

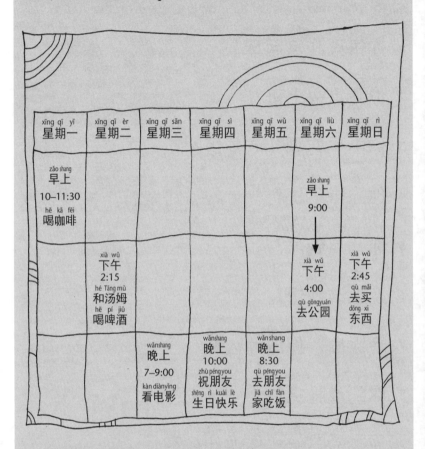

Lǐ Fēng xīng qī yī zuò shén me
1. 李凤星期一做什么?

Tā xīng qī èr xià wǔ hé shuí hē pí jiǔ
2. 他星期二下午和谁喝啤酒?

Tā xīng qī jǐ qù kàn diàn yǐng　Jǐ diǎn
3. 他星期几去看电影? 几点?

Tā shén me shí hou zhù péng you shēng rì kuài lè
4. 他什么时候祝朋友生日快乐?

5. Tā xīng qī wǔ wǎnshang bā diǎn bàn zài nǎ 'r chī fàn
他星期五晚上八点半在哪儿吃饭？

6. Tā zhōu mò zuò shén me
他周末做什么？

7. Tā xīng qī liù qù mǎi dōng xi ma
他星期六去买东西吗？

Check your answers at the back of the book.

14 Try constructing a similar schedule for yourself with your own plans filled in.

xīng qī yī 星期一	xīng qī èr 星期二	xīng qī sān 星期三	xīng qī sì 星期四	xīng qī wǔ 星期五	xīng qī liù 星期六	xīng qī rì 星期日

3 Making a date

Key expressions: Making arrangements to go out

To make a simple suggestion:

Nǐ xiǎng qù kàn diàn yǐng ma
你想去看电影吗?

Would you like to go to
a film/movie?

xiǎng bú tài xiǎng bù xiǎng
想 / 不太想 / 不想

yes/not really/no

To suggest a time:

Nǐ xiǎng shén me shí hou qù
你想什么时候去?

When would you like
to go?

Xīng qī liù wǎn shang kě yǐ ma
星期六晚上可以吗?

Would Saturday night
be ok?

Xià wǔ sān diǎn zěn me yàng
下午三点怎么样?

How/What about 3pm?

kǒng pà bù xíng   dāng rán   hǎo de
恐怕不行 / 当然 / 好的

I'm afraid not/of course/
ok

To ask for preference:

Nǐ shuō nǎ ge hǎo
你说哪个好?

Which one do you prefer?

To confirm a date:

Bú jiàn bú sàn
不见不散。

See you there. (lit. no see, no leave)

15 Xiao Wang and Xiao Li would like to go out to see a movie
together but they've both got a busy weekend. Listen to their
conversation and how they finally manage to agree on a time.

Xiao Wang:
小李，我听说周末有新电影，
你想去看吗？

Xiao Li:
好啊。你想什么时候去？

Xiao Wang:
星期六下午三点可以吗？

Xiao Li:
星期六下午我要去买东西，恐怕不
行。星期天我有时间，要么我们星
期天去吧！星期天有票吗？

Xiao Wang:
有，上午十一点半或者下午四点
一刻。你说哪个好？

Xiao Li:
下午的吧，看完电影我们还可以
一起去吃晚饭。

Xiao Wang:
好主意。那么我们星期天下午
四点见，怎么样？

Xiao Li:
好，不见不散。

New words and phrases: Making a date

想	xiǎng	would like to; to want to
当然	dāngrán	of course
说	shuō	to talk; to say
新	xīn	new
可以	kěyǐ	can; could; to be able to
要	yào	to need to; to want to
恐怕	kǒngpà	to be afraid
不行	bùxíng	not possible; no way
时间	shíjiān	time
要么	yàome	or; either ... or ...
票	piào	ticket
或者	huòzhě	or; alternatively
完	wán	to finish; to complete
还	hái	also; in addition to
主意	zhǔyi	idea
那么	nàme	in that case; then
不见不散	bújiànbúsàn	used to confirm a date (lit. no see, no leave)

Language notes

3.1 *Saying 'yes' and 'no' in Chinese*

When asked a 'yes or no' question in Chinese, you don't usually answer with the actual word 'yes' (是 **shì**) or 'no' (不 **bù**). Instead, the 'yes' and 'no' is provided by confirming the information being asked. For example, imagine you ask a Chinese person, 'Are you busy?' (你忙吗? **Nǐ máng ma?**) The Chinese person would reply 忙 **máng** (busy, meaning 'yes') or 不忙 **bù máng** (not busy, meaning 'no'). Consider the following examples:

Míng tiān shì nǐ de shēng rì ma
明天是你的生日吗?
Is tomorrow your birthday?

Shì   Bú shì
是 / 不是。
Yes/No.

Nǐ yǒu dì di ma
你有弟弟吗?
Do you have younger brothers?

Yǒu   Méi yǒu
有 / 没有。
Yes/No.

Tā gōng zuò ma
他工作吗?
Does he work?

Gōng zuò   Bù gōng zuò
工作 / 不工作。
Yes/No.

Jīn tiān nǐ qù kàn diàn yǐng ma
今天你去看电影吗?
Are you going to watch the film today?

Qù   Bú qù
去 / 不去。
Yes/No.

3.2 *The use of exclamation words 啊 and 吧*
a   ba

In Chinese, a lot of exclamation words are used to express emotions. These words are predominantly at the end of a sentence and have neutral tones. Here we introduce the exclamations 啊 **a** and 吧 **ba**.

啊 **A** is used to express a strong emotion and enforce the meaning of the word used before it, either positive or negative.

Shì a	Hǎo a	Duì a
是啊!	好啊!	对啊!
That's right!	Excellent!	That's right!

吧 **Ba**, on the other hand, is usually used at the end of a proposal or suggestion to make it sound less blunt and direct. It can be roughly translated as 'shall we?' or 'please'.

Jiào wǒ Xiǎomíng ba
叫我小明吧!
Please, call me Xiaoming!

Wǒ men míng tiān qù ba
我们明天去吧!
Shall we go tomorrow?/
Let's go tomorrow.

yī
3.3 *The use of* 一 *to indicate a brief action*

Verb + yī + verb is a structure used to indicate brief actions.

kàn yí kàn	shuō yi shuō	xiǎng yi xiǎng
看一看	**说一说**	**想一想**
to have a look	to talk about	to think about

chá yì chá	shì yí shì	wèn yí wèn
查一查	**试一试**	**问一问**
to have a check	to have a try	to ask about

When used to give instructions, this structure also softens the tone of the instruction or order, making the sentence more polite. It is interchangeable with the structure **verb + yí xià** (see Unit 3, Language note 2.2). In spoken Chinese, the 一 yī can even be omitted. Just repeat the verb for the same effect, for example:

看看 kàn kan, **说说** shuō shuo.

Practice

16 Answer the following questions in English, based on the dialogue in Exercise 15:

1. What did Xiao Wang suggest doing?
2. Why couldn't Xiao Li go on Saturday afternoon?
3. What time did Xiao Wang and Xiao Li eventually agree to meet?

17 On the recording someone asks you to go out and do various things. Listen and reply to each of the requests, agreeing to go or politely declining.

1.
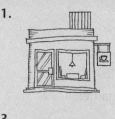

2.

3.

4.

18 How do you say the following in Chinese? Check your answers in the Answers section.

1. Let me have a look.
2. Let me think about it.
3. Let her have a try.
4. Let me talk about my job for a bit.
5. He would just like to check the time quickly.

Learning Chinese characters

Xué hàn zì
学汉字

How Chinese characters are formed (2)

In Unit 5, we looked at 'meaning plus meaning' characters. Now let's look at 'meaning plus sound' characters.

These types of character are also formed with two different components ('radicals' or characters). Usually, one component indicates the meaning of the new character and the other indicates its possible pronunciation. Occasionally, the second component may contribute to the meaning as well as the sound. But be careful as the tones may change and the pronunciation may not be exactly the same.

Meaning radical	+	Sound	=	New character

Meaning radical + Sound =   New character

辶
to walk far

口
to enclose

月
body parts

饣
food

女
female

禾
farm

氵
water

扌
hand

yuán
元

jǐ
几

jiā
家

mò
莫

yuǎn
远
far

yuán
园
garden

jī
肌
skin

jī
饥
hungry

jià
嫁
to marry

jià
稼
grain

mò
漠
desert

mō
摸
to touch

As you can see, it is important to recognize some basic radicals and simple characters. Radicals contain a fixed meaning and in the later units we will focus on some of the most common radicals. They will enable you get a rough idea of the meaning of the whole character.

Write the characters in the text

19 Try writing the following characters using the stroke order indicated.

点 diǎn o'clock	丨	卜	卜	占	占	点	点	点	点
分 fēn minute	丿	八	今	分					
半 bàn half	丶	丷	丷	㐅	半				
上 shàng to be on	丨	卜	上						
下 xià to be off	一	丁	下						
午 wǔ noon	丿	𠂉	𠂉	午					
晚 wǎn to be late	丨	刀	月	日	日	日	日	晚	晚
	晚	晚							

去 qù to go	一	十	土	去	去			
吃 chī to eat	丶	口	口	吖	吃	吃		
看 kàn to watch	一	二	三	手	禾	看	看	看	看
玩 wán to play	一	二	于	王	玗	玗	玗	玩	
做 zuò to make	丿	亻	仁	什	什	估	估	做	做
	做	做						
饭 fàn cooked rice	丿	勹	饣	饣	饣	饭	饭		
睡 shuì to sleep	丨	刀	月	月	目	目	盱	盱	盱
	盱	睡	睡	睡				
买 mǎi to buy	一	乛	乛	买	买	买		
要 yào to want	一	一	二	西	西	西	要	要	要

Recognize the characters in the text

20 Match the Chinese character captions with the pictures. Note that there is one extra caption.

1. _____   2. _____   3. _____

4. _____   5. _____

a. 吃饭   b. 看电视   c. 去公园玩

d. 做饭   e. 上班   f. 睡觉

21 Circle the words you can identify and write out their meanings in English. One has already been done for you.

teacher

我	是	老	师	很	儿
他	你	好	吃	忙	子
叫	们	早	下	工	作
小	明	上	午	不	妈
今	天	中	饭	去	妈
女	英	国	人	看	书

Chinese traditional festivals

There are many traditional Chinese festivals. They are all based on the lunar calendar and thus the dates vary from year to year. The biggest and the most important Chinese festival is the Spring Festival, also known as Chinese New Year, when people usually celebrate for 15 days. This involves a lot of traditional Chinese food, such as dumplings, spring rolls, fish, oranges and rice cakes. Each food carries a particular meaning, usually expressing good wishes and expectations for the New Year. People will usually wear red for good luck, set off fireworks, and visit family and friends. At the end of the Spring

 Festival, there is a Lantern Festival. People make their own lanterns and hang them in their houses. They also gather together and have Chinese character quizzes (a game where you have to guess what character a simple poem is based on). The traditional food to eat during the Lantern Festival is sweet rice balls. Other festivals include the Dragon Boat Festival, Qingming Festival (Tomb Sweeping), Moon Festival and Chongyang Festival (Double Ninth). You came across some of these in Unit 5.

In the past, people would only have days off work during the Spring Festival. However, in 2008, the Chinese government decided to set national holidays for each traditional festival. It was felt that this would further promote and preserve Chinese traditional customs and culture.

7 Shopping

ì qī kè   Gòu wù
弟七课   购物

In this unit, you will learn:
- How to ask for and understand prices
- About shopping for everyday items in Chinese
- How words are formed (1)
- About the art of bargaining in China

Getting the pronunciation right

Pīn yīn liàn xí
拼音练习

For a complete list of the sound combinations in Mandarin Chinese, see the Appendix (page 306). A recording of all the sounds is available at: www.palgrave.com/modernlanguages/xiang.

It is important to pronounce the sound combinations as accurately as possible. The key is to say them over and over and over again. We will continue to work on these from this unit on and also introduce some more culturally-oriented activities, such as reading Chinese poems, tongue twisters and song lyrics.

1 Listen and mark the tones on the following syllables:

1. ma   **2.** fu   **3.** bu   **4.** me   **5.** pou   **6.** mu
7. pa   **8.** pian   **9.** jun   **10.** qu

2 Listen and write down the words you hear in Pinyin with tones:

1. _____   2. _____   3. _____

4. _____   5. _____

3 Fun time: Tongue twisters are very popular in China, especially with schoolchildren. Try the following one which plays with the tones. Good luck!

Mā má mǎ mà
妈麻马骂   **Mother, hemp, horse, to scold**

Mā ma zhòng má
妈妈种麻，   Mother grows hemp,

wǒ qù fàng mǎ
我去放马，   I go to graze the horse,

mǎ chī le má
马吃了麻，   the horse eats the hemp,

mā ma mà mǎ
妈妈骂马。   mother scolds the horse.

**Communicating
in Chinese**

Hàn yǔ jiāo liú
汉语交流

1 Understanding Chinese currency

Zhōng guó qián bì
中国钱币

 4 The Chinese currency is the 人民币 **rénmínbì** (RMB or ¥). It has three units rather than the two found in most Western countries. The basic unit is the **yuán** (formal) / **kuài** (informal). The smallest unit is the **fēn**, which is 0.01 of a **yuán**. However, there is also a middle unit, which is 0.1 of a **yuán**, and is called the **jiǎo** (formal) / **máo** (informal). It is important to remember to say 5 **jiǎo** rather than 50 **fēn**. Only the informal spoken forms will be used on the audio.

100 RMB	**50 RMB**

yì bǎi yuán   yì bǎi kuài
一百元 / 一百块

wǔ shí yuán   wǔ shí kuài
五十元 / 五十块

20 RMB	10 RMB
èr shí yuán　èr shí kuài 二十元 / 二十块	shí yuán　shí kuài 十元 / 十块
5 RMB	**2 RMB**
wǔ yuán　wǔ kuài 五元 / 五块	liǎng yuán　liǎng kuài 两元 / 两块
0.5 RMB	**0.2 RMB**
wǔ jiǎo　wǔ máo 五角 / 五毛	liǎng jiǎo　liǎng máo 两角 / 两毛
0.1 RMB	**0.05 RMB**
yì jiǎo　yì máo 一角 / 一毛	wǔ fēn 五分
0.02 RMB	**0.01 RMB**
liǎng fēn 两分	yì fēn 一分

The final monetary unit is often omitted from the end of a price in spoken Mandarin, especially if a larger unit has already been mentioned (e.g. ¥2.5 **liǎng kuài wǔ**). When there is no 角 jiǎo / 毛 máo unit, but there is a 分 fēn unit (e.g. ¥2.05 **liǎng kuài líng wǔ**), you should say the zero placeholder.

New words and phrases: Understanding Chinese currency

元	yuán	a monetary unit in RMB, ¥1.00
块	kuài	same as yuan but more informal
角	jiǎo	a monetary unit in RMB, ¥0.10
毛	máo	same as jiao but more informal
分	fēn	a monetary unit in RMB, ¥0.01
块	kuài	(measure word, for piece, slice, etc.)

Practice

5 **a.** Listen to the audio and write down the sequence in which you hear the following prices.

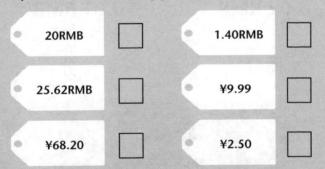

20RMB	☐	1.40RMB	☐
25.62RMB	☐	¥9.99	☐
¥68.20	☐	¥2.50	☐

b. Try saying the amounts listed below out loud. Check your answers in the Answers section.

| 20RMB | 100RMB | 12.30RMB | 76.01RMB |
| ¥234.99 | ¥1000 | ¥23.40 | ¥45.88 |

6 Liu Hong has overspent this week, and is trying to remember everything she has bought.

a. Listen to Liu Hong going through her list and write down the sequence of the items as she says them in the pictures below.

b. Listen again and fill in the four missing prices.

c. Complete the description of each picture giving the item and price. The first one has been done for you. (If you cannot remember how measure words work, have another look through Unit 4.) Check your answers at the back of the book.

Yì bēi kā fēi liǎng kuài wǔ máo
一杯咖啡两块五毛。

Yì běn shū
一本书_____。

Yí jiàn máo yī
一件毛衣_____。

Yì zhāng diàn yǐng piào
一张电影票_____。

Yí kuài dàn gāo
一块蛋糕_____。

_____。

_____。

_____。

2 How much?

Duō shǎo qián
多少钱?

> ### Key expressions: Asking for and giving prices
>
> *To ask what someone wants to buy and to respond when asked:*
>
> Nǐ yào mǎi shén me
> 你要买什么?
> What do you want to buy?
>
> Wǒ yào mǎi yì bēi kā fēi
> 我要买一杯咖啡。
> I want to buy a cup of coffee.
>
> Yǒu kě lè ma
> 有可乐吗?
> Do you have Coke?
>
> Hái yào bié de ma
> 还要别的吗?
> Do you want anything else?
>
> *To ask for and give a price:*
>
> Duō shǎo qián
> 多少钱?
> How much?
>
> Yí gòng duō shǎo qián
> 一共多少钱?
> How much altogether?
>
> Yì bēi kě lè duō shǎo qián
> 一杯可乐多少钱?
> How much is a glass of Coke?
>
> Yì bēi kě lè wǔ kuài
> 一杯可乐五块。
> A glass of Coke is 5RMB.
>
> *To pay and give change:*
>
> Zhè shì shí kuài
> 这是十块。
> This/Here is 10RMB.
>
> Gěi nǐ shí kuài
> 给你十块。
> (I) give you 10RMB.
>
> Zhǎo nǐ wǔ kuài
> 找你五块。
> Here's your 5RMB change.

7 You are going to hear four dialogues taking place in different shops. Pay particular attention to how you ask for the price in Chinese: 多少钱? **Duō shǎo qián ?**

a. In a bakery

Nǐ hǎo   wǒ yào mǎi
A: 你好，我要买

miàn bāo
面包。

Hǎo de   Yào jǐ ge
B: 好的。要几个?

Liǎng ge   duō shǎo qián
A: 两个，多少钱?

Liù kuài
B: 六块。

b. In a kiosk

Nǐ hǎo   yì píng kuàng quán shuǐ
A: 你好，一瓶矿泉水。

Hǎo de   Sān kuài
B: 好的。三块。

Yǒu yóu piào ma
A: 有邮票吗?

Yǒu
B: 有。

Duō shǎo qián
A: 多少钱?

Liǎng kuài yì zhāng
B: 两块一张。

Hǎo   wǒ mǎi sì zhāng
A: 好，我买四张。

Yí gòng shí yì kuài
B: 一共十一块。

Gěi nǐ wǔ shí
A: 给你五十。

Hǎo   zhǎo nǐ sān shí jiǔ kuài
B: 好，找你三十九块。

c. In a book store

Xiān sheng   zhè běn shū duō shǎo qián
A: 先生，这本书多少钱?

Sān shí bā kuài sì máo   Hái yào bié de ma
B: 三十八块四毛。还要别的吗?

Bú yào le   Xiè xie
A: 不要了。谢谢。

d. In a fast-food shop

A: 小姐，你要买什么？
Xiǎo jiě   nǐ yào mǎi shén me

B: 一个汉堡，一杯可乐，一共多少钱？
Yí ge hàn bǎo   yì bēi kě lè   yí gòng duō shǎo qián

A: 汉堡五块二一个，可乐三块一杯，
Hàn bǎo wǔ kuài èr yí ge   kě lè sān kuài yì bēi
一共八块二。
yí gòng bā kuài èr

B: 这是十块。
Zhè shì shí kuài

A: 好，找你一块八。谢谢。
Hǎo   zhǎo nǐ yí kuài bā   Xiè xie

New words and phrases: Asking for and giving prices

面包	miànbāo	bread
钱	qián	money
矿泉水	kuàngquánshuǐ	mineral water
水	shuǐ	water
邮票	yóupiào	stamp
给	gěi	to give
找	zhǎo	to give change back
别的	biéde	other (things)
小姐	xiǎojiě	Miss; young lady
汉堡	hànbǎo	burger
可乐	kělè	Coke

Please note that the meaning of 小姐 **Xiǎojiě** (Miss) has changed in some big cities in China over the last few years and now has the negative connotation of 'prostitute'. Of course, this does not affect its use in official settings and the term is widely used with no negative connotations outside of the big cities. It is also fine when a surname is used before the title.

Language notes

2.1 *The question words* 几 *jǐ and* 多少 *duō shǎo*

几 **Jǐ** is always used with a measure word and usually refers to an amount less than ten. 多少 **Duōshǎo** is used when the amount is assumed to be ten or more and the measure word can be omitted in the question.

Nǐ yǒu jǐ běn shū
你有几本书?
How many books do you have?

Wǒ yǒu sān běn shū
我有三本书。
I have three books.

Nǐ yǒu duō shǎo qián
你有多少钱?
How much money do you have?

Wǒ yǒu bā shí kuài qián
我有八十块钱。
I have 80RMB.

2.2 *Sentence order when asking about prices*

These three sentence orders are all correct and can all be used to ask for and give a unit price:

Yì bēi pí jiǔ duō shǎo qián
一杯啤酒多少钱?

Yì bēi pí jiǔ sì kuài wǔ
一杯啤酒四块五。

Pí jiǔ duō shǎo qián yì bēi
啤酒多少钱一杯?

Pí jiǔ sì kuài wǔ yì bēi
啤酒四块五一杯。

Pí jiǔ yì bēi duō shǎo qián
啤酒一杯多少钱?

Pí jiǔ yì bēi sì kuài wǔ
啤酒一杯四块五。

How much is a glass of beer?

It's ¥4.50 for a glass of beer.

Practice

8 Answer the following questions based on Exercise 7.

Miàn bāo duō shǎo qián yí ge
1. 面包多少钱一个?

Yì zhāng yóu piào duō shǎo qián
2. 一张邮票多少钱?

Yì běn shū duō shǎo qián
3. 一本书多少钱?

Yí ge hàn bǎo hé yì bēi kě lè   yí gòng duō shǎo qián
4. 一个汉堡和一杯可乐，一共多少钱?

9 Listen to three short shopping dialogues. Decide if the following statements are true 对 **duì** or false 不对 **bú duì**.

Situation a

Yì bēi kě lè sān kuài liù
1. 一杯可乐三块六。   _____

Tā yào yì bēi kě lè
2. 她要一杯可乐。   _____

Situation b

Tā mǎi liǎng ge miàn bāo hé sì kuài dàn gāo
1. 她买两个面包和四块蛋糕。   _____

Yí gòng shí bā kuài jiǔ máo
2. 一共十八块九毛。   _____

Situation c

Yí jiàn máo yī liǎng bǎi qī shí wǔ kuài
1. 一件毛衣两百七十五块。   _____

Tā yào mǎi máo yī   bú yào mǎi xié
2. 她要买毛衣，不要买鞋。   _____

10 Look at the pictures below and enquire about the price of
each object. Either work with a partner who gives the price or
say the price out loud yourself. You will find some suggested
questions and responses in the Answers section.

1. ¥40.00

2. ¥10.00

3. ¥15.00

4. ¥230.00

5. ¥9.99

6. ¥3.50

7. ¥599.99

8. ¥7.50

9. ¥360.00

11 Role play: Create a short dialogue between a customer and
a sales assistant in the following situations. Work with a partner
or take both roles yourself.

- Buying food in a fast food restaurant
- Buying some drinks at a kiosk
- Buying clothes and shoes in a department store

3 Too expensive!

Tài guì le
太贵了!

Key expressions: Bargaining

To ask for a cheaper price:

Tài guì le
太贵了!
Too expensive!

Zài pián yi   yì diǎn ba
再便宜一点吧!
A bit cheaper please!

To suggest a price:

Wǔ shí kuài   zěn me yàng   Wǔ shí kuài   hǎo ma
五十块，怎么样? / 五十块，好吗?
How about ¥50?

To refuse or accept a price:

bù xíng
不行
no way

hǎo ba
好吧
ok

Wǒ yào le
我要了。
I will take it.

Wǒ bú yào le
我不要了。
I will leave it.

---

12 You can bargain in most markets and small shops in China. In this dialogue Xiao Li is negotiating with a shop assistant over a vase. Pay attention to how to negotiate the price. What is the outcome of their discussion?

shop assistant:
Xiǎo jiě xiǎng mǎi shén me
小姐想买什么?

Xiao Li:
Zhè ge huā píng duō shǎo qián
这个花瓶多少钱?

shop assistant:
Sān bǎi kuài
三百块。

Xiao Li:
Sān bǎi kuài　　Tài guì le　　Liǎng bǎi kuài
三百块？太贵了！两百块，
zěn me yàng
怎么样？

shop assistant:
Bù xíng　　nǐ kàn　　zhè ge huā píng duō piàoliang
不行，你看，这个花瓶多漂亮!
Liǎng bǎi bā　　hǎo ma
两百八，好吗？

Xiao Li:
Zài pián yi　yì diǎn ba
再便宜一点吧!

shop assistant:
Hǎo ba　　hǎo ba　　yì kǒu jià
好吧，好吧，一口价，
liǎng bǎi wǔ mài gěi nǐ
两百五卖给你。

Xiao Li:
Hǎo　　wǒ yào le　　Gěi nǐ qián
好，我要了! 给你钱。

shop assistant:
Hǎo　　xià cì zài lái
好，下次再来。

So the final price is 250RMB. Did you get it?

New words and phrases: Bargaining

一点	yìdiǎn	a little bit
售货员	shòuhuòyuán	shop assistant
花瓶	huāpíng	vase
贵	guì	expensive
多	duō	so; really

漂亮	piàoliang	pretty; beautiful
再	zài	again
便宜	piányi	cheap
一口价	yìkǒujià	final price (lit. one mouth price)
卖	mài	to sell
下次	xiàcì	next time

In Chinese, 'to buy' is 买 **mǎi** and 'to sell' is 卖 **mài**, and when you put these two characters together, the resulting word 买卖 **mǎimài** means 'to trade' or 'to do business'. It literally means to buy and then to sell. The words 买 **mǎi** and 卖 **mài** show how important tones are in Chinese. You obviously don't want to confuse people in terms of whether you are wanting to buy or sell!

Language notes

Tài   le
3.1 太 ··· 了 *construction*

太 **Tài** + **adjective** + 了 **le** is a very common construction in Chinese. It indicates an excess of something.

tài hǎo le	tài duō le	tài lèi le	tài guì le
太好了	太多了	太累了	太贵了
great	too much/many	too tired	too expensive

tài pián yi le	tài piàoliang le	tài dà le	tài xiǎo le
太便宜了	太漂亮了	太大了	太小了
so cheap	so beautiful	too big	too small

3.2 *Making suggestions in Chinese*

There are many short phrases you can use to make a suggestion or ask someone's opinion in Chinese. State your suggestion first, and then add these short phrases to probe for an opinion:

zěn me yàng
怎么样?
How about it?

xíng ma
行吗?
Is that ok?

hǎo ma
好吗?
Is that ok?

Sān bǎi wǔ shí kuài   zěn me yàng
三百五十块，怎么样?
How about ¥350?

Zài pián yi diǎn   xíng ma
再便宜点，行吗?
How about a bit cheaper?

Wǒ men míng tiān qù hē kā fēi   hǎo ma
我们明天去喝咖啡，好吗?
Shall we go for a coffee tomorrow?

Practice

13 How do you say the following in Chinese?

1. Too expensive!

3. A bit cheaper!

2. How about ¥300?

4. Final price, ¥50!

14 Now imagine you are going to a market. Take part in the dialogue on the recording, speaking after the prompts. You will hear the correct answers after each pause.

Learning Chinese characters

Xué hàn zì
学汉字

How words are formed (1)

A word in Chinese is usually constructed with two or three characters and, in that case, each character only represents one syllable. In this unit, we will introduce ways that Chinese noun words and adjective words can be formed from a combination of single characters.

Construction of nouns

1. noun + noun

niú nǎi
牛奶 milk
= cow + milk

diàn huà
电话 telephone
= electricity + conversation

diàn shì
电视 television
= electricity + vision

shǒu biǎo
手表 watch
= hand + clock

2. adjective + noun

xiǎo xué
小学 primary school
= small + learning

gōngyuán
公园 park
= public + garden

dà xué
大学 university
= big + learning

dà rén
大人 adult
= big + person

3. verb + noun

xué sheng
学生 student
= to study + young person

xué fèi
学费 tuition fee
= to study + expenses

qù nián
去年 last year
= to go + year

yǎn yuán
演员 actor
= to act + person

4. adjective + adjective

dà xiǎo
大小 size =
big + small

hǎo dǎi
好歹 rightness, justice
= good + bad

lǎo shào
老少 people
= old + young

kùn nan
困难 difficulty
= sleepy + hard

Construction of adjectives

1. adjective + adjective

měi lì
美丽 beautiful
= beautiful + beautiful!

míng liàng
明亮 bright
= bright + bright!

gāo dà
高大 huge
= tall + big

xióng wěi
雄伟 magnificent
= male + great

2. adjective + noun

tián mì
甜蜜 sweet
= sweet + honey

kōng dòng
空洞 empty; hollow
= empty + cave

3. adjective + verb

hǎo chī
好吃 delicious
= good + to eat

hǎo kàn
好看 good looking
= good + to look at

nán dǒng
难懂 difficult = difficult +
to understand

nán tīng
难听 bad sounding
= difficult + to listen

4. verb + noun

shū xīn
舒心 satisfied; pleased
= to spread out + heart

shùn lì
顺利 smooth
= to go in the same
direction + profit

5. verb + adjective

fēi kuài
飞快 very fast
= to fly + fast

níng zhòng
凝重 imposing
= to condense + heavy

As you can see, the ways in which Chinese words are formed
are very logical and meaningful. Each character has its own
meaning but a word is usually a combination of two or more
single characters. Learning some basic Chinese characters will
also allow you to guess at the meaning of unknown words
that contain those characters, as the meaning of the single
characters usually remains unchanged.

Recognize the characters in the text

15 Write the characters for each of these items on the correct label in the picture:

1. 汉堡   2. 矿泉水   3. 面包   4. 可乐
5. 鞋   6. 毛衣   7. 啤酒   8. 蛋糕

Write the characters in the text

16 Try writing the following characters using the stroke order indicated.

元 **yuán** (Chinese currency)	一	二	于	元				
块 **kuài** (Chinese currency)	一	十	圠	圤	圠	垆	块	

毛 máo (Chinese currency)	´	二	三	毛				
多 duō many, much	´	ク	タ	多	多	多		
少 shǎo few, little	`	八	小	少				
钱 qián money	´	广	上	乍	钅	钅	钅	钱	钱
	钱							
给 gěi to give	´	乡	纟	纟	纠	纵	纶	给	给
找 zhǎo to give change back	一	十	才	扌	找	找	找		
想 xiǎng would like to	一	十	オ	木	朾	相	相	相	相
	相	想	想	想				
漂亮 piào liang beautiful	`	``	氵	汀	泸	沪	沜	洒
	漂	漂	漂	漂	漂			
	`	二	广	市	亭	亭	高	亭	亮

贵 guì expensive	丶	冖	口	中	虫	尹	弗	贵	贵
便宜 piányi cheap	丿	亻	亻	仁	佰	佰	佰	伊	便
	丶	丷	宀	宀	宀	宁	宜	宜	
卖 mài to sell	一	十	士	击	幸	去	卖	卖	
次 cì time (refers to frequency of action)	丶	冫	丷	汐	次	次			
再 zài again	一	冂	丏	丹	再	再			

The art of bargaining

For Chinese people, bargaining is not only a way of getting the best price but also a way of socializing. The key to bargaining is to know how to 'make friends'. Walking down Huaihai Road in Shanghai, you will hear salesmen saying: 'Bags, watches, my friend, I can sell one to you more cheaply.' But you are hardly their friend! The reverse strategy works well when you are trying to bargain. Try saying 交个朋友嘛！便宜点！ **Jiāo ge péngyou ma! Piányi diǎn!** (Let's be friends! A bit cheaper!) or 我下次带朋友来！ **Wǒ xiàcì dài péngyou lái!** (I will bring my friends next time).

8 Eating and drinking

Dì bā kè　　Cān yǐn
第八课　餐饮

In this unit, you will learn:
- How to order simple drinks and coffees
- About eating out in a restaurant in China and reading a menu
- How Chinese words are formed (2)
- About the food culture in China

Getting the pronunciation right

Pīn yīn liàn xí
拼音练习

Following on from Unit 7, let's continue working on tones and sound combinations.

1 Listen and mark the tones on the following syllables:

1. ge　　**2.** nin　　**3.** jia　　**4.** la　　**5.** ri　　**6.** jiu
7. dui　　**8.** hou　　**9.** gei　　**10.** lian

2 Listen and write down the word you hear in Pinyin with tones:

1. _____　**2.** _____　**3.** _____

4. _____　**5.** _____

3 Fun time: Chinese poetry has a long history, and there are different forms and features of poetry from the different dynasties. Poetry was most popular in the Tang (AD 618–907) and Song (AD 960–1279) dynasties. In this unit, you will learn one of the most popular poems from the Tang dynasty by one of the greatest Chinese romantic poets, Li Bai.

Lǐ Bái de   jìng yè sī
李白的《静夜思》：

Chuáng qián míng yuè guāng
床 前 明 月 光 ，   The moonlight in front of the bed,

yí shì dì shàng shuāng
疑 是 地 上 霜 。   Suspect it is the frost on the ground.

Jǔ tóu wàng míng yuè
举 头 望 明 月 ，   One raises his head to watch the moon,

dī tóu sī gù xiāng
低 头 思 故 乡 。   Looks down and misses his home town.

The poet was trying to express his sadness at being away from home during the Moon Festival, a very special time when a family is supposed to be together.

| Communicating in Chinese | Hàn yǔ jiāo liú 汉语交流 |

1 What would you like to drink?   Nín hē shén me
                                          您喝什么？

Key expressions: **Ordering drinks**

To offer someone a drink:

Nín hē   diǎn   shén me   Liǎng wèi hē   diǎn   shén me
您喝（点）什么？/ 两位喝（点）什么？/

Jǐ wèi hē   diǎn   shén me
几位喝（点）什么？
What would you/you two/you (plural) like to drink?

Nín yào jiā nǎi yóu ma   Nín yào jiā bīng kuài 'r ma
您要加奶油吗？   您要加冰块儿吗？
Would you like (to add) cream? Would you like (to add) ice?

Qǐng shāo děng
请稍等。
Just a minute.

Méi wèn tí
没问题。
No problem.

To ask for a drink:

Wǒ yào yì bēi kā fēi
我要一杯咖啡。
I want a cup of coffee.

Lái yì píng pí jiǔ
来一瓶啤酒。
Please bring a bottle of beer.

Kě yǐ gěi wǒ men chá ma
可以给我们茶吗？
Could you give us tea?

Yǒu mei yǒu kā fēi
有没有咖啡？
Do you have coffee?

Jiā nǎi bú jiā táng
加奶，不加糖。
Please add milk but no sugar.

---

4 See if you can match the English with the Chinese. They sound quite similar!

1. Coca-Cola **2.** Champagne **3.** Whisky **4.** Rum
5. Vodka **6.** Soda **7.** Cappuccino **8.** Brandy

wēi shì jì
a. 威士忌

fú tè jiā
b. 伏特加

bái lán dì
c. 白兰地

lǎng mǔ jiǔ
d. 朗姆酒

sū dá shuǐ
e. 苏打水

xiāng bīng
f. 香槟

kě kǒu kě lè
g. 可口可乐

kǎ bù qí nuò
h. 卡布奇诺

You may have been surprised at just how easy Exercise 4 was. All of these words sound familiar because they were imported from English, so they mimic the English pronunciation. This happens mostly with foreign names, places (as in Unit 3) and imported products. In these cases, the Chinese characters function purely as a way of representing sounds, not meanings.

5　Listen to the following two short dialogues in a bar.

Dialogue a

Nǐ hǎo
A: 你好。

Nǐ hǎo　　Liǎng píng Qīng dǎo　pí　jiǔ
B: 你好。两瓶青岛啤酒，

yì　bēi hóng pú tao jiǔ
一杯红葡萄酒。

Sì　shí wǔ kuài
A: 四十五块。

Gěi　　　xiè　xie
B: 给，谢谢。

Dialogue b

Liǎng wèi xiǎo jiě　hē shén me
A: 两位小姐喝什么？

Yì　bēi wēi shì　jì　jiā bīng kuài
B: 一杯威士忌加冰块。

Wǒ yào yì bēi kě lè jiā fú
C: 我要一杯可乐加伏

tè　jiā
特加。

6 Order your drink in response to the waiter on the recording. First order yourself a glass of beer, and then replay the recording and order yourself a bottle of wine. If you are working with a partner, take turns to act out the scene as customer and waiter.

7 Now listen to the following two dialogues in a café.

Dialogue a

Zǎo shang hǎo   Nǐ men yào diǎn shén me
A: 早上好。你们要点什么?

Yì bēi zhōng bēi ná tiě   yí ge
B: 一杯中杯拿铁,一个

huǒ tuǐ sān míng zhì
火腿三明治。

Yì bēi dà bēi kǎ bù qí nuò
C: 一杯大杯卡布奇诺

hé yí kuài qiǎo kè lì dàn gāo
和一块巧克力蛋糕。

Hǎo de   qǐng shāo děng
A: 好的,请稍等。

Kě yǐ gěi wǒ men liǎng bēi shuǐ ma
B: 可以给我们两杯水吗?

Hǎo de   méi wèn tí
A: 好的,没问题。

Dialogue b

Nǐ hǎo   yì bēi rè qiǎo kè lì   dài zǒu
A: 你好,一杯热巧克力,带走。

Nín yào jiā nǎi yóu ma
B: 您要加奶油吗?

Yào   xiè xie
A: 要,谢谢。

8 As before, order your drink in response to the waiter on the recording. Order a medium cappuccino to take away.

9 Finally, listen to the following dialogue in a Chinese tea house.

Xià wǔ hǎo   Jǐ wèi hē diǎn shén me
A: 下午好。几位喝点什么?

Wǒ men liǎng ge yào yì hú mò lì huā chá
B: 我们两个要一壶茉莉花茶。

Hǎo
A: 好。

Yǒu mei yǒu Lóng jǐng lǜ chá
C: 有没有龙井绿茶?

Yǒu
A: 有。

Hǎo   lái yì bēi
C: 好,来一杯。

Hái yào bié de ma
A: 还要别的吗?

Zài lái yì pán diǎn xīn
D: 再来一盘点心。

Hǎo   qǐng shāo děng
A: 好,请稍等。

10 Now order a pot of green tea and a plate of Chinese snacks. Respond to the waitress on the recording as before.

New words and phrases: Ordering drinks

青岛	Qīngdǎo	(a coastal city in China famous for its beer)
啤酒	píjiǔ	beer

红	hóng	red
葡萄	pútao	grapes
酒	jiǔ	alcohol, alcoholic drinks
葡萄酒	pútaojiǔ	wine
位	wèi	person (polite measure word)
威士忌	wēishìjì	whisky
加	jiā	to add
冰块（儿）	bīngkuài('r)	ice cube
伏特加	fútèjiā	vodka
中	zhōng	medium; middle
拿铁	nátiě	latte
火腿	huǒtuǐ	ham
三明治	sānmíngzhì	sandwich
卡布奇诺	kǎbùqínuò	cappuccino
热	rè	hot
巧克力	qiǎokèlì	chocolate
请	qǐng	please
稍等	shāoděng	just a minute (lit. a bit wait)
没问题	méiwèntí	no problem
带走	dàizǒu	to take away

奶油	nǎiyóu	cream
奶	nǎi	milk
糖	táng	sugar
壶	hú	a pot of (measure word)
茉莉花茶	mòlìhuāchá	jasmine flower tea
龙井	Lóngjǐng	(a region in Hangzhou famous for its tea)
绿茶	lǜchá	green tea
茶	chá	tea
盘	pán	a plate of (measure word)
点心	diǎnxīn	snacks

Language notes

1.1 *'Please' in Chinese*

Just as often happens in English, 'please' comes in front of the verb in Chinese:

Qǐng jìn
请进!   Please come in.

Qǐng zuò
请坐!   Please sit down.

However, you need to remember two differences. First, in Chinese, 'please' can only be used at the beginning of a sentence, not at the end as in English. So, in English you can say 'Can I have some water, please?', but in Chinese you have to say 请给我一瓶水，可以吗? Qǐng gěi wǒ yì píng shuǐ, kěyǐ ma? (Please give me some water, is that ok?). Second, 请 qǐng is usually used in very formal and official situations. It's not often used between close friends and family members. In fact, it would usually be quite inappropriate to use 请 qǐng in everyday situations as it would be seen as putting distance between you and the people you are close to. If you want to make a request in an informal situation and you don't want to be too bold, you can always add 好吗? **hǎo ma?** or 可以吗? **kěyǐ ma?** (Is that ok?) to the end of your request to make it softer.

1.2 *Verb + not + verb questions*

In Unit 2 (page 27) you saw how to form yes/no questions using the question particle 吗 **ma**. In this unit, you will learn an alternative question form using the **verb + not + verb** construction. Note that 不 **bù** and 没 **méi** are usually toneless in this structure.

Statement :	Wǒ shì Yīng guó rén 我是英国人。	I am British.
Question form 1 :	Nǐ shì Yīng guó rén ma 你是英国人吗?	Are you British?
Question form 2 :	Nǐ shì bu shì Yīng guó rén 你是不是英国人?	Are you (or are you not) British?
Statement :	Tā hē hóng pú tao jiǔ 他喝红葡萄酒。	He drinks red wine.
Question form 1 :	Tā hē hóng pú tao jiǔ ma 他喝红葡萄酒吗?	Does he drink red wine?
Question form 2 :	Tā hē bu hē hóng pú tao jiǔ 他喝不喝红葡萄酒?	Does he drink (or not drink) red wine?
Statement :	Wǒ men yǒu kā fēi 我们有咖啡。	We have coffee.
Question form 1 :	Nǐ men yǒu kā fēi ma 你们有咖啡吗?	Do you have coffee?
Question form 2 :	Nǐ men yǒu mei yǒu kā fēi 你们有没有咖啡?	Do you have (or not have) coffee?

Practice

 11 Listen to four dialogues and indicate which of the following items are ordered each time:

1.

啤酒   MILTON BRANDY   VODKA ◊

☐   ☐   ☐

2.

☐   ☐   ☐

3.

水

☐   ☐   ☐

4.

☐   ☐   ☐

12 Think about the different ways you can order drinks. How would you order the following in Chinese? Say your order for each out loud and then listen to the audio for some suggested answers.

1.

2.

3.

4.

5.

6.

13 Role play: Imagine you are in a Chinese tea house. Create a conversation with a partner or on your own. In your conversation, find out if the tea house serves English tea, and how much a plate of Chinese snacks costs.

14 Change the following sentences into yes/no questions using the **verb + not + verb** construction.

1. Tā yào yì bēi kā fēi
他要一杯咖啡。

2. Tā shì Měi guó rén
她是美国人。

3. Wǒ yǒu sān ge mèi mei
我有三个妹妹。

4. Wǒ men shuō Zhōng wén
我们说中文。

5. Wǒ de pí jiǔ jiā bīng kuài
我的啤酒加冰块。

6. Tā men jiā yǒu Zhōng guó chá
他们家有中国茶。

2 What dishes do you recommend?

Nǐ kě yǐ tuī jiàn shén me cài
你可以推荐什么菜?

Key expressions: Eating in a restaurant

To get a table:

Nǐ men jǐ wèi
你们几位?

How many of you are there?

Yǒu yù dìng ma
有预定吗?

Do you have a reservation?

Yǒu liǎng ge rén de zhuō zi ma
有两个人的桌子吗?

Have you got a table for two people?

Qǐng gēn wǒ lái
请跟我来。

Please follow me.

To ask for specialities:

Nǐ men yǒu shén me tè sè cài
你们有什么特色菜?

What specialities do you have?

Nǐ kě yǐ tuī jiàn shén me cài
你可以推荐什么菜?

What dishes do you recommend?

To express likes and dislikes:

Wǒ xǐ huan chī yú
我喜欢吃鱼。

I like (eating) fish.

Wǒ bù xǐ huan chī ròu
我不喜欢吃肉。

I don't like (eating) meat.

To ask for and pay the bill:

Láo jià   qǐng jié zhàng
劳驾，请结帐。

Excuse me, the bill please.

Kě yǐ yòng xìn yòng kǎ ma
可以用信用卡吗?

May I use a credit card?

Duì bu qǐ   wǒ men zhǐ shōu
对不起，我们只收
xiàn jīn
现金。

Sorry, we only accept cash.

Qǐng gěi wǒ shōu jù
请给我收据。

Please give me a receipt.

15 Liu Hong and two of her colleagues go to a local restaurant after a busy day at work. Listen to their interactions with the waiter, from getting a table to paying the bill.

a. They arrive at the restaurant and the waiter greets them:

waiter:
Huān yíng guāng lín　Qǐng wèn　　nǐ men jǐ wèi
欢迎光临。请问，你们几位？
Yǒu yù dìng ma
有预定吗？

Liu Hong:
Méi yǒu　　Yǒu mei yǒu sān ge rén de zhuō zi
没有。有没有三个人的桌子？

waiter:
Yǒu　　qǐng gēn wǒ lái
有，请跟我来。

Liu Hong:
Hǎo　　xiè xie
好，谢谢。

b. The waiter takes them to a table and they start to order drinks:

waiter:
Qǐng kàn cài dān　　Nǐ men xiān hē diǎn shén me
请看菜单。你们先喝点什么？

Xiao Zhang:
Yí guàn kě lè
一罐可乐。

Liu Hong:
Wǒ yào yì bēi chéng zhī
我要一杯橙汁。

Xiao Li:
Yǒu mei yǒu Bǎi wēi pí jiǔ
有没有百威啤酒？

waiter:
Duì bu qǐ　　wǒ men zhǐ yǒu Qīng dǎo hé
对不起，我们只有青岛和
Hǔ pái pí jiǔ
虎牌啤酒。

Xiao Li:
Nà jiù lái yì píng Qīng dǎo pí jiǔ ba
那就来一瓶青岛啤酒吧。

waiter:
Hǎo　　qǐng shāo děng
好，请稍等。

c. Now they order their food:

Nǐ men de yǐn liào lái le Kě yǐ diǎn cài le ma
waiter: 你们的饮料来了。可以点菜了吗？

Kě yǐ Lái yí ge yú xiāng ròu sī yí ge
Liu Hong: 可以。来一个鱼香肉丝，一个
hóng shāo niú ròu bāo Wǒ men xǐ huan chī hǎi xiān
红烧牛肉煲。我们喜欢吃海鲜，
nǐ kě yǐ tuī jiàn shén me cài
你可以推荐什么菜？

Wǒ men de táng cù yú hé chǎo yóu yú dōu hěn bú cuò
waiter: 我们的糖醋鱼和炒鱿鱼都很不错。

Hǎo liǎng ge dōu yào Zài lái sān ge rén de mǐ fàn
Xiao Li: 好，两个都要。再来三个人的米饭。

Hǎo qǐng shāo děng
waiter: 好，请稍等。

d. After a while, the waiter has served all the dishes:

Nǐ men de cài qí le qǐng màn yòng
waiter: 你们的菜齐了，请慢用。

Hǎo xiè xie
Xiao Zhang: 好，谢谢。

e. After the meal, they ask for the bill:

Liu Hong:
Láo jià   qǐng jié zhàng
劳驾，请结帐。

waiter:
Yí gòng sān bǎi èr shí qī
一共三百二十七。

Liu Hong:
Kě yǐ yòng xìn yòng kǎ ma
可以用信用卡吗?

waiter:
Duì bu qǐ   wǒ men zhǐ shōu xiàn jīn
对不起，我们只收现金。

Liu Hong:
Gěi nǐ   qǐng gěi wǒ shōu jù
给你，请给我收据。

waiter:
Hǎo de   méi wèn tí
好的，没问题。

New words and phrases: Eating in a restaurant

特色	tèsè	specialty (refers to food, art, skills)
欢迎光临	huānyíngguānglín	(your presence is) welcome
预定	yùdìng	to reserve; to book
桌子	zhuōzi	table
跟	gēn	to follow
菜单	càidān	menu
罐	guàn	a can of (measure word)
橙汁	chéngzhī	orange juice
百威啤酒	Bǎiwēipíjiǔ	Budweiser beer
虎牌啤酒	Hǔpáipíjiǔ	Tiger beer

对不起	duìbuqǐ	sorry
那	nà	in that case
就	jiù	just
饮料	yǐnliào	beverage
点菜	diǎncài	to order
鱼香肉丝	yúxiāngròusī	shredded pork with fish flavour
肉	ròu	meat
喜欢	xǐhuan	to like
红烧	hóngshāo	braised in soy sauce (a way of cooking)
牛肉	niúròu	beef
煲	bāo	(dishes cooked in a pot, like a stew)
海鲜	hǎixiān	seafood
推荐	tuījiàn	to recommend
糖醋	tángcù	sweet and sour flavour
鱼	yú	fish
炒	chǎo	to stir fry
鱿鱼	yóuyú	squid
米饭	mǐfàn	boiled rice
齐	qí	complete; ready

请慢用	qǐngmànyòng	please enjoy (lit. please use slowly)
劳驾	láojià	excuse me
结帐	jiézhàng	bill; check
用	yòng	to use
信用卡	xìnyòngkǎ	credit card
收	shōu	to receive; to accept
只	zhǐ	only
都	dōu	both, all
现金	xiànjīn	cash
收据	shōujù	receipt
冷	lěng	cold
冷盘	lěngpán	cold dishes (usually served as starters)
烤	kǎo	to roast; roasted
鸭	yā	duck
份	fèn	a portion of (measure word)
豆腐	dòufu	bean curd; tofu
羊肉	yángròu	lamb
汤	tāng	soup
可是	kěshì	but

> ℹ️ 炒鱿鱼 **Chǎo yóuyú** is the name of a dish meaning 'stir-fried squid', but it is also used as slang to mean 'to fire someone'! This is because in the past, when people were fired, they had to pack up their things and wrap them up to take with them. When squid is stir fried, it curls up and looks like wrapped-up belongings.

Language notes

2.1 *The position of adverbs in Chinese*

You have met a range of Chinese adverbs so far:

xiān		yě		zhǐ	
先	first	也	also	只	only

màn		dōu	
慢	slowly	都	both

Unlike in English, adverbs always need to go *before* the verb in Chinese. Read the following examples and pay particular attention to the position of the adverbs.

Tā xiān qù Zhōngguó
他**先**去中国。
He will go to China first.

Wǒ yě xǐhuan chī qiǎokèlì
我**也**喜欢吃巧克力。
I also like eating chocolate.

Wǒmen zhǐ yǒu yí ge nǚ ér
我们**只**有一个女儿。
We only have one daughter.

Nǐmen qǐng màn yòng
你们请**慢**用。
Please enjoy. (Please use (eat) slowly.)

Tāmen dōu shì xuésheng
他们**都**是学生。
They are both (or all) students.

2.2 *Use of the* nà jiù 那就··· ba 吧 *construction*

This sentence construction can be used for making an
alternative suggestion or decision. It can be translated as 'In
that case, let's … then'.

Nà jiù hē lǜ chá ba
那就喝绿茶吧!   In that case, let's drink green tea then.

Nà jiù xiàn zài qù ba
那就现在去吧!   In that case, let's go now then.

Nà jiù zài jiā chī fàn ba
那就在家吃饭吧!   In that case, let's eat at home then.

Nà jiù shuōZhōngwén ba
那就说中文吧!   In that case, let's speak Chinese then.

2.3 *Change of status using the particle* le 了

The addition of the particle 了 **le** to any type of verb describing
a situation or condition indicates that a new condition or state
of affairs has materialized. Look at these examples from the
dialogues and see how the situation has changed:

Nǐ men de yǐn liào lái le
你们的饮料来了。   Your drinks have arrived.

(Indicating the drinks were not here previously.)

Kě yǐ diǎn cài le ma
可以点菜了吗?   Can (I) take your order now?

(Indicating the speaker knows that the customer was not ready
previously.)

Nǐ men de cài qí le
你们的菜齐了。   Your food is complete.

(Indicating that all of the food had not been served until this point.)

It is also common to use 了 **le** after adjectives for the same
function.

Nǐ de wǎn fàn hǎo le
你的晚饭好了。   Your dinner is ready. (It wasn't before.)

Miàn bāo guì le
面包贵了。   Bread is expensive. (It wasn't before.)

Shuǐ rè le
水热了。   The water is warm. (It wasn't before.)

Practice

16 Look at the following menu and say what you would like
to eat. Note that Pinyin is not provided in this exercise as you
will not see Pinyin on any menu in China. This is a good chance
to read through the characters carefully and try to remember
the key words for food and drink. You will be able to find the
translation at the back of the book.

冷盘
烤鸭 . . . . 20.00 元 / 份
冷豆腐 . . . . 15.00 元 / 份

热炒
红烧牛肉 . . . . 20.00 元 / 份
鱼香肉丝 . . . . 20.00 元 / 份
羊肉煲 . . . . 25.00 元 / 份
糖醋鱼 . . . . 18.00 元 / 份

汤
海鲜汤 . . . . 25.00 元 / 份

饮料
茶 . . . . 3.00 元 / 壶   可乐 . . . . 3.50 元 / 瓶
啤酒 . . . . 5.00 元 / 瓶

17 How do you say the following in Chinese? First try matching the sentences with their Chinese counterparts and then cover up the Chinese and try to work them out for yourself.

1. I have a reservation for three people.

a. Wǒ kě yǐ yòng xìn yòng kǎ ma
我可以用信用卡吗?

2. Do you have a table for two?

b. Wǒ bú chī niú ròu
我不吃牛肉。

3. What dish do you recommend?

c. Wǒ bú xǐ huan yú
我不喜欢鱼。

4. I don't like fish.

d. Yǒu liǎng ge rén de zhuō zi ma
有两个人的桌子吗?

5. I don't eat beef.

e. Wǒ men zhǐ yào liǎng ge rén de mǐ fàn
我们只要两个人的米饭。

6. We only want rice for two.

f. Wǒ yù dìng le sān wèi
我预定了,三位。

7. The bill, please.

g. Nǐ kě yǐ tuī jiàn shén me cài
你可以推荐什么菜?

8. May I use a credit card?

h. Qǐng gěi wǒ shōu jù
请给我收据。

9. Please give me a receipt.

i. Qǐng jié zhàng
请结帐。

18 Listen to the conversation and choose which answers are correct:

1. Does the man have a reservation?
   a. yes   **b.** no   **c.** yes, but it's at 8pm not 7pm

2. For how many people in total?
   a. two   **b.** three   **c.** four

3. What does the man want to drink?
   a. tea   **b.** Coke   **c.** wine

4. Which of the following statements is true?
   a. the woman doesn't like fish   **b.** the woman doesn't eat fish
   c. the woman thinks the fish is too expensive

5. How much is the bill?
   a. ¥250   **b.** ¥345   **c.** ¥180

Learning Chinese characters

Xué hàn zì
学汉字

How words are formed (2)

In the previous unit, you discovered how nouns and adjectives can be formed in Chinese. In this unit, we will focus on verbs.

1. verb + verb

tīng shuō
听说 to hear someone say = to listen + to speak

tīng dǒng
听懂 to understand (by listening) = to listen + to understand

jiào huàn
叫唤 to call, to shout = to call + to call

kàn jian
看见 to see = to look + to see

2. verb + noun

chī fàn
吃饭 to eat = to eat + rice

zǒu lù
走路 to walk = to walk + road

kāi huì
开会 to have a meeting = to open + meeting

shuō huà
说话 to speak = to speak + conversation

3. adjective + verb

huān yíng
欢迎 to welcome = happy + to welcome

gāo chàng
高唱 to sing happily = high + to sing

huàn xiǎng
幻想 to imagine = unreal + to think

kuáng wǔ
狂舞 to dance wildly = crazy + to dance

Write the characters in the text

19 Try writing the following characters using the stroke order indicated.

酒 jiǔ alcohol	丶	丶	氵	沪	沪	沪	沔	洒	酒
	酒								
奶 nǎi milk	ㄑ	乆	女	奶	奶				
糖 táng sugar	丶	丷	半	米	米	米	籵	籵	籵
	籵	籵	糖	糖	糖	糖	糖		
醋 cù vinegar	一	厂	冂	丙	丙	酉	酉	酉	酐
	酐	酢	酢	醋	醋	醋			
茶 chá tea	一	一	艹	艹	苁	苁	苓	茶	茶
菜 cài vegetable	一	一	艹	艹	艹	苹	苹	苹	苹
	茅	菜							
肉 ròu meat	丨	冂	冂	内	肉	肉			
鱼 yú fish	丿	夕	夕	鸟	鱼	角	鱼	鱼	

牛 niú cow	ノ	⺊	仁	牛				
羊 yáng sheep	⸝	⸜	⸍	⸌	兰	羊		
鸭 yā duck	⎮	口	日	日	甲	甲	甲ク	甲勺	鸭
	鸭								
鸡 jī chicken	フ	又	汉	鸡	鸡	鸡	鸡		
海鲜 hǎixiān seafood (sea + delicious)	⸝	⸟	氵	氵	汇	泛	海	海	海
	海								
	⸝	⸝	⸜	勹	色	角	鱼	鱼	鱼
	鱼ノ	鱼⸍	鱼⸌	鲜	鲜				
汤 tāng soup	⸝	⸟	氵	汀	汙	汤	汤		
冷 lěng cold	⸝	⸟	冫	八	夳	冷	冷		
热 rè hot	一	十	扌	扐	执	执	执	热	热
	热								

Chinese food and eating out in a guest–host setting

Food has always been an important part of Chinese culture. There are eight different styles of cuisine in mainland China, which vary a lot from the north to the south. If you are adventurous, you should try local dishes wherever you go. Even if you do not want to try a particular dish, it is still a good idea to show a bit of curiosity by asking how the dishes are prepared. It all helps to make a good impression with the host.

Eating out in China is relatively cheap and it is a major means of socializing, building interpersonal relationships, celebrating any event, and opening or closing a business deal. If you are invited by a Chinese family, it's always good to take presents. If you are taken out to a restaurant, always let the host order the food and never start eating until the host has touched their chopsticks first. You will find that saying 'I am full' never really works in China and the host will keep putting food on your plate. The wisest thing to do is simply not to finish the food already on your plate! This shows the generosity of the host. It is important to invite your Chinese host out in return. This is a polite gesture that will further build your relationship.

You are likely to be treated to some 白酒 báijiǔ (lit. white alcohol) by your Chinese host. The host may make a toast in your honour and say 干杯 gān bēi (cheers, lit. dry the glass).

Dates, time, shopping and restaurants

Communicating in Chinese

Hàn yǔ jiāo liú
汉语交流

1 Listen and match the appropriate information for each person's birthday based on what you hear. The first one has been done for you:

~~today~~	58 年 04 月 12 日	Wednesday
tomorrow	78 年 09 月 12 日	~~Saturday~~
yesterday	~~93 年 11 月 08 日~~	Sunday
today	81 年 03 月 07 日	Friday

Xiao Wang:
today
93 年 11 月 08 日
Saturday

Xiao Zhang:
_____
_____
_____

Xiao Li:
_____
_____
_____

Xiao Chen:
_____
_____
_____

2 Listen to a few short dialogues and decide whether the following statements are true or false.

Dialogue a
1. The time now is 7:45pm. _____
2. Today is Sunday. _____
3. The movie starts at 9pm. _____

Dialogue b
1. Xiao Li goes to work at 8am every day. _____
2. He has lunch at 12:30pm. _____
3. He goes for walks and goes shopping over the weekend. _____

Dialogue c
1. They had previously agreed to go for a coffee this afternoon. _____
2. Xiao Chen cannot go now because she's too tired. _____
3. They will go to see a movie at 3pm tomorrow. _____

3 Describe your daily routine and weekly plans. Try to use the following words:

měi tiān	qǐ chuáng	shàng bān	xià wǔ	huí jiā
每天	起床	上班	下午	回家

yǒu shí	cháng	cóng dào	de shí hou	yì bān
有时	常	从⋯到⋯	⋯的时候	一般

shuì jiào	kàn diàn yǐng	mǎi dōng xi	hē kā fēi	hòu
睡觉	看电影	买东西	喝咖啡	后

4 Listen and write down the price for each of these items:

1. _____   2. _____   3. _____

4. _____   5. _____   6. _____

5 How would you say the following in Chinese?

1. How much is it?   5. Here's the money.
2. Too expensive!   6. What would you like to buy?
3. How about ¥85?   7. Be a bit cheaper!
4. I will take it.

6 How would you order the following food and drink?

1.   2.   3. 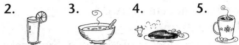   4.   5.   6.

There are different ways of saying these; some sample answers are given in the back of the book.

7 Role play: You and your friend are eating out in a restaurant. Look at the menu below and create a conversation on your own or with a partner.

冷盘
烤鸭 · · · · · · · · · · · · · · 20.00 元 / 份
冷豆腐 · · · · · · · · · · 15.00 元 / 份

热炒
红烧牛肉 · · · · · · · · 20.00 元 / 份
鱼香肉丝 · · · · · · · · 20.00 元 / 份
羊肉煲 · · · · · · · · · · 25.00 元 / 份
糖醋鱼 · · · · · · · · · · 18.00 元 / 份

汤
海鲜汤 · · · · · · · · · · 25.00 元 / 份

饮料
茶 · · · · · · 3.00 元 / 壶   可乐 · · · · 3.50 元 / 瓶
啤酒 · · · · 5.00 元 / 瓶

8 Read the following text and then answer the questions:

Míng tiān shì èr líng yī líng nián shí yī yuè sān hào　　shì wǒ
明天是二零一零年十一月三号，是我

hǎo péng you Dà wèi de shēng rì　　Dà wèi shì Yīng guó rén　　tā zài
好朋友大为的生日。大为是英国人，他在

Zhōng guó xué xí Zhōng wén　　Tā jīn nián èr shí bā suì le　　shǔ jī
中国学习中文。他今年二十八岁了，属鸡。

Zhè shì tā dì yī cì zài Zhōng guó guò shēng rì　　Wǒ xiǎng qǐng tā jīn
这是他第一次在中国过生日。我想请他今

wǎn lái wǒ jiā guò tā de shēng rì
晚来我家过他的生日。

Jīn tiān shì xīng qī liù　　kě shì wǒ hěn máng　　Zǎo shang
今天是星期六，可是我很忙。早上，

cóng jiǔ diǎn dào shí èr diǎn　　wǒ qù mǎi dōng xi　　Wǒ gěi Dà wèi
从九点到十二点，我去买东西。我给大为

mǎi le yí ge dà dàn gāo hé yí jiàn máo yī　　Máo yī yǒu yì diǎn
买了一个大蛋糕和一件毛衣。毛衣有一点

guì　　kě shì hěn piào liang　　wǒ hěn xǐ huan　　Wǒ hái mǎi le hěn
贵，可是很漂亮，我很喜欢。我还买了很

duō cài　　Xià wǔ liǎng diǎn bàn　　wǒ hé Dà wèi qù kàn diàn yǐng
多菜。下午两点半，我和大为去看电影。

Wǎn shang　　wǒ de mā ma zuò le hěn duō cài　　yǒu niú ròu　　yǒu
晚上，我的妈妈做了很多菜，有牛肉，有

hǎi xiān　　Bà ba hái mǎi le liǎng píng pú tao jiǔ　　Wǒ de hěn duō
海鲜。爸爸还买了两瓶葡萄酒。我的很多

péng you men dōu lái le wǒ jiā　　Wǒ men chī le shēng rì dàn gāo
朋友们都来了我家。我们吃了生日蛋糕，

měi ge rén dōu hěn gāo xìng
每个人都很高兴！

1. Míng tiān jǐ yuè jǐ hào
明天几月几号？

2. Dà wèi shì nǎ guó rén
大为是哪国人？

3. Tā jīn nián duō dà
他今年多大？

4. Jīn tiān xīng qī jǐ
今天星期几？

5. Wǒ jīn tiān zǎo shang mǎi le shén me
"我"今天早上买了什么？

6. Shén me yǒu yì diǎn guì
什么有一点贵？

7. Tā men jǐ diǎn qù kàn diàn yǐng
他们几点去看电影？

8. Bà ba mǎi le shén me
爸爸买了什么？

9. Tā men wǎn shang zuò le shén me
他们晚上做了什么？

10. Měi ge rén dōu zěn me yàng
每个人都怎么样？

Getting the pronunciation right

Pīn yīn liàn xí
拼音练习

9 Listen and write the initials:

_____ao   _____o   _____e   _____i   _____un

_____ün   _____ang   _____ing   _____en   _____ia

_____ua   _____uo   _____ie   _____uo   _____ian

_____eng   _____iao   _____iang   _____iong   _____uan

_____ong   _____iu   _____uang

10 Listen and write the finals:

zh_____	c_____	z_____	s_____
sh_____	ch_____	n_____	l_____
g_____	k_____	ch_____	j_____
q_____	x_____	p_____	r_____
y_____	w_____	t_____	m_____
zh_____	k_____	q_____	f_____

11 Listen and circle the tones:

1. zhāng   zháng   zhǎng   zhàng
2. qiāng   qiáng   qiǎng   qiàng
3. chuō   chuó   chuǒ   chuò
4. shū   shú   shǔ   shù
5. xūn   xún   xǔn   xùn
6. shījiān   shíjiān   shǐjiàn   shíjiàn
7. guānhuāi   guánhuái   guǎnhuài   guànhuài
8. huīyī   huíyì   huǐyì   huìyì
9. zhīsháng   zhíshāng   zhǐsháng   zhìshāng
10. yūnchuán   yúnchuān   yǔnchuán   yùnchuán

12 Listen and mark the correct tones.

xuexi   qingkuang   jiankang

chenggong   xiangxiang   zanshi

laoshi   qiangpo   zuanshi

Learning Chinese characters

Xué hàn zì
学汉字

13 Read the following text and then decide if the given statements are true or false.

我是英国人。我是学生，我在中国学习中文。我有一个好朋友，他叫小明。他是中国人。我们一起住在大学。星期一和星期三，我们很忙。周末我们常去看电影，喝咖啡。

这个星期六是中国的国庆节。我们下午去公园玩，晚上八点去吃北京烤鸭。中国菜很好吃，也不太贵。我也喜欢中国茶。在北京买东西很便宜。明天我想去买书和邮票。明年四月我打算去上海旅行，一定很有意思。

1. I am studying Chinese at a university in China. _____
2. I have a very good English friend. _____
3. We are very busy on Mondays and Fridays. _____
4. This Saturday is my birthday. _____
5. We will have roast duck on Saturday evening. _____
6. I like Chinese food and Chinese tea. _____
7. I want to go for coffee tomorrow. _____
8. I plan to travel around China next May. _____

14 Write a brief 'things to do' list in Chinese for next week, with days, dates, times and activities.

9 Transport and directions

第九课

Jiāo tōng hé fāng wèi
交通和方位

In this unit, you will learn:
- How to get around in China: by taxi, bus and train
- How to ask for and give directions
- About some common radicals in Chinese characters
- About transport in China

Getting the pronunciation right

Pīn yīn liàn xí
拼音练习

In this unit, you will do some more advanced Pinyin practice with a focus on words starting with the first tone. You will also learn a couple of traditional Chinese tongue twisters as a challenge!

1 Combinations with the first tone: Try to pronounce the following words on your own first, and then listen to the audio. Go over it again and again until you are used to the pattern.

The first tone + the first tone

kāfēi	jīntiān	chūntiān	tīngshuō	xiāngyān
coffee	today	spring	hear (that)	cigarette

The first tone + the second tone

Zhōngguó	Yīngguó	Zhōngwén	Yīngwén	shēngcí
China	Britain	Chinese	English	new words

The first tone + the third tone

hēibǎn	**shēntǐ**	**fēngjǐng**	**jīnglǐ**	**kāishǐ**
blackboard	body	scenery	manager	to start

The first tone + the fourth tone

gōngzuò	**yīnyuè**	**shūdiàn**	**gāoxìng**	**tiānqì**
job	music	bookshop	happy	weather

The first tone + the neutral tone

tāmen	**māma**	**xiānsheng**	**xiūxi**	**gēge**
they	mother	Mr	to rest	older brother

2 Sound discrimination: Some Chinese sounds may sound similar to you, especially when they are combined in certain ways. In this exercise, focus on the sounds j, q, x, z, c and s, which are usually considered to be difficult for beginners:

jīqì	**qīzǐ**	**xuéxí**	**cèsuǒ**	**zérèn**
machine	wife & child	to study	toilet	responsibility

sījī	**zúqiú**	**jiérì**	**zuǒ**	**zǒu**
driver	football	holiday	left	to walk

3 Fun time: You already tried saying a Chinese tongue twister in Unit 7. Now you will learn another classic one focusing on tones as well as the sound distinction of 's' and 'sh'.

Sì hé shí
四和十   **4 and 10**

Sì shì sì   shí shì shí
四是四 , 十是十 ,   4 is 4, 10 is 10,

shí sì shì shí sì   sì shí shì sì shí
十四是十四 , 四十是四十 ,   14 is 14, 40 is 40,

bú yào bǎ shí sì shuō chéng sì shí
不要把十四说成四十 ,   don't say 14 as 40,

yě bú yào bǎ sì shí shuō chéng shí sì
也不要把四十说成十四。   and don't say 40 as 14.

Communicating in Chinese
Hàn yǔ jiāo liú
汉语交流

1 Beijing Hotel, please
Qù Běi jīng Fàn diàn
去北京饭店

Key expressions: **Travel by taxi, bus and train**

To take a taxi:

Nǐ qù nǎ 'r
你去哪儿?
Where do you (want to) go?

Shī fu qù Běi jīng Fàn diàn
师傅，去北京饭店。
Master, go to (the) Beijing Hotel.

Běi jīng Fàn diàn dào le
北京饭店到了。
We've arrived at (the) Beijing Hotel.

To take a bus:

Yī zhāng qù Běi jīng Fàn diàn de piào
一张去北京饭店的票。
A ticket to (the) Beijing Hotel.

Qǐngwèn jǐ zhàn
请问，几站?
How many stops does it take?

Zài Běi jīng Fàn diàn xià chē
在北京饭店下车。
Get off at (the) Beijing Hotel.

To get a train ticket:

Shén me shí hou zǒu
什么时候走?
When does it leave?

Shén me shí hou dào Běi jīng
什么时候到北京?
When does it arrive at Beijing?

Yǒu shén me qū bié
有什么区别?
What's the difference?

Jǐ hào zhàn tái
几号站台?
Which platform?

---

4 A lot of Chinese words can be broken down into individual words or characters which represent part of the meaning of the final word, such as the days of the week and the months of the year. The basic transport words are also formed in this manner.

The general word for vehicle is 车 **chē**, and new words are created by adding characters in front of it. Look at the following pictures and see how the meanings of the characters for the different vehicles break down.

zì xíng chē
自行车
self-ride + vehicle

huǒ chē
火车
fire + vehicle

qì chē
汽车
steam + vehicle

gōng gòng qì chē
公共汽车
public + car

chū zū chē
出租车
for rent + vehicle

mó tuō chē
摩托车
phonetic
(imported word)

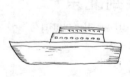

lún chuán
轮船
wheel + boat

fān chuán
帆船
sail + boat

fēi jī
飞机
flying + machine

5 Listen to a short conversation about taking a taxi. Pay attention to the simple structure used to say where you want to go: 师傅，去 Shīfu, qù....

Zuò chū zū chē
（坐出租车）:

A: Nǐ hǎo   xiǎo jiě   Nǐ qù nǎ ´r
你好，小姐。你去哪儿?

B: Shī fu   qù Běi jīng Fàn diàn
师傅，去北京饭店。

A: Hǎo
好。

...

(after 15 minutes)

A: Xiǎo jiě   Běi jīng Fàn diàn dào le
小姐，北京饭店到了。

B: Duō shǎo qián
多少钱?

A: Sān shí kuài
三十块。

B: Gěi nǐ   xiè xie
给你，谢谢。

6 Imagine you want to go to the Great Wall (长城 Cháng chéng) and you have just called a taxi. Tell the driver where you want to go in Chinese, either out loud on your own or with a partner.

7 Now listen to a conversation on a bus. Listen for how to ask for a bus ticket.

Zuò gōng gòng qì chē
（坐公共汽车）:

A: Nǐ hǎo   yì zhāng qù Shàng hǎi Bó wù guǎn de piào
你好，一张去上海博物馆的票。

Liǎng kuài
B: 两块。

Hǎo   Qǐng wèn   jǐ zhàn
A: 好。请问，几站？

Sān zhàn   zài Rén mín Guǎngchǎng xià chē   Dào le wǒ jiào nǐ
B: 三站，在人民广场下车。到了我叫你。

Tài xiè xie le
A: 太谢谢了。

Bú yòng xie
B: 不用谢。

8 Now, imagine you want to go to the Great Wall again, but by bus this time. Ask for two tickets for you and a friend. Also find out how many stops it takes to get there.

 9 The following conversation takes place at a train station. Listen for the ways of asking and giving departure and arrival times.

Zài huǒ chē zhàn
（在火车站）：

Nǐ hǎo   wǒ xiǎng yào liǎng zhāng qù Guì lín de huǒ chē piào
A: 你好，我想要两张去桂林的火车票。

Shén me shí hou zǒu
B: 什么时候走？

Zuì hǎo míng tiān xià wǔ sì diǎn zuǒ yòu
A: 最好明天下午四点左右。

Yǒu   cì   míng tiān xià wǔ sān diǎn chū fā   hé   cì
B: 有 51 次，明天下午三点出发，和 81 次，
míng tiān xià wǔ wǔ diǎn bàn chū fā de huǒ chē   Nǐ yào nǎ ge
明天下午五点半出发的火车。你要哪个
shí jiān de piào
时间的票？

Yǒu shén me qū bié   Shén me shí hou dào Guì lín
A: 有什么区别？什么时候到桂林？

Dōu shì wǎnshang shí diǎn dào   Bú guò   cì shì tè kuài
B: 都是晚上十点到。不过，81 次是特快，
suǒ yǐ bǐ   cì pǔ kuài kuài liǎng ge xiǎo shí   piào jià yě guì
所以比 51 次普快快两个小时，票价也贵
wǔ shí kuài
五十块。

Nà jiù mǎi liǎng zhāng   cì de piào ba
A: 那就买两张 81 次的票吧。

Hǎo   Yí gòng liù bǎi èr shí kuài
B: 好。一共六百二十块。

Jǐ hào zhàn tái
A: 几号站台？

Liù hào zhàn tái
B: 六号站台。

Guilin

10 According to the conversation in Exercise 9, what is the
difference between train no. 51 and train no. 81? First give
your answer in English and then try to express your answer in
Chinese.

New words and phrases: Travel by taxi, bus and train		
师傅	shīfu	master (just a polite way to address people you do not know)
坐	zuò	to take (a bus, train, etc.); to sit
饭店	fàndiàn	hotel
博物馆	bówùguǎn	museum
站	zhàn	(bus) stop
人民广场	Rénmín Guǎngchǎng	People's Square

下车	xiàchē	to get off
火车	huǒchē	train
火车站	huǒchēzhàn	train station
桂林	Guìlín	(a city in Southern China)
最好	zuìhǎo	the best; ideally
左右	zuǒyòu	about, approximately (lit. left and right)
次	cì	no., # (only refers to trains)
出发	chūfā	to depart
区别	qūbié	difference
不过	búguò	however, but
特快	tèkuài	express train
普快	pǔkuài	standard train
所以	suǒyǐ	therefore
比	bǐ	compared with
快	kuài	fast
小时	xiǎoshí	hour
票价	piàojià	ticket fee
站台	zhàntái	platform

NB: The modes of transport in Exercise 4 are also key new words for this section.

Language notes

1.1 *Verbal attributive with* 的 de

Attributives come in different forms. Their function is to describe and define nouns. In this unit, you will learn how *verbal* attributives are used. A verbal attributive gives added description or definition to a noun through a verb. Here's an example from the dialogue:

yì zhāng qù Shàng hǎi Bó wù guǎn de piào
一张**去上海博物馆的**票
a ticket (that goes) to Shanghai Museum

When using verbal attributives, 的 **de** has to be placed between the verbal attributive and the noun it is describing, and the noun always comes last. Here are some more examples from the dialogues:

Wǒ xiǎng yào liǎng zhāng qù Guì lín de huǒ chē piào
我想要两张**去桂林的**火车票。
I would like to buy two tickets (that go) to Guilin

míng tiān xià wǔ wǔ diǎn bàn chū fā de huǒ chē
明天下午五点半**出发的**火车
a train which leaves at 5:30 tomorrow afternoon

As you may have already noticed, the sentence order is different from English. In English, the extra description of the noun is expressed (or implied at least) via a clausal phrase after the noun – 'tickets *that go to Guilin*'. In Chinese, however, a verbal attributive is used *in front of* the noun (the same position as an adjective), so it is literally '*go to Guilin* tickets'. Here are a few more examples:

Mā ma zuò de fàn hěn hào chī
妈妈**做的**饭很好吃。
The food that mum makes is delicious.

Mǎi miàn bāo de xué sheng jiào Xiǎo míng
买面包**的**学生叫小明。
The student who buys the bread is called Xiaoming.

1.2 *Comparative form with* 比 ^{bǐ}

The basic structure for comparing two entities A and B is:

A + 比 ^{bǐ} (compared with) + B + **adjective**

Here are some examples:

Kā fēi bǐ chá guì
咖啡比茶贵。   Coffee is more expensive than tea.

Nǐ men bǐ tā kuài
你们比她快。   You (pl.) are faster than her.

Zhōng guó bǐ Yīng guó dà
中国比英国大。   China is bigger than Britain.

A and B can also be in the form of a phrase or a clause. B is
usually kept in its minimum form for comparative purposes.

Wǒ mǎi de kā fēi bǐ nǐ mǎi de   kā fēi   guì
我买的咖啡比你买的（咖啡）贵。
The coffee I bought was more expensive than yours.

Qù Běi jīng lǚ xíng de rén bǐ qù Shàng hǎi   lǚ xíng   de
去北京旅行的人比去上海（旅行）的
rén   duō
（人）多。
More people travel to Beijing than to Shanghai.

Practice

11 How do you say the following in Chinese?

1. I would like to buy a train ticket to Shanghai.
2. When does the train depart?
3. When does the train arrive?
4. Which platform is it?
5. Train no. 10 is ¥100 more expensive than train no. 5.

12 You have just arrived in Beijing and there are a few tourist sites you want to visit.

a. Call a taxi to go to each place and ask how much it will cost each time.

b. Buy a bus ticket to each place and ask how many stops the journey will take each time.

Cháng chéng
1. 长城 Great Wall

Yí hé yuán
2. 颐和园 Summer Palace

Gù gōng
3. 故宫 Forbidden City

Ào yùn cūn
4. 奥运村 Olympic Village

You can check your answers at the back of the book.

13 Listen to a conversation where Tom books a train ticket. Based on what you hear, select the correct answers to these questions:

1. When does Tom want to leave?

shí yuè sān hào
a. 十月三号

shí yuè shí sān hào
b. 十月十三号

shí yuè sān shí hào
c. 十月三十号

2. Where is Tom going to?

Běi jīng
a. 北京

Shàng hǎi
b. 上海

Nán jīng
c. 南京

3. When does the train arrive?

   a. 8:30pm   **b.** 8:45pm   **c.** 8:15pm

4. How much is the ticket?

   a. ¥530   **b.** ¥350   **c.** ¥335

5. Which platform does the train leave from?

   a. 6   **b.** 8   **c.** 12

14 Look at the following pictures and try to describe them with the comparative form using the adjectives provided. The first one has been done for you.

1.

kuài
快 fast

màn
慢 slow

Sān hào gōng gòng qì chē bǐ liù hào kuài
三号公共汽车比六号快。
Bus no. 3 is faster than no. 6.

Liù hào gōng gòng qì chē bǐ sān hào màn
六号公共汽车比三号慢。
Bus no. 6 is slower than no. 3.

2.

máng
忙 busy

xián
闲 free

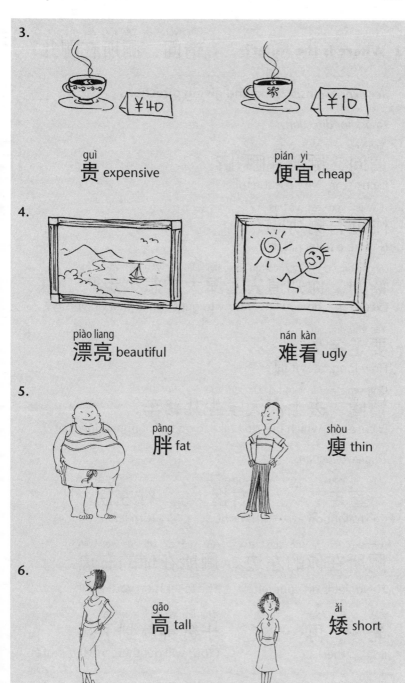

3.

guì
贵 expensive

pián yi
便宜 cheap

4.

piào liang
漂亮 beautiful

nán kàn
难看 ugly

5.

pàng
胖 fat

shòu
瘦 thin

6.

gāo
高 tall

ǎi
矮 short

2 Where is the toilet?

Qǐngwèn   cè suǒ zài nǎ ´r
请问，厕所在哪儿?

Key expressions: **Asking and giving directions**

To ask for directions:

Qǐngwèn   cè suǒ zài nǎ ´r
请问，厕所在哪儿?
Excuse me, where is the toilet?

Fù jìn yǒu cè suǒ ma
附近有厕所吗?
Is there a toilet nearby?

Qǐngwèn   nǐ zhī dao qù Shàng hǎi Dà xué zěn me zǒu
请问，你知道去上海大学怎么走?
Excuse me, do you know how to get to Shanghai University?

Yào zǒu duō jiǔ
要走多久?
How long does it take?

Qǐngwèn   qù Shàng hǎi Dà xué zuò jǐ   lù chē
请问，去上海大学坐几路车?
Excuse me, which bus do I take to go to Shanghai University?

To give directions:

yì zhí zǒu	wǎng yòu guǎi	wǎng zuǒ guǎi
一直走	往右拐	往左拐
go straight on	turn right	turn left

Cè suǒ zài nǐ de zuǒ bian	Cè suǒ zài nǐ de yòu bian
厕所在你的左边。	厕所在你的右边。
The toilet is on your left.	The toilet is on your right.

xiān zài	Shí fēn zhōng jiù dào le
先…，再…	十分钟就到了。
first ..., then ...	(You) will get there in 10 minutes.

15 Listen to four short dialogues where people ask directions to various places. Try to understand the dialogues with the help of the new word list and the maps.

Dialogue a: At a restaurant

Nǐ hǎo   qǐng wèn
A: 你好，请问，

cè suǒ zài nǎ ′r
厕所在哪儿？

Qiánmian yòu bian dì èr jiān jiù shì
B: 前面右边第二间就是。

Xiè xie
A: 谢谢。

Dialogue b: At a university campus

Tóng xué   nǐ zhī dao xué xiào tú shū guǎn zài nǎ ′r
A: 同学，你知道学校图书馆在哪儿？

Zhī dao   tú shū guǎn zài cān tīng de zuǒ bian
B: 知道，图书馆在餐厅的左边，

bàn gōng lóu de hòu mian
办公楼的后面。

Xiè xie   Xué xiào fù jìn yǒu chāo shì ma
A: 谢谢。学校附近有超市吗？

Yǒu   cóng xué xiào chū qù wǎng zuǒ guǎi   zǒu wǔ fēn zhōng jiù
B: 有，从学校出去往左拐，走五分钟就

yǒu yí ge chāo shì
有一个超市。

Tài hǎo le   Xiè xie nǐ
A: 太好了！谢谢你。

Bú yòng xiè
B: 不用谢。

Dialogue c: On the street

A: 师傅，请问，去和平电影院怎么走?
Shī fu   qǐng wèn   qù Hé píng Diàn yǐng yuàn zěn me zǒu

B: 一直走，到第一个路口往右
Yì zhí zǒu   dào dì yī ge lù kǒu wǎng yòu
拐。和平电影院就在你的
guǎi   Hé píng Diàn yǐng yuàn jiù zài nǐ de
左边，马路的对面。
zuǒ bian   mǎ lù de duì miàn

A: 要走多久?
Yào zǒu duō jiǔ

B: 十分钟就到了。
Shí fēn zhōng jiù dào le

Dialogue d: At a bus stop

A: 小姐，请问，去上海大学坐几路车?
Xiǎo jiě   qǐng wèn   qù Shàng hǎi Dà xué zuò jǐ lù chē

B: 上海大学很远，恐怕你得换车。
Shàng hǎi Dà xué hěn yuǎn   kǒng pà nǐ děi huàn chē

A: 怎么换?
Zěn me huàn

B. 你可以先坐 10 路车，到人民广场下车，
Nǐ kě yǐ xiān zuò   lù chē   dào Rén mín Guǎng chǎng xià chē
再换 20 路车，或者可
zài huàn   lù chē   huò zhě kě
以在那儿换地铁
yǐ zài nà 'r huàn dì tiě
一号线。
yí hào xiàn

A: 谢谢。
Xiè xie

New words and phrases: Asking and giving directions

厕所	cèsuǒ	toilet
哪儿	nǎ'r	where (= 哪里 nǎ li)
知道	zhīdao	to know
前面	qiánmian	at the front
右边	yòubian	right-hand side
第一	dìyī	first
第二	dì'èr	second
间	jiān	(measure word for rooms)
就	jiù	exactly; just
学校	xuéxiào	school
大学	dàxué	university
图书馆	túshūguǎn	library
餐厅	cāntīng	restaurant
左边	zuǒbian	left-hand side
办公楼	bàngōnglóu	office building
后面	hòumian	behind
附近	fùjìn	nearby
超市	chāoshì	supermarket
出去	chūqù	to exit; to go outside

往	wǎng	towards
左	zuǒ	left
拐	guǎi	to turn
走	zǒu	to walk
分钟	fēnzhōng	minute (duration of time)
和平	hépíng	peace
电影院	diànyǐngyuàn	cinema
一直	yìzhí	straight
路口	lùkǒu	crossroad
右	yòu	right
马路	mǎlù	road; street
对面	duìmiàn	opposite
多久	duōjiǔ	how long (time)
路	lù	no., # (only refers to buses)
车	chē	bus; car; vehicle
远	yuǎn	far; far away
得	děi	to have to; must
换	huàn	to change
地铁	dìtiě	underground, subway
线	xiàn	line

In the northern part of China, especially in Beijing, people tend to have a particular accent where they add an 儿 **er** sound to the end of words. For example, you may hear 这儿 **zhè'r** instead of 这里 **zhèlǐ**; or 画儿 **huà'r** instead of 画 **huà**. The meanings of the words do not change. This is mainly used in informal and spoken Mandarin Chinese.

Language notes

2.1 *Expressing position and location*

Words to express position are formed by taking nouns indicating directions, such as:

qián	hòu	páng	zuǒ
前 (front)	后 (behind)	旁 (beside)	左 (left)

yòu	běi	nán	dōng
右 (right)	北 (north)	南 (south)	东 (east)

xī	shàng	xià	
西 (west)	上 (above)	下 (below)	

and then adding one of these suffixes:

miàn	biān
面 (face)	边 (side).

Please note that these suffixes may keep or lose the original tone depending on the word. So you need to learn the word as a whole.

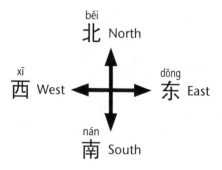

1. The location of place A can be expressed using either of the following two patterns:

- A + 在 zài (to be located) + **location**

  Cè suǒ zài qiánmian
  厕所在前面。
  The toilet is at the front.

  Dì tiě zài zuǒ bian
  地铁在左边。
  The underground is on the left.

- **location** + 有 yǒu (there is/are) + A

  Duì miàn yǒu yí ge tú shū guǎn
  对面有一个图书馆。
  There is a library opposite.

  Tā hòu mian yǒu sì ge rén
  他后面有四个人。
  There are four people behind him.

2. Indicating the location of A in terms of its position relative to B can be expressed using the following pattern:

- A + 在 zài (to locate) + B (的 de) **location**

  (The 的 **de** can be omitted in spoken Chinese.)

  Wǒ de jiā zài dà xué de dōng bian
  我的家在大学的东边。
  My house is to the east of the university.

  Cān tīng zài diàn yǐng yuàn de yòu bian
  餐厅在电影院的右边。
  The restaurant is on the right of the cinema.

2.2 Using the prepositions 从 cóng and 到 dào

The prepositions 从 **cóng** and 到 **dào** can be used to express not only time but also location. The preposition 从 **cóng** is used to indicate a starting point; whereas the preposition 到 **dào** indicates a terminal point or destination of the movement verbs.

Cóng zhè lǐ zǒu dào wǒ jiā bù yuǎn
从这里走到我家不远。
It's not far to walk to my house from here.

Cóng xué xiào zuò sān hào gōng gòng qì chē   dào Rén mín Guǎng chǎng xià chē
从学校坐三号公共汽车，到人民广场下车。
Take bus No 3 from the school and get off at the People's Square.

2.3 *Using imperatives*

Imperatives are used for giving orders or instructions – 'Take the bus', 'Get off at People's Square'. They are normally used in face-to-face interactions, therefore the person being addressed can be omitted as it is obvious who is meant. 请 **Qǐng** can be added at the beginning for politeness in a formal situation and 吧 **ba** can be added at the end for politeness in an informal situation.

Qǐng zuò
请坐! Please sit down.

Qǐng hē chá
请喝茶! Please have some tea.

Zuò ba
坐吧! Have a seat.

Hē chá ba
喝茶吧! Have some tea.

It is not necessarily rude in Chinese if you don't use 请 **qǐng** or 吧 **ba**. It very much depends on the context as well as your tone of voice.

In guest–host situations, duplicated imperatives are often used by the host to express the warmth of the invitation. For example:

Zuò zuò zuò
坐，坐，坐!
Sit, sit, sit!

Chī chī chī
吃，吃，吃!
Eat, eat, eat!

Hē hē hē
喝，喝，喝!
Drink, drink, drink!

Lái lái
来，来!
Come, come!

Practice

16 Look at the following pictures and complete the sentences, first with Pinyin, and then try Chinese characters if you can.

Cè suǒ zài cān tīng de
1. 厕所在餐厅的＿＿＿＿＿＿。

Tú shū guǎn zài　　　　　　de hòu mian
2. 图书馆在＿＿＿＿＿＿的后面。

Chāo shì　　　　　xué xiào de
3. 超市＿＿＿＿＿＿学校的＿＿＿＿。

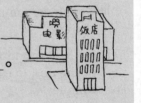

Diàn yǐng yuàn　　　　yǒu yí ge
4. 电影院＿＿＿＿有一个＿＿＿＿。

Wǒ de jiā
5. 我的家＿＿＿＿＿＿＿＿＿＿＿。

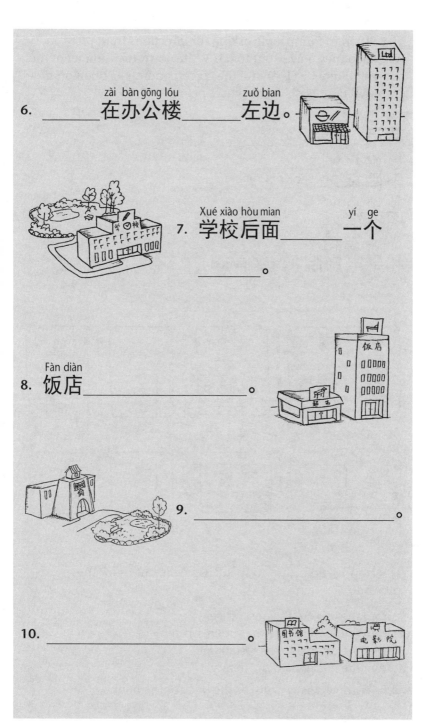

6. _____ 在办公楼 _____ 左边。
zài bàn gōng lóu zuǒ bian

7. 学校后面 _____ 一个
Xué xiào hòu mian yí ge
_____ 。

8. 饭店 _____ 。
Fàn diàn

9. _____ 。

10. _____ 。

17 Listen to four people asking for directions from point X. Where do they each want to go? Write down the number of the relevant dialogue (1–4) and the corresponding location on the map (A–D) for each of the places below:

chāo shì
超市 (supermarket) _____

Zhōng guó Yín háng
中国银行 (Bank of China) _____

tú shū guǎn
图书馆 (library) _____

Hé píng Diàn yǐng yuàn
和平电影院 (Peace Cinema) _____

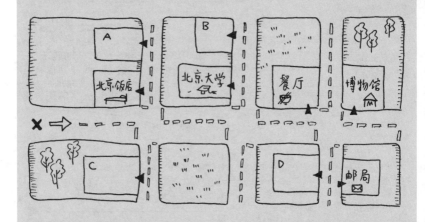

18 Now it's your turn to speak. Give directions for the following:

1. from the bank to the post office
2. from the university to the supermarket
3. from the cinema to the restaurant
4. from the museum to the library

Some sample answers are at the back of the book.

Learning Chinese characters

Common radicals in Chinese characters (1)

As already discussed in previous units, radicals indicate partial meaning of characters. You also need to be able to identify the radicals in order to look a character up in a Chinese dictionary as they are ordered by radical and then number of strokes. From this unit on, you will learn some of the most commonly used radicals with their meanings and sample characters.

口 "口" 'mouth' character on its own, refers to anything to do with the mouth

chī 吃 (to eat)　hē 喝 (to eat)　jiào 叫 (to call)　ma 吗 (question mark)

火 "火" 'fire' character on its own, refers to anything to do with fire

kǎo 烤 (to roast)　shāo 烧 (to burn)　bāo 煲 (to stew)　chǎo 炒 (to fry)

氵 "水" 'water' character on its own, refers to anything to do with water

hé 河 (river)　hǎi 海 (sea)　hú 湖 (lake)　xǐ 洗 (to wash)

木 "木" 'wood' character on its own, refers to anything to do with wood or trees

lín 林 (woods)　yǐ 椅 (chair)　chuáng 床 (bed)　zhuō 桌 (desk)

忄 "心" 'heart' character on its own, refers to feelings and emotions

nín 您 (the polite 'you'; to address the person with one's heart)

xiǎng 想 (to think of)　qíng 情 (emotion)　sī 思 (to miss)

女 "女" 'female' character on its own, refers to a female or anything related to females

mā
妈 (mother)

mèi
妹 (younger sister)

jiě
姐 (older sister)

lǎo
姥 (grandmother)

When a single character functions as a radical in another character, it is usually written slightly differently to allow for the balance of the whole character. It may even be written differently depending on whether it appears at the side or bottom of the character (e.g. see the 'heart' radical).

Recognize some basic street signs

Stop

Slow

Write the characters in the text

19 Try writing the following characters using the stroke order indicated.

左 **zuǒ** left	一	ナ	ナ	ナ	左			
右 **yòu** right	一	ナ	ナ	右	右			
前 **qián** front	丶	㇏	丷	广	疒	肖	肖	前	前
后 **hòu** behind	㇒	厂	斤	斤	后	后			
东 **dōng** east	一	七	东	东	东			
西 **xī** west	一	亡	万	丙	两	西			
南 **nán** south	一	十	冇	冇	内	肉	南	南	南
北 **běi** north	㇒	二	才	北	北				

路 lù road	丶	口	口	尸	尸	足	足	跒	跁
	趵	趵	路	路					
往 wǎng towards	丿	彳	彳	彳	彳	行	往	往	
拐 guǎi to turn	一	十	扌	扌	护	护	拐	拐	
坐 zuò to sit, to take (bus)	丿	人	𠆢	𠆢	𡗗	坐	坐		
边 biān side	丁	力	为	边	边				
哪儿 nǎ'r where	丶	口	口	叮	叮	呐	哬	哪	哪
	丿	儿							
面 miàn surface	一	丆	丆	丏	而	而	而	面	面

远	一	二	于	元	元	沅	远		
yuǎn far									
近	一	厂	斤	斤	斤	近	近		
jìn close									

Getting around in China

Bicycles are still the most common form of transport for day-to-day journeys. There are around 300 million bicycles being ridden in China. However, nowadays for longer distances, with the expansion of cities as well as the economic growth, more and more people are buying cars instead of riding bikes or relying on public transport. In China people drive on the right-hand side of the road, the same as in continental Europe and the United States but the opposite of Britain and Japan.

China Rail (中国铁路 **Zhōngguó Tiělù**) is the biggest and busiest rail network in the world and links all the major towns and cities in China. You can buy different types of train tickets. For short trips, you can usually choose between a hard seat (硬座 **yìngzuò**) and a soft seat (软座 **ruǎnzuò**). A hard seat is like a bench and a soft seat is a soft upholstered seat. For a longer journey, you could choose between a hard-sleeper (硬卧 **yìngwò**) and a soft-sleeper (软卧 **ruǎnwò**). The difference here is the type of mattress provided and the number of bunks per compartment. Travelling by train gives you a chance to interact with Chinese people as well as to enjoy the beautiful views along the way.

unit 10

Staying in a hotel

Dì shí kè Zhù fàn diàn
第十课 住饭店

In this unit, you will learn:

- How to check into a hotel
- How to make simple requests and describe situations
- About some more common radicals in Chinese characters
- About hotels and properties in China

Getting the pronunciation right

Pīn yīn liàn xí
拼音练习

In this unit, you will continue to do some more advanced Pinyin practice with a focus on words starting with the second tone. You will also learn a few slang expressions and famous sayings which reveal the traditional philosophy and values of Chinese culture!

1 Combinations with the second tone: Pronounce the following words on your own first, and then listen to the audio. Go over it until you feel comfortable with the patterns.

The second tone + the first tone

míngtiān	**shíjiān**	**shíyī**	**zuótiān**	**qiánbāo**
tomorrow	time	eleven	yesterday	wallet

The second tone + the second tone

xuéxí	**yínháng**	**zúqiú**	**Déguó**	**yóujú**
to study	bank	football	Germany	post office

The second tone + the third tone

nín hǎo	**píngguǒ**	**yóuyǒng**	**píjiǔ**	**cídiǎn**
hello	apple	to swim	beer	dictionary

The second tone + the fourth tone

búcuò	**tóngshì**	**háishì**	**zázhì**	**chéngshì**
not bad	colleague	or	magazine	city

The second tone + the neutral tone

shénme	**péngyou**	**érzi**	**míngzi**	**háizi**
what	friend	son	name	child

2 Sound discrimination: As you saw in the last unit, some Chinese sounds may sound similar to you, especially when they are combined in certain ways. In this section, focus on the sounds zh, ch, sh, z, c, s, j and x, which are usually considered to be difficult for beginners:

chá	**hùzhào**	**fángjiān**	**yàoshi**
tea	passport	room	key

xūyào	**dēngjìbiǎo**	**xiē**	**jiàoxǐng**
to need	registration form	some	to make up

xíngli	**jìcún**	**shàngcì**	**shǒujī**
luggage	to deposit	last time	mobile phone

3 Fun time: The Chinese language is rich and culturally oriented. Learning a few slang words and famous sayings will not only really impress the Chinese people you speak to but will also increase your understanding of the language and culture. The following are just a small selection of the most popular expressions, so just listen and pick the ones that you find most interesting or enlightening!

Kù	Méi mén	Guài bu de
酷!	**没门!**	**怪不得!**
Cool!	No way!	No wonder!

chī xiāng

吃香

'to taste delicious'

This refers to someone or something that is popular.

Tiān wú jué rén zhī lù

天无绝人之路!

'There is no totally blocked road for people.'

This means that all things will be worked out eventually.

Yǒu qíng rén zhōng chéng juàn shǔ

有情人终成眷属。

'May couples in love eventually be together.'

This is usually used as a good wish to couples.

Zhǐ yào gōng fu shēn   tiě chǔ mó chéng zhēn

只要功夫深，铁楮磨成针。

'As long as there is enough effort, an iron stick can be ground into a needle.'

This means that with determination and hard work, one can achieve what is believed to be impossible.

Dà zhàng fu yì yán jì chū   sì mǎ nán zhuī

大丈夫一言既出，四马难追。

'A real man says one word, four horses cannot drag it back.'

This refers to a principle whereby people to stick to their word and their promises.

Yì nián zhī jì zài yú chūn   yí rì zhī jì zài yú chén

一年之计在于春，一日之计在于晨。

'A year's plan happens in spring, a day's plan happens in the morning.'

This is all about the importance of planning.

| Communicating in Chinese | Hàn yǔ jiāo liú 汉语交流 |

1 I've booked a room

Wǒ yù dìng le yí ge fáng jiān
我预定了一个房间

Key expressions: **Checking into a hotel**

To say what kind of room you want:

Wǒ yù dìng le yí ge dān rén shuāng rén fáng jiān
我预定了一个单人 / 双人房间。
I've reserved a single/double room.

Wǒ shì zài wǎng shang dìng de
我是在网上订的。
I booked it online.

Wǒ zhù sān ge wǎn shang
我住三个晚上。
I am staying for three nights.

Qǐng wèn fáng jiān lǐ dài kōng tiáo ma
请问，房间里带空调吗？
Does the room include air conditioning?

What you might hear when you check in:

Qǐng wèn nín guì xìng
请问，您贵姓？
What's your surname?

Qǐng nín bǎ hù zhào gěi wǒ kàn yí xià
请您把护照给我看一下。
Could you please show me your passport?

Qǐng nín tián yí xià zhè zhāng dēng jì biǎo
请您填一下这张登记表。
Could you please fill in this registration form?

Zhè shì nín de fáng jiān yào shi
这是您的房间钥匙。
This is your room key.

4 Look at the different types of rooms below and try to read them out loud in Chinese.

dān rén fáng jiān
单人房间
single room

shuāng rén fáng jiān
双人房间
double room

dài wèi shēng jiān
带卫生间
with bathroom

dài kōng tiáo
带空调
with air conditioning

dài wú xiàn shàng wǎng
带无线上网
with wireless internet

bāo zǎo cān
包早餐
includes breakfast

5 How do you say the following in Chinese? Say them out loud and then check the answers at the back of the book.

1. I want a single room with bathroom.
2. I want a double room with wireless internet.
3. I don't want a single room. I want a double room.
4. I want a double room with air conditioning.

6 Listen to a guest checking into a hotel and have a go at
answering the questions that follow to see how much you've
understood. Don't worry if you need to listen several times over.

Zhang:
Xiǎo jiě   nǐ hǎo   Wǒ yù dìng le yí ge fáng jiān
小姐，你好。我预定了一个房间。

Receptionist:
Hǎo   xiān sheng   qǐng wèn   nín guì xìng
好，先生，请问，您贵姓？

Zhang:
Wǒ xìng Zhāng   jiào Zhāng Míng   Wǒ shì zài wǎng shang dìng
我姓张，叫张明。我是在网上订
le yí ge dān rén fáng jiān   Wǒ zhù sān ge wǎn shang
了一个单人房间。我住三个晚上。

Receptionist:
Hǎo de   qǐng shāo děng   Wǒ chá yí xià   Yǒu le
好的，请稍等。我查一下。有了，
nín de fáng jiān shì sān líng qī hào fáng jiān   zài sān
您的房间是三零七号房间，在三
lóu   Qǐng nín bǎ hù zhào gěi wǒ kàn yí xià   rán
楼。请您把护照给我看一下，然
hòu tián yí xià zhè zhāng dēng jì biǎo
后填一下这张登记表。

Zhang:
Hǎo   gěi nǐ   Fáng jiān dài wú xiàn shàng wǎng ma
好，给你。房间带无线上网吗？

Receptionist:
Dài   Zhè shì nín de yào shi   Zǎo cān shì cóng qī
带。这是您的钥匙。早餐是从七
diǎn dào shí diǎn bàn   Diàn tī zài dà tīng de yòu bian
点到十点半。电梯在大厅的右边。

Zhang:
Hǎo   xiè xie
好，谢谢。

1. What is the guest's name?
2. What kind of room has he booked?
3. How many nights is he staying?
4. What's his room number?
5. Does the room have wireless internet?
6. When is breakfast served?

New words and phrases: Checking into a hotel

房间	fángjiān	room
网上	wǎngshang	on the internet
订	dìng	to book; to confirm
单人	dānrén	single person
双人	shuāngrén	two people/couple
空调	kōngtiáo	air conditioning
卫生间	wèishēngjiān	bathroom
查	chá	to check
楼	lóu	floor/storey
把	bǎ	(grammar word – see Language note 1.1)
护照	hùzhào	passport
填	tián	to fill in (a form)
登记表	dēngjìbiǎo	registration form
带	dài	to include; to have with
无线上网	wúxiànshàngwǎng	wireless internet
钥匙	yàoshi	key
电梯	diàntī	lift/elevator
大厅	dàtīng	lobby
包	bāo	to include

Language notes

1.1 *The use of the* 把 *structure*

bǎ

把 **Bǎ** is a grammar word in Chinese (known as a co-verb) and is normally used in the sentence pattern:

bǎ

A + 把 + B + Verb + Result

It is one of the most common structures in Chinese. It indicates a certain action is carried out towards B (a person or thing) by A (a person or thing) which emphasizes the following:

1. A is the active subject
2. B is the passive object
3. The condition or position of B therefore will be/has changed due to A's action

Qǐng nín bǎ nín de hù zhào gěi wǒ kàn yí xià

请您把您的护照给我看一下。   Could you please
   A   B   V+R   let me take a look at
                                      your passport?

Wǒ bǎ kě lè hē le

我把可乐喝了。   I drank the Coke.
A   B   V+R

Tā huì bǎ fáng jiān yù dìng le

他会把房间预定了。   He will reserve the room.
A   B   V+R

In example 3, although the sentence is in the future tense, 了 **le** is needed to indicate that the result of A's action is completed.

le

1.2 了 *indicating completion of an action*

The particle 了 **le** is used as a completion aspect indicator in Chinese. It follows an action verb to show that the action has been completed. It can express both that an action was completed (simple past tense, e.g. I went to China) and that an action has taken place (present perfect tense, e.g. I have been to China) depending on the context.

Tā qù le xué xiào
他去了学校。   He went to school.

Wǒ yù dìng le   yí ge dān rén fáng jiān
我预定了一个单人房间。   I have booked a single room.
                                 (*or:* I booked a single room.)

Wǒ hē le sān bēi chá
我喝了三杯茶。   I drank three cups of tea.

Practice

7 Listen to a few short sentences and then choose the correct English translation for each.

1. **a.** I have booked a single room with bathroom.
   b. I have booked a double room with bathroom.
   c. I have booked a single room with breakfast.

2. **a.** I am staying for 3 days.
   b. I am staying for 3 weeks.
   c. I am staying for 2 weeks.

3. **a.** Could you please let me have a look at your room?
   b. Could you please let me have a look at your passport?
   c. Could you please let me have a look at your key?

4. **a.** Breakfast is from 5:00 to 10:00am.
   b. Breakfast is from 6:00 to 11:30am.
   c. Breakfast is from 6:30 to 11:00am.

5. **a.** Your room is 307, on the third floor.
   b. Your room is 403, on the fourth floor.
   c. Your room is 304, on the third floor.

6. **a.** I would like to book a room.
   b. I have booked a room online.
   c. I have booked a room on the phone.

Steamed filled rice buns –
a typical Chinese breakfast

8 Look at the following pictures and write as many sentences about them as you can. Try to use the words provided and use the first person 'I'. There are some sample answers at the back of the book.

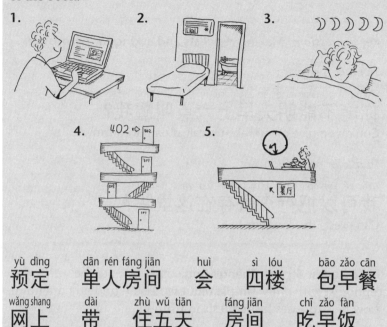

yù dìng	dān rén fáng jiān	huì	sì lóu	bāo zǎo cān
预定	单人房间	会	四楼	包早餐

wǎng shang	dài	zhù wǔ tiān	fáng jiān	chī zǎo fàn
网上	带	住五天	房间	吃早饭

Wǒ zài wǎng shang yù dìng le yí ge fáng jiān
e.g. 我在网上预定了一个房间。

9 Change the following sentences using the 把 **bǎ** structure. The first one has been done for you.

Tā yù dìng le fáng jiān   Tā bǎ fáng jiān yù dìng le
1. 他预定了房间。 → 他**把**房间预定了。

Wǒ hē le kā fēi
2. 我喝了咖啡。

Mā ma huì zuò zǎo fàn
3. 妈妈会做早饭。

Wǒ chá le yí xià hù zhào
4. 我查了一下护照。

Tā qǐng wǒ men qù Zhōng guó le
5. 他请我们去中国了。

Tā gěi le wǒ yào shi
6. 他给了我钥匙。

Wáng xiān sheng tián le dēng jì biǎo
7. 王先生填了登记表。

Wǒ kě yǐ bǎ xíng li
2 Can I keep
my luggage here?
我可以把行李
jì cún zài zhè lǐ ma
寄存在这里吗?

Key expressions: **Making requests and asking for permission**

To make a request:

Nǐ néng bu néng míng tiān zǎo shang liù diǎn jiào xǐng wǒ
你能不能明天早上六点叫醒我?
Could you give me a wake-up call at 6am tomorrow?

To ask for permission:

Wǒ kě yǐ bǎ xíng li jì cún zài zhè lǐ ma
我可以把行李寄存在这里吗?
Can I keep this luggage here?

---

10 The guest 张明 **Zhāng Míng** comes back to the receptionist with a few simple requests. Listen and pay attention to how he expresses his requests in Chinese.

Xiānsheng nín hǎo   Nín xū yào xiē shén me
Receptionist: 先生,您好。您需要些什么?

Nǐ néng bu néng míng tiān zǎo shang liù diǎn jiào xǐng wǒ
Zhang: 你能不能明天早上六点叫醒我?

Dāng rán kě yǐ   Nín zhù jǐ hào fáng jiān
Receptionist: 当然可以。您住几号房间?

fáng jiān
Zhang: 307 房间。

Hǎo de   méi wèn tí   Nín hái xū yào shén me
Receptionist: 好的,没问题。您还需要什么?

Wǒ kě yǐ bǎ xíng li jì cún zài zhè lǐ ma
Zhang: 我可以把行李寄存在这里吗?

Receptionist:
Dāng rán kě yǐ   Zhè shì nín de xíng li pái
当然可以。这是您的行李牌。

Zhang:
Tài xiè xie le
太谢谢了。

New words and phrases: Hotel services

需要	xūyào	to need
些	xiē	some
能	néng	can; to be able to
叫醒	jiàoxǐng	to wake (somebody) up
行李	xíngli	luggage
寄存	jìcún	to deposit; to keep
行李牌	xínglipái	luggage tag

Language note

néng   kě yǐ
2.1 *Use of* 能 *and* 可以

Both 能 **néng** (can, to be able to) and 可以 **kěyǐ** (may) can be used to express permission and possibility in the sense of someone being able to do something on a particular occasion.

To give and ask for permission:

Nǐ kě yǐ   néng bǎ xíng li jì
你可以 / 能把行李寄
cún zài zhè lǐ
存在这里。

You may keep your luggage here.

Wǒ kě yǐ   néng shuō Yīng wén ma
我可以 / 能说英文吗?   May I speak English?

To express possibility:

Nǐ míng tiān kě yǐ   néng lái ma
你明天可以 / 能来吗?   Can you come tomorrow?

Tā kě yǐ   néng zài dà xué zhù
她可以 / 能在大学住。   She can stay at the university.

However, **能 néng** (can, to be able to) also expresses general and physical ability:

Nǐ néng kàn dào tā ma
你能看到他吗?   Can you see him?

Wǒ néng yí cì hē sān bēi pí jiǔ
我能一次喝三杯啤酒。   I can drink three glasses of beer at once.

Practice

11 Listen to the requests on the audio and number the corresponding pictures in the order you hear them. The first one has been done for you.

a. _____   b. _____   c. __1__   d. _____

e. _____   f. _____   g. _____   h. _____

12 Now try to make the following requests in Chinese:

1. Ask for some coffee
2. Ask for a morning call at 7am
3. Ask if you can leave your luggage at the hotel
4. Ask if you can reserve a room on the internet
5. Ask if you can stay for a week
6. Ask if you can take a look at the room

Check your answers at the back of the book.

3 I can't find my bag

Wǒ de bāo bú jiàn le
我的包不见了

Key expressions: **Describing a situation**

Wǒ zài Zhōng guó de shí hou
我在中国的时候…

When I was in China ...

gāng   bù jiǔ   jiù
刚…（不久），…就…

just ..., and then (not long after) ...

Wǒ de bāo bú jiàn le   Yǒu   hái yǒu
我的包不见了。   有…还有…

I lost my bag.   There is/are ... and there is/are also ...

xìng hǎo   zhōng yú
幸好…   终于…

fortunately ...   finally ...

kě néng   Jiù zài zhè ge shí hou
可能…   就在这个时候…

maybe ...   Just at that moment ...

---

13 Listen to Alice talking about her previous travel experience in China. You might want to go through the new words first before you try to understand what happened and how it was resolved.

Tiananmen Gate, Beijing

Wǒ shàng cì zài Zhōng guó lǚ xíng de shí hou　　　 zhù zài Běi jīng
我上次在中国旅行的时候，住在北京

Fàn diàn　　Nà tiān　　wǒ qù le yín háng　gāng huí fàn diàn　　jiù
饭店。那天，我去了银行，刚回饭店，就

fā xiàn wǒ de bāo 　　　　　　　bú jiàn le　　Wǒ de bāo lǐ yǒu
发现我的包 　　不见了。我的包里有

wǒ de hù zhào 　　　　　　　　měi jīn hé　　　　rén mín bì
我的护照 ，300 美金和 1000 人民币

，
hái yǒu yì běn tōng xùn lù
还有一本通讯录

hé yí ge shǒu jī 　　　　　Wǒ zhǎo le hěn jiǔ hái shì méi
和一个手机 。我找了很久还是没

zhǎo dào　　fēi cháng zháo jí
找到，非常着急。

幸好，我终于想到我可能把包忘在出
Xìng hǎo　　wǒ zhōng yú xiǎng dào wǒ kě néng bǎ bāo wàng zài chū

租车上 了。前台小姐很热心，
zū chē shàng　　　　　　　　　le　　Qián tái xiǎo jiě hěn rè xīn

马上打电话给出租车公司。
mǎ shàng dǎ diàn huà gěi chū zū chē gōng sī

就在这个时候，那位出租车司机出现
Jiù zài zhè ge shí hou　　nà wèi chū zū chē sī jī chū xiàn

了，手里拿着我的包！我非常感谢那位出
le　shǒu lǐ ná zhe wǒ de bāo　Wǒ fēi cháng gǎn xiè nà wèi chū

租车司机和前台小姐的帮助!
zū chē sī jī hé qián tái xiǎo jiě de bāng zhù

New words and phrases: I can't find my bag

上次	shàngcì	last time; the previous time
那天	nàtiān	on that day
刚 … 就 …	gāng … jiù …	just … then …
发现	fāxiàn	to discover
包	bāo	bag (general term)
里	lǐ	in, inside
美金	měijīn	US dollars
人民币	rénmínbì	RMB, Chinese currency
通讯录	tōngxùnlù	address book
手机	shǒujī	mobile phone/cell phone

找	zhǎo	to look for
找到	zhǎodào	to find
非常	fēicháng	extremely, very
着急	zháojí	to be worried
幸好	xìnghǎo	fortunately
可能	kěnéng	maybe, perhaps
终于	zhōngyú	finally, at the end
想到	xiǎngdào	to think of; to think about
忘	wàng	to forget
前台	qiántái	reception; front desk
热心	rèxīn	warm-hearted
马上	mǎshàng	at once; immediately
打电话	dǎdiànhuà	to make a phone call
司机	sījī	driver
出现	chūxiàn	to appear; to show
手	shǒu	hand
拿	ná	to take; to carry
感谢	gǎnxiè	to thank
帮助	bāngzhù	help; assistance

Language notes

3.1 *Use of ...* 的时候 *(when ..., while ...)*
de shí hou

This structure is used as a time clause, translated as 'when …' or 'while …' in English.

Wǒ xǐ huan zài xué xí de shí hou hē chá
我喜欢在学习**的时候**喝茶。

I like drinking tea when I am studying.

Tā zài Zhōngguó de shí hou hái bú rèn shi wǒ
他在中国**的时候**还不认识我。

He didn't know me yet when he was in China.

Míngtiān nǐ lái de shí hou bǎ wǒ de shū yě dài lái
明天你来**的时候**把我的书也带来。

Also bring the book when you come tomorrow.

The only thing you need to be careful of is that, as you may have already noticed, the order of the sentence differs in Chinese and English. The time expression needs to be placed at the beginning of the sentence in Chinese.

3.2 *Use of* 刚···, ···就··· *(just ..., and then ...)*
gāng   jiù

This sentence structure indicates the short time period between two actions or events. The sentence in the dialogue
那天，我去了银行，刚回饭店，就发现我的包不见了 **Nàtiān, wǒ qù le yínháng, gāng huí fàndiàn, jiù fāxiàn wǒ de bāo bú jiàn le** means: 'That day, I went to the bank. I'd just got back to the hotel, and then found that my bag was gone.' Here are more examples of how it's used:

Wǒ gāng huí jiā   tā men jiù lái le
我**刚**回家，他们**就**来了。

Not long after I got home, they came.

Wǒ gāngzhǎo tā   tā jiù chū xiàn le
我**刚**找他，他**就**出现了。

Not long after I started to look for him, he appeared.

3.3 *Use of 'verb +* 到 *'*
dào

到 **Dào** (to reach somewhere, to arrive) acts as a complement when it follows another verb, indicating a direction or a result and manner.

e.g. Indicating a direction:

zǒu
走 to walk

zǒu dào wǒ de jiā
走到我的家 to walk to my house

kāi
开 to drive

kāi dào Běi jīng
开到北京 to drive to Beijing

e.g. Indicating a result and manner:

kàn
看 to look (does not mean you actually see anything)

kàn dào
看到 to see (to have seen)

tīng
听 to listen (does not mean you actually hear anything)

tīng dào
听到 to hear (to have heard)

zhǎo
找 to look for

zhǎo dào
找到 to find (to have found)

xiǎng
想 to think

xiǎng dào
想到 to think of (sth.) (to have thought of)

3.4 *Use of 'verb +* 着 *'*
zhe

着 **Zhe** is used directly after a verb and it usually refers to the continuing state of an action. In the dialogue, it is used to express when one action occurs at the same time as another. Therefore, the sentence 就在这个时候，那位出租车司机出现在了饭店前台，手里还拿着我的包 **Jiù zài zhè ge shíhou, nà wèi chūzūchē sījī chūxiàn zài le fàndiàn qiántái, shǒu lǐ hái ná zhe wǒ de bāo** means: 'Just at that moment, the taxi driver appeared at the hotel reception, carrying my bag in his hand.'

Here are some more examples:

Tā hē zhe kā fēi zǒu huí jiā
他喝着咖啡走回家。   He walked back home while drinking a coffee.

Wǒ men kàn zhe diàn shì chī fàn
我们看着电视吃饭。   We ate while watching TV.

Practice

14 Answer the following questions based on Exercise 13.

shàng cì zài Zhōng guó lǚ xíng de shí hou
1. Alice 上次在中国旅行的时候，
zhù zài nǎ 'r le
住在哪儿了？

Nà tiān   tā xiān qù le nǎ 'r
2. 那天，她先去了哪儿？

Tā shén me shí hou fā xiàn tā de bāo bú jiàn le
3. 她什么时候发现她的包不见了？

Tā de bāo lǐ yǒu shén me
4. 她的包里有什么？

Qián tái xiǎo jiě rè xīn ma
5. 前台小姐热心吗？

Tā kě néng bǎ bāo wàng
6. 她可能把包忘
nǎ 'r le
哪儿了？

Shuí chū xiàn zài le qián tái
7. 谁出现在了前台？
Nà ge rén shǒu lǐ ná zhe shén me
那个人手里拿着什么？

15 Complete the sentences using these words and phrases:

de shí hou   gāng   jiù   yǒu   hái yǒu
…的时候   刚…，…就…   有…还有…

zhōng yú   kě néng   mǎ shàng
终于   可能   马上

Wǒ zhǎo le yí ge xià wǔ   zhǎo dào le nà běn shū
1. 我找了一个下午，_____ 找到了那本书。

Tā   wǎn shang qù Shàng hǎi
2. 他 _____ 晚上去上海。

Fáng jiān lǐ   diàn shì kōng tiáo   diàn huà
3. 房间里 _____ 电视，空调，_____ 电话。

Nǐ zài Zhōng guó   shuō Zhōng wén le ma
4. 你在中国 _____ 说中文了吗?

Nǐ kě yǐ   jiù lái ma
5. 你可以 _____ 就来吗?

Tā   lái dà xué   wǒ men   rèn shi le
6. 她 _____ 来大学，我们 _____ 认识了。

16 Look at the following pictures and try to write out the sequence of events. The first one has been done for you.

1.

2.

Qù nián   Zhāng xiān sheng zhù zài
去年，张先生住在
Běi jīng Fàn diàn
北京饭店。

Learning Chinese characters

Xué hàn zì
学汉字

Common radicals in Chinese characters (2)

日 `日` 'sun' character on its own, refers to words to do with the sun, or days and times, which are related as they indicate the movement of the sun

míng
明 (bright)

xīng
星 (star)

wǎn
晚 (late)

shí
时 (time)

亻 `人` 'person' character on its own, refers to things related to people

nǐ
你 (you)

tā
他 (he)

xiū
休 (to rest)

zhòng
众 (group of people)

月 ˝月˝ 'moon' character on its own, refers to things related to the moon or to body parts

qī
期 (period of time)

péng
朋 (friend – it is believed that friends are like two moons that support each other)

liǎn
脸 (face)

jiǎo
脚 (feet)

车 ˝车˝ 'vehicle' character on its own, refers to anything to do with transport

lún
轮 (wheel)

liàng
辆 (measure word for vehicle)

kù
库 (parking)

zhuǎn
转 (to turn)

讠 ˝言˝ 'speech' character on its own, refers to speech or talking

shuō
说 (to say)

sù
诉 (to complain)

rèn shi
认识 (to recognize, to tell)

shī
诗 (poem)

钅 ˝金˝ 'metal' character on its own, refers to metal products or objects

zhēn
针 (needle)

tiě
铁 (iron)

zhōng
钟 (clock)

qián
钱 (money)

A rural hotel

Write the characters in the text

17 Try writing the following characters using the stroke order indicated.

把 **bǎ** (grammar word)	一	扌	扌	扣	扣	扣	把		
查 **chá** to check	一	十	才	木	朩	杏	杏	杳	查
能 **néng** can	厶	厶	刍	刍	肖	肖	育	能	能
	能								
找 **zhǎo** to look for	一	扌	扌	扌	扒	找	找		
忘 **wàng** to forget	丶	二	亡	产	忘	忘	忘		
拿 **ná** to hold	丿	人	人	人	全	合	仝	仝	拿
	拿								
刚 **gāng** just	丨	冂	冈	冈	刚	刚			
就 **jiù** then	丶	二	亠	产	古	亨	京	京	京
	就	就	就						

	`	⺊	⺌	户	户	庐	房	房	

房间
fángjiān
room

	`	丨	门	门	间	间	间		

单
dān
single

	`	⺌	⺍	兴	兯	单	単	单	

双
shuāng
pair

フ	又	邓	双						

Hotels in China

There are many hotels in China ranging from 1-star guesthouses to 5-star international hotel chains. You will come across many different words for 'hotel'. For example, big hotels are usually called 饭店 fàndiàn, 大酒店 dàjiǔdiàn, 酒店 jiǔdiàn and 宾馆 bīnguǎn; relatively local or medium-sized hotels may be called 旅店 lǚdiàn or 旅馆 lǚguǎn; and some institutes may have their own guesthouses or smaller hotels, which may be called 招待所 zhāodàisuǒ. In the larger hotels, all employees are expected to be able to speak English and you will be able to enjoy a range of services such as transport bookings, travel information and currency exchange. If you would like to experience something more traditionally Chinese, many old courtyard-style homes have now been turned into hotels and hostels.

Hotel in Sanya, Hainan Island

Usually there isn't a problem finding a place to stay without booking in advance. However, if you don't know a city well, it is advisable to book online before you get there, and this may also mean you find some good deals or discounts. During the high season (usually spring and autumn), you can always book hotels through travel agencies around the country. Some websites that may be helpful are: www.elong.com and www.ctrip.com. At airports in the big cities there is always information on hotels, or travel agencies that may be able to help you to get good value hotels.

If you stay in a Chinese hotel, tipping is not usually expected. However, in the big cities, some hotels and restaurants have adopted this custom.

The numbering of the hotel floors/storeys is the same as in the United States and different from the UK. So what is known as the ground floor in the UK is actually the first floor in China.

*Sofitel Jin Jiang Oriental
Pudong Hotel, Shanghai*

11

Leisure and hobbies

Dì shí yī kè   Xiū xián hé ài hào
第十一课　休闲和爱好

In this unit, you will learn:
- How to talk about activities you like and dislike
- How to make simple comparisons
- How to give reasons
- About even more common radicals in Chinese characters
- About lifestyles and leisure activities in China

Getting the pronunciation right

Pīn yīn liàn xí
拼音练习

In this unit, you will continue to do some more advanced Pinyin practice, this time with a focus on words starting with the third tone. You will also learn another very famous Classical Chinese poem!

1 Combinations with the third tone: Try to pronounce the following words on your own first, and then listen to the audio. Keep going over it until you get used to the patterns.

The third tone + the first tone

lǎoshī	zuǒbiān	xiǎoshuō	yǔtīan	jiǎndān
teacher	left side	novel	rainy day	simple

The third tone + the second tone

xiǎoshí	yǔyán	nǚ'ér	qǐchuáng	wǎngqiú
hour	language	daughter	to get up	tennis

The third tone + the third tone (Remember the tone change: 3rd + 3rd = 2nd + 3rd)

nǐhǎo	**kěyǐ**	**yǔfǎ**	**xiǎojiě**	**xǐzǎo**
hello	can	grammar	miss	to take a bath

The third tone + the fourth tone

nǚshì	**qǐngwèn**	**kǒngpà**	**nǎilào**	**bǎobèi**
madam	excuse me	afraid	cheese	treasure

The third tone + the neutral tone

xǐhuan	**wǒmen**	**zěnme**	**yǐzi**	**jiějie**
to like	we	how	chair	older sister

2 Sound discrimination: In this section, focus on the sounds in, ing, zh, ch, sh, z, c and s, which are usually considered to be difficult for beginners:

yīnyuè	**yīnwèi**	**píngshí**	**qīngliáng**
music	because	usually	cool

wǔtīng	**huánjìng**	**zuòfàn**	**fàngsōng**
disco	environment	to cook	relaxing

zhīshi	**zàishuō**	**cídiǎn**	**sānshí**
knowledge	in addition	dictionary	thirty

Traditonal fan dancing – a Chinese hobby

3 Fun time: You already read a poem in Unit 8. On the next page is another – it is one of the most popular poems from the Tang dynasty and was written by Li Shen.

Lǐ Shēn de mǐn nóng
李绅的《悯农》

Chú hé rì dāng wǔ
锄禾日当午，
Working in the field when it's midday,

hàn dī hé xià tǔ
汗滴禾下土，
sweat drops on the soil underneath the grain,

shuí zhī pán zhōng cān
谁知盘中餐，
who can tell from the food on the plate,

lì lì jiē xīn kǔ
粒粒皆辛苦。
that every single piece is such hard work.

The poet was trying to describe the tough working conditions for farmers and this was later used as an educational poem to stop children wasting food.

Hàn yǔ jiāo liú
Communicating in Chinese
汉语交流

Wǒ xǐ huan yóu yǒng
1 I like swimming
我喜欢游泳

Key expressions: Expressing likes and dislikes

To say what you like:

Wǒ xǐ huan yóu yǒng
我喜欢游泳。
I like swimming.

Wǒ gèng xǐ huan dǎ lán qiú
我更喜欢打篮球。
I prefer playing basketball.

Wǒ zuì xǐ huan tīng yīn yuè
我最喜欢听音乐。
I like listening to music the most.

To say what you dislike:

Wǒ bù xǐ huan kàn jīng jù
我不喜欢看京剧。
I don't like watching Beijing opera.

Wǒ gèng bù xǐ huan yě cān
我更不喜欢野餐。
I dislike having picnics even more.

Wǒ zuì bù xǐ huan tī zú qiú
我最不喜欢踢足球。
I like playing football the least.

4 Xiao Li describes his likes and dislikes. Complete the following sentences with the help of the audio and the activity vocabulary below and over the page.

1. Wǒ xǐ huan
我喜欢 _____ 。

4. Wǒ gèng bù xǐ huan
我更不喜欢 _____ 。

2. Wǒ bù xǐ huan
我不喜欢 _____ 。

5. Wǒ zuì xǐ huan
我最喜欢 _____ 。

3. Wǒ gèng xǐ huan
我更喜欢 _____ 。

6. Wǒ zuì bù xǐ huan
我最不喜欢 _____ 。

a.

kàn jīng jù
看京剧
to watch Beijing opera

b.

pān yán
攀岩
to rock-climb

c.

yě cān
野餐
to have a picnic

d.

kàn diàn shì
看电视
to watch TV

e.

yóu yǒng
游泳
to go swimming

f.

dǎ lán qiú
打篮球
to play basketball

g.

tī zú qiú
踢足球
to play football

h.

tīng yīn yuè
听音乐
to listen to music

i.

kàn shū
看书
to read

j.

kàn diàn yǐng
看电影
to watch movies

k.

chàng kǎ lā
唱卡拉 OK
to sing Karaoke

l.

bèng dí
蹦迪
to go clubbing

m.

zài wǎng shang liáo tiān
在网上聊天
to chat on the internet

n.

mǎi dōng xi
买东西
to go shopping

o.

hē kā fēi
喝咖啡
to have coffee

The activities and hobbies in Exercise 4 are your **New words and phrases** for this section.

| Language note |

1.1 *The use of* 更 gèng *and* 最 zuì

To indicate the *comparative* form or preference, use the intensifier 更 gèng (more) in front of an adjective or verb.

Wǒ xǐ huan jīng jù   wǒ gèng xǐ huan yóu yǒng
我喜欢京剧，我**更**喜欢游泳。
I like Beijing opera. I like swimming more.

Bà ba hěn gāo xìng   mā ma gèng gāo xìng
爸爸很高兴，妈妈**更**高兴。
Father is happy. Mother is happier.

Tā bǐ tā gèng duì kàn shū yǒu xìng qù
她比他**更**对看书有兴趣。
She's more interested in reading than he is.

Wǒ gèng xiǎng hē kā fēi
我**更**想喝咖啡。
I prefer drinking coffee.

To indicate the *superlative* form, use the intensifier 最 **zuì** (the most) in front of an adjective or verb (usually a verb describing a state that lasts a long time, such as 喜欢 **xǐhuan**).

Wǒ jīn tiān zuì máng
我今天**最**忙。   I am most busy today.

Wǒ zuì xǐ huan mǎi dōng xi
我**最**喜欢买东西。   I like shopping the most.

Shàng hǎi rén zuì duō
上海人**最**多。   Shanghai has the most people.

Practice

5 Liu Hong is going through the series of pictures in Exercise 4, telling you whether she likes or dislikes these sports and activities. Draw ☺ next to each activity she likes, and ☹ next to those she doesn't. Draw ☺ ☺ for the things she likes best, and ☹ ☹ for those activities she really dislikes.

6 Which activities and sports do you like and dislike? Use these basic phrases and change the underlined words to suit your own likes and dislikes. Talk to a partner or simply say it all out loud to yourself!

Wǒ xǐ huan kàn jīng jù
我喜欢看<u>京剧</u>。

Wǒ bù xǐ huan pān yán
我不喜欢<u>攀岩</u>。

wǒ gèng xǐ huan yě cān
我更喜欢<u>野餐</u>。

Wǒ gèng bù xǐ huan kàn diàn shì
我更不喜欢<u>看电视</u>。

Wǒ zuì xǐ huan yóu yǒng
我最喜欢<u>游泳</u>。

Wǒ zuì bù xǐ huan dǎ lán qiú
我最不喜欢<u>打篮球</u>。

2 I'm not interested in Beijing opera

Wǒ duì jīng jù méi xìng qù
我对京剧没兴趣

Key expressions: **Expressing interest and conditions**

To say if something interests you or not

Wǒ duì kàn diàn yǐng yǒu xìng qù
我对看电影有兴趣。

Wǒ duì mǎi dōng xi méi xìng qù
我对买东西没兴趣。

I am interested in watching films.

I am not interested in shopping.

To express conditions:

Rú guǒ   jiù
如果…，就…

Tiān gōng bú zuò měi
天公不作美…

If ..., then ...

If the circumstances don't permit ...
(lit. If the gods don't make things easy).

7 Listen to two friends discussing their plans for the weekend and try to understand what they each like and dislike.

Míng tiān zhōu mò   nǐ xiǎng zuò xiē shén me
A: 明天周末，你想做些什么？

Wǒ zuì xǐ huan kàn jīng jù   Wǒ tīng shuō zhè ge xīng qī Běi jīng
B: 我最喜欢看京剧。我听说这个星期北京
jīng jù tuán lái Shàng hǎi yǎn chū   wǒ xiǎng qù kàn kan   Nǐ xiǎng
京剧团来上海演出，我想去看看。你想
bu xiǎng yì qǐ qù
不想一起去？

Bù le   wǒ duì jīng jù méi xìng qù   Wǒ gèng xǐ huan hù wài
A: 不了，我对京剧没兴趣。我更喜欢户外
huó dòng   Rú guǒ míng tiān tiān qì hǎo   wǒ hé jǐ ge péng you
活动。如果明天天气好，我和几个朋友
xiǎng qù pān yán   rán hòu yě cān
想去攀岩，然后野餐。

B:
Zhēn bú cuò
真不错。

A:
Shì a　　　bú guò　　rú guǒ tiān gōng bú zuò měi　　jiù zhǐ hǎo
是啊，不过，如果天公不作美，就只好
zài jiā kàn diàn shì le
在家看电视了。

New words and phrases: I'm not interested in Beijing opera

团	tuán	group; team
演出	yǎnchū	to perform
不了	bùle	not really (used to decline an invitation)
户外	hùwài	outdoor
活动	huódòng	activity
天气	tiānqì	weather
天公	tiāngōng	the gods
作美	zuòměi	to make things easy
只好	zhǐhǎo	to have to; to have no choice but to

rú guǒ   jiù
2.1 *To express conditions with* 如果···, 就··· *(if ..., then ...)*

The structure 如果 **rúguǒ** ..., 就 **jiù** ...' (if ..., then ...) can be
used to express conditions and possibilities just as in English.

Rú guǒ nǐ xǐ huan chá   wǒ men jiù hē chá
如果你喜欢茶，我们**就**喝茶。
If you like tea, then we will drink tea.

Rú guǒ nǐ jīn tiān máng   nǐ jiù bié lái le
如果你今天忙，你**就**别来了。
If you are busy today, then you don't need to come.

Rú guǒ tiān qì bù hǎo   wǒ men jiù bú qù yě cān le
如果天气不好，我们**就**不去野餐了。
If the weather's bad, we won't go for a picnic.

8 Listen to a dialogue between four friends. Complete the
sentences about what they like and dislike doing in their spare
time.

xǐ huan   bù xǐ huan
Xiao Wang: 喜欢 _____，不喜欢 _____

xǐ huan   gèng xǐ huan
Xiao Zhang: 喜欢 _____，更喜欢 _____

zuì xǐ huan   zuì bù xǐ huan
Xiao Li: 最喜欢 _____，最不喜欢 _____

duì   yǒu xìng qù
Xiao Liu: 对 _____ 有兴趣，

duì   méi xìng qù
            对 _____ 没兴趣

9 Look at the pictures below and describe each set with comparative and superlative forms. The first one has been done for you.

1.

Tā xǐ huan hē
她喜欢喝
kā fēi
咖啡。

Tā gèng xǐ huan
她更喜欢
hē chá
喝茶。

Tā zuì xǐ huan hē
她最喜欢喝
rè qiǎo kè lì
热巧克力。

2.

3.

4.

3 My leisure activities

Wǒ de xiū xián huó dòng
我的休闲活动

> ### Key expressions: *Reasons and time frequency*
>
> *To express opinions and reasons:*
>
> | wǒ jué de | yīn wèi | tè bié shì |
> |---|---|---|
> | 我觉得… | 因为… | 特别是… |
> | I feel/think ... | because ... | especially ... |
>
> | ér qiě | zài shuō | jì   yòu |
> |---|---|---|
> | 而且… | 再说… | 既…又… |
> | in addition ... | moreover ... | not only ... but also ... |
>
> *To express frequency:*
>
> | yǒu shí | yǒu shí | cháng cháng | ǒu ěr |
> |---|---|---|---|
> | 有时…, | 有时… | 常常… | 偶尔… |
> | sometimes ..., | sometimes ... | often ... | occasionally ... |
>
> | yī   jiù | měi   dōu | měi   yí cì |
> |---|---|---|
> | 一…就… | 每…都… | 每…一次 |
> | ... as soon as ... | every ... | once every |

10 Listen to Ming talking about his leisure activities.

Wǒ zài yì jiā diàn nǎo gōng sī gōng zuò   píng shí gōng zuò hěn
我在一家电脑公司工作，平时工作很

máng Wǒ yì yǒu kōng jiù qù yùn dòng Suǒ yǒu de yùn dòng wǒ dōu
忙。我一有空就去运动。所有的运动我都

xǐ huan   yīn wèi yùn dòng jì néng duàn liàn shēn tǐ   yòu hǎo wán
喜欢，因为运动既能锻炼身体，又好玩。

Wǒ xǐ huan yóu yǒng   tè bié shì xià tiān de shí hou   Wǒ yě xǐ
我喜欢游泳，特别是夏天的时候。我也喜

huan dǎ lán qiú Kě shì   wǒ zuì xǐ huan tī zú qiú Měi ge
欢打篮球。可是，我最喜欢踢足球。每个

xīng qī wǒ dōu hé péng you men tī yí cì zú qiú
星期我都和朋友们踢一次足球。

Rú guǒ gōng zuò tài lèi   wǒ xǐ huan zài jiā kàn shū   yīn wèi
如果工作太累，我喜欢在家看书，因为
kàn shū hěn fàng sōng   ér qiě kě yǐ xué dào hěn duō zhī shi   Wǒ yě
看书很放松，而且可以学到很多知识。我也
cháng tīng yīn yuè   hé péng you zài wǎng shang liáo tiān
常听音乐，和朋友在网上聊天。

Zhōu mò de shí hou   wǒ yǒu shí qù mǎi dōng xi   yǒu shí qù
周末的时候，我有时去买东西，有时去
hē kā fēi   ǒu ěr qù kàn chǎng diàn yǐng huò chàng kǎ lā
喝咖啡，偶尔去看场电影或唱卡拉 OK。
Wǒ bù xǐ huan kàn diàn shì   wǒ jué de kàn diàn shì jì làng fèi
我不喜欢看电视，我觉得看电视既浪费
shí jiān yòu wú liáo   Wǒ yě bù xǐ huan bèng dí   yīn wèi wǔ tīng tài
时间又无聊。我也不喜欢蹦迪，因为舞厅太
chǎo le   zài shuō huán jìng yě bù hǎo   yǒu tài duō rén chōu yān
吵了，再说环境也不好，有太多人抽烟。

11 Based on the passage in Exercise 10, decide if the following
statements are 对 **duì** (true) or 不对 **bú duì** (false).

hěn xǐ huan yùn dòng
1. Ming 很喜欢运动。

Tā zuì xǐ huan dǎ lán qiú
2. 他最喜欢打篮球。

Měi ge xīng qī tā dōu tī zú qiú
3. 每个星期他都踢足球。

Tā jué de kàn shū hěn fàng sōng
4. 他觉得看书很放松。

Tā cháng cháng kàn diàn yǐng
5. 他常常看电影。

Tā bù xǐ huan kàn diàn shì yīn wèi diàn shì tài chǎo le
6. 他不喜欢看电视因为电视太吵了。

Tā bù xǐ huan yǒu hěn duō rén chōu yān de dì fang
7. 他不喜欢有很多人抽烟的地方。

New words and phrases: My leisure activities

平时	píngshí	normally
一 … 就 …	yī … jiù …	as soon as …
运动	yùndòng	sports
所有的	suǒyǒude	all
因为	yīnwèi	because
既 … 又 …	jì … yòu …	both … and …
锻炼	duànliàn	to do exercise
身体	shēntǐ	body; health
好玩	hǎowán	good fun; fun
特别	tèbíe	especially
夏天	xiàtiān	summer
打	dǎ	to hit; to punch
可是	kěshì	but
踢	tī	to kick
放松	fàngsōng	relaxing; relaxed
而且	érqiě	in addition
学到	xuédào	to learn; to acquire
知识	zhīshi	knowledge

有时···,	yǒushí...,	sometimes ...,
有时···	yǒushí...	sometimes ...
偶尔	ǒu'ěr	occasionally
场	chǎng	(measure word for movies)
无聊	wúliáo	boring
舞厅	wǔtīng	disco; dance hall
吵	chǎo	noisy
再说	zàishuō	further more (lit. again say)
环境	huánjìng	environment
抽烟	chōuyān	to smoke (cigarettes)
觉得	juéde	to think; to feel
电脑	diànnǎo	computer (lit. electronic brain)
浪费	làngfèi	to waste; waste
地方	dìfang	place

Language notes

3.1 *Use of* 每··· 都··· *(every...)*
měi dōu

The adjective 每 **měi** (every) is normally followed by a measure word and it is also usually linked with the adverb 都 **dōu** (all).

Wǒ men měi ge rén dōu xǐ huan zú qiú
我们**每个人都**喜欢足球。 Every one of us likes football.

Měi běn shū dōu hěn wú liáo
每本书**都**很无聊。

Every book is boring.

Tā měi tiān dōu qù yùn dòng
他**每**天**都**去运动。

He plays sport every day.

Wǒ měi ge xīng qī sān dōu huí jiā chī
我**每**个星期三**都**回家吃
wǔ fàn
午饭。

I go home for lunch every
Wednesday.

3.2 *To describe frequency*

有时 Yǒushí (sometimes), **常常** chángcháng (often) and
偶尔 ǒu'ěr (occasionally) are some of the adverbs that can
be used to describe the frequency of doing something. These
adverbs need to be used in front of verbs as they express times.

Wǒ yǒu shí zài gōng sī chī wǔ fàn
我**有时**在公司吃午饭。

I sometimes have lunch at
the company.

Tā chángcháng hē jiǔ
他**常常**喝酒。

He drinks often.

Wǒ bà ba ǒu ěr chōu yān
我爸爸**偶尔**抽烟。

My dad smokes occasionally.

měi   cì
You can also use the pattern **每** ··· ··· **次** to express
frequency in a measured way.

Tā měi nián qù Zhōng guó liù cì
他**每年**去中国**六次**。

He goes to China six times
a year.

Wǒ měi ge xīng qī tī liǎng cì zú qiú
我**每个星期**踢**两次**足球。

I play football twice a week.

Wǒ men měi sān tiān kàn yí cì diàn yǐng
我们**每三天**看**一次**电影。

We watch a movie every
three days.

3.3 Use of 一 yī … 就 jiù … (as soon as)

The pattern 一 **yī** … 就 **jiù** … means 'as soon as'. Both words are followed by action verbs. Note that the order of the sentence is different from English.

Wǒ men yì huí jiā jiù chī fàn
我们一回家**就**吃饭。
We ate dinner as soon as we got home.

Tā yí dào Zhōng guó jiù xué Zhōng wén
他一到中国**就**学中文。
He studied Chinese as soon as he arrived in China.

3.4 Use of 既 jì … 又 yòu … (both … and …)

The sentence pattern 既 **jì** … 又 **yòu** … means 'not only … but also' and it is used in the same way as in English. It can follow adjectives or verbs.

Tā jì máng yòu lèi
他**既**忙**又**累。
He's not only busy but also tired.

Wǒ jì xǐ huan zú qiú yòu
我**既**喜欢足球**又**
xǐ huan lán qiú
喜欢篮球。
I like not only football but also basketball.

Practice

12 Rearrange the words to form a proper sentence. The first one has been done for you.

yóu yǒng   zuì   wǒ   de   xǐ huan   shì   yùn dòng
1. 游泳   最   我   的   喜欢   是   运动

Wǒ zuì xǐ huan de yùn dòng shì yóu yǒng
我最喜欢的运动是游泳。

tā   hěn   gōng zuò   píng shí   máng
2. 他   很   工作   平时   忙

3.

jué de   tā   yǒu yì si   jì   yòu   kàn shū

觉得   她   有意思   既…又…   看书

fàng sōng

放松

4.

wǒ men   hǎo   yě cān   yī   jiù   tiān qì   qù

我们   好   野餐   一…就…   天气   去

5.

tā   měi gè   hé   wǔ tīng   xīng qī   qù   péng you

她   每个   和   舞厅   星期   去   朋友

yí cì   dōu

一次   都

Check your answers at the back of the book.

13 Role play: You and a Chinese friend are discussing hobbies and sports. Create a short dialogue by yourself or with a partner.

14 Listen to a few people talking about their hobbies and leisure activities. Write down what they each like to do and mark how often they do them. Note that each person may mention more than one activity. The first one has been done for you.

Name	Activity	Every day	Once a week	Three times a week	Once every two weeks
Zhang	swim drink coffee	 X		X	
Li					
Liu					
Wang					
Chen					

15 Look at the following pictures. Say which of the activities you like and describe how often you do them. Discuss this with a partner if you can, or if you're alone, talk out loud!

Learning Chinese characters

Xué hàn zì
学汉字

Common radicals in Chinese characters (3)

衤 "衣" 'clothes' character on its own, refers to anything related to clothing

qún	kù	bèi	chèn
裙 (skirt)	裤 (trousers)	被 (quilt)	衬 (shirt)

艹 "草" 'grass' character on its own, refers to anything to do with plants or vegetables

cài	huā	píng	chá
菜 (vegetables in general)	花 (flower)	苹 (apple)	茶 (tea)

马 ˋ马ˊ   'horse' character on its own, refers to anything
            to do with horses

shǐ
驶 (to drive fast)   jià
驾 (to drive)   jī
骑 (to ride)

chuǎng
闯 (to break into [horse inside])

虫 ˋ虫ˊ   'insect' character on its own, refers to anything
            to do with insects or animals in rivers or seas

bàng
蚌 (freshwater mussel)   shé
蛇 (snake)   yǐ
蚁 (ant)   xiā
虾 (shrimp)

犭 ˋ犬ˊ   'dog' character on its own, refers to animals
            (mammals) in general

māo
猫 (cat)   gǒu
狗 (dog)   hóu
猴 (monkey)   shī
狮 (lion)

鸟 ˋ鸟ˊ   'bird' character on its own, refers to anything
            related to birds

jī
鸡 (chicken)   yā
鸭 (duck)   gē
鸽 (dove)   é
鹅 (goose)

Playing majiang

Playing Chinese chess

Write the characters in the text

16 Try writing the following characters using the stroke order indicated.

更 gèng more	一	冖	冂	帀	百	更	更		
最 zuì the most	丶	冂	冃	日	旦	昻	昻	昻	昻
	昻	最	最						
聊 liáo to chat	一	厂	丆	冃	耳	耳	耴	耴	耴
	聊	聊							
听 tīng to listen	丶	口	口	口	听	听	听		
唱 chàng to sing	丶	口	口	唱	唱	唱	唱	唱	唱
	唱	唱							
打 dǎ to hit	一	扌	扌	扌	打				
踢 tī to kick	丶	口	口	呈	足	足	足	跙	踢
	踢	踢	踢	踢	踢	踢			

因为 yīnwèi because	丨	冂	冃	囝	囷	因		
	丶	⺀	为	为				
喜欢 xīhuan to like	一	十	士	吉	吉	吉	直	直	直
	壴	喜	喜						
	丁	又	冴	欢	欢	欢			
每 měi every	丿	⺁	仁	勾	每	每	每		
都 dōu both, all	一	十	土	耂	耂	者	者	者	都
	都								
有时 yǒushí sometimes	一	ナ	才	右	有	有			
	丨	冂	月	日	日一	时	时		

Leisure activities and entertainment in China

There are many activities for people of all age groups in China. Older people tend to do taiqi (a Chinese martial art), play Chinese chess in the park, go for walks and listen to local operas. The younger generation plays majiang (mahjong) with friends or relatives at weekends and during festivals. Majiang is the most popular game in China. It requires four players and has complex rules. Young people also enjoy going out for meals or going shopping in the evening after work. There are many 24-hour restaurants, 24-hour convenience stores, and night clubs and bars. Major department stores close at 10pm.

There are also places to relax such as hair salons, foot massage parlours and public baths. This might sound strange to a foreigner, but if you ever experience the service in a hair salon in China, you will understand why this is so. You will get an appointment for one hour to 'dry-wash' your hair along with a head and shoulder massage, all for a good price. The public baths are also a huge entertainment complex usually with their own restaurant, games rooms, karaoke and massage room, along with the different types of baths.

Also, there are a lot of Chinese people who are interested in more traditional cultural activities such as calligraphy, Chinese traditional painting, kite making, paper cutting and playing traditional Chinese instruments. Sports are popular with everyone, especially basketball, table tennis and bowling. This is even more true since the Beijing Olympics.

As a foreigner in China, you can find out what's happening in the city through local English magazines and newspapers. Of course, this is easier in big cities like Shanghai and Beijing. If you go to a western-style coffee shop in Shanghai or Beijing, you can easily find those magazines or newspapers for free. They list all kinds of events, bars, international restaurants and clubs. If you really want to experience the Chinese way of socializing, it's worthwhile going to a traditional tea house where you can enjoy some small snacks with various Chinese teas.

unit

12 Making phone calls

Dì shí èr kè   Dǎ diàn huà
第十二课　打电话

In this unit, you will learn:
- How to make a phone call
- How to make enquiries and solve problems
- About even more common radicals in Chinese characters
- About making phone calls in China

Getting the pronunciation right

Pīn yīn liàn xí
拼音练习

In this unit, you will do some more Pinyin practice with a focus on words starting with the fourth tone. You will also learn two very popular Chinese songs for celebrating birthdays and the New Year!

1 Combinations with the fourth tone: First try to pronounce the following words by yourself, and then listen to the audio. Go over it again and again until you feel comfortable with the pattern.

The fourth tone + the first tone

shàngbān	**qìchē**	**chànggē**	**rìqī**	**kànshū**
to work	bus	to sing	date	to read

The fourth tone + the second tone

wàipó	**kèrén**	**kèwén**	**fùxí**	**qùnián**
grandma	guest	text	to review	last year

The fourth tone + the third tone

diànyǐng	**tiàowǔ**	**xiàwǔ**	**xià yǔ**	**shàngwǔ**
movie	to dance	afternoon	to rain	morning

The fourth tone + the fourth tone

yùdìng	**shàngkè**	**shuìjiào**	**duànliàn**	**hànzì**
to reserve	to have lessons	to sleep	to exercise	Chinese characters

The fourth tone + the neutral tone

xièxie	**piàoliang**	**kuàizi**	**mèimei**	**dìdi**
thanks	pretty	chopsticks	younger sister	younger brother

2 Sound discrimination: Now focus on the sounds b, p, zh, ch, sh, z, c and s, which are usually considered to be difficult for beginners:

zuǒbian	**zhàopiān**	**gàosu**	**qīngchǔ**
left side	photo	to tell	clearly

zhèyàng	**cāngkù**	**cuò**	**sīrén**
this way	storage	wrong	private

yìzhí	**zhànxiàn**	**zuòyè**	**zhù**
always	occupied	homework	to wish

3 Fun time: Chinese people love singing! Going to karaoke is one of the most popular leisure activities in China. I am sure you will find a chance to use the following two songs for New Year and birthday celebrations. The good news is that tones aren't pronounced while singing. So, give it a go and sing along with the audio.

New Year song

Xīn nián hǎo ya　　xīn nián hǎo ya
新年好呀，　新年好呀，
Happy new year, happy new year,

zhù hè dà jiā xīn nián hǎo
祝贺大家新年好！
Wishing everyone a happy new year.

Wǒ men chàng gē   wǒ men tiào wǔ
我们唱歌，我们跳舞，

We are singing, we are dancing,

zhù hè dà jiā xīn nián hǎo
祝贺大家新年好!

to wish everyone a happy new year.

Birthday song

Zhù nǐ shēng rì kuài lè
祝你生日快乐，

Wishing you a happy birthday,

zhù nǐ shēng rì kuài lè
祝你生日快乐，

wishing you a happy birthday,

zhù nǐ shēng rì kuài lè
祝你生日快乐，_____ ，

wishing you a happy birthday, (name),

zhù nǐ shēng rì kuài lè
祝你生日快乐!

wishing you a happy birthday!

Communicating in Chinese

Hàn yǔ jiāo liú
汉语交流

Liú Hóng zài ma
刘红在吗?

1 Is Liu Hong there?

Key expressions: **Making and answering phone calls**

To make phone calls:

Wèi   Liú Hóng zài ma
喂! 刘红在吗?
Hello! Is Liu Hong in?

Tā   Tā shén me shí hou huí lai
他 / 她什么时候回来?
When will he/she be back?

Má fan nín gào su tā   tā gěi wǒ huí ge diàn huà
麻烦您告诉他 / 她给我回个电话。
May I ask you to tell him/her to call me back?

Má fan nín qǐng tā   tā gěi wǒ huí ge diàn huà
麻烦您请他 / 她给我回个电话。
May I ask you to ask him/her to call me back?

To answer phone calls:

Wǒ jiù shì
我就是。
Speaking.

Qǐngwèn nín shì nǎ wèi
请问您是哪位?
May I ask who's calling?

Qǐng jiǎng
请讲。
Go ahead. (lit. please speak)

Nǐ yǒu shén me shì
你有什么事?
What's the call regarding?

Duì bu qǐ   tā   tā bú zài
对不起, 他 / 她不在。
Sorry, he/she's not in.

Yào bu yào liú yán
要不要留言?
Do you want to leave a message?

Nín shuō màn diǎn   wǒ jì yí xià
您说慢点, 我记一下。
Speak more slowly and I will note it down.

---

4 You are going to hear three short telephone conversations. Listen and then decide whether the statements that follow them are true or false. Listen as many times as you want.

a. A telephone conversation between Xiaoming and his mother

Wèi   Xiǎomíng
Mother: 喂! 小明?

Wèi   Mā ma a
Xiaoming: 喂! 妈妈啊,
shén me shì a
什么事啊?

Nǐ bà ba dào jiā le ma
Mother: 你爸爸到家了吗?

Tā hái méi ne
Xiaoming: 他还没呢!

Mother:
Gào su nǐ bà ba wǒ jīn tiān xué xiào yǒu shì   yào wǎn
告诉你爸爸我今天学校有事，要晚
diǎn huí lai   Nǐ men xiān chī
点回来。你们先吃
wǎn fàn ba   bié děng wǒ le
晚饭吧，别等我了。

Xiaoming:
Hǎo de   Mā ma zài jiàn
好的。妈妈再见。

Mother:
Zài jiàn
再见。

Now decide if the following are true or false:

Bà ba dào jiā le
1. 爸爸到家了。 _____

Mā ma yào wǎn diǎn huí lai
2. 妈妈要晚点回来。 _____

Mā ma jiào Xiǎomíng hé bà ba děng tā huí jiā chī wǎn fàn
3. 妈妈叫小明和爸爸等她回家吃晚饭。 _____

b. A telephone conversation between Zhang Tian and Xiaoyun

Zhang Tian:
Wèi   Liú Hóng zài ma
喂！刘红在吗？

Xiaoyun:
Duì bu qǐ   tā bú zài   Qǐng wèn nín shì nǎ wèi
对不起，她不在。请问您是哪位？

Zhang Tian:
Wǒ shì tā de péng you   jiào Zhāng Tiān   Qǐng wèn tā
我是她的朋友，叫张天。请问她
shén me shí hou huí lai
什么时候回来？

Xiaoyun:
Wǒ bù zhī dao   Tā qù mǎi dōng xi le   kě néng
我不知道。她去买东西了，可能
wǎn shang huí lai   Nín yào bu yào liú yán
晚上回来。您要不要留言？

Zhang Tian: Má fan nín qǐng tā gěi wǒ huí ge diàn huà　Wǒ de
麻烦您请她给我回个电话。我的

diàn huà hào mǎ shì
电话号码是 63726582。

Xiaoyun: Nín shuō màn diǎn　wǒ jì yí xià
您说慢点，我记一下。

Zhang Tian: 6-3-7-2-6-5-8-2。

Xiaoyun: Hǎo de　wǒ huì gào su tā de
好的，我会告诉她的。

Zhang Tian: Xiè xie nǐ　Zài jiàn
谢谢你。再见。

Now decide if the following are true or false:

Liú Hóng bú zài jiā
1. 刘红不在家。_____

Zhāng Tiān shì Liú Hóng de gē ge
2. 张天是刘红的哥哥。_____

Xiǎo yún zhī dao Liú Hóng huì wǎnshang huí lai
3. 小云知道刘红会晚上回来。_____

Zhāng Tiān bú yào liú yán
4. 张天不要留言。_____

Zhāng Tiān shuō huì zài dǎ diàn huà gěi Liú Hóng de
5. 张天说会再打电话给刘红的。_____

c. A telephone conversation between two colleagues Xiao Zhang and Xiao Li

Xiao Zhang: Wèi　Xiǎo Lǐ zài ma
喂！小李在吗？

Xiao Li: Wǒ jiù shì　Qǐngwèn nín shì něi wèi
我就是。请问您是哪位？

Xiao Zhang: Wǒ shì Shàng hǎi fēn diàn de XiǎoZhāng
我是上海分店的小张。

Xiao Li:
Ò   Xiǎo Zhāng a   nǐ yǒu shén me shì
哦，小张啊，你有什么事？

Xiao Zhang:
Wǒ men Wáng jīng lǐ ràng wǒ wèn yí xià Měi guó nà li
我们王经理让我问一下美国那里
de yàng pǐn dào le ma
的样品到了吗？

Xiao Li:
Wǒ yě bú tài qīng chǔ a   Zhè yàng ba   wǒ qù
我也不太清楚啊。这样吧，我去
cāng kù chá yí xià   wǒ guò yì huì 'r dǎ gěi nǐ
仓库查一下，我过一会儿打给你。

Xiao Zhang:
Tài hǎo le   Xiè xie
太好了。谢谢。

Now decide if the following are true or false:

Xiǎo Zhāng zài Běi jīng gōng zuò
1. 小张在北京工作。＿＿＿＿

Wáng jīng lǐ xiǎng zhī dao cóng Měi guó lái de yàng pǐn yǒu mei yǒu dào
2. 王经理想知道从美国来的样品有没有到。
＿＿＿＿

Xiǎo Lǐ xiān qù cāng kù zài dǎ diàn huà gěi Xiǎo Zhāng
3. 小李先去仓库再打电话给小张。＿＿＿＿

New words and phrases: Making and answering phone calls

喂	wèi	hello (pronounced as a second tone on the phone)
事	shì	matter; issue; thing
还	hái	still (also 'in addition to')
告诉	gàosu	to tell
晚	wǎn	late; to be late
留言	liúyán	to leave a message

给	gěi	to (also 'to give')
记	jì	to take note; to write down
就	jiù	(grammar word for emphasis); (also 'just', 'exactly')
分店	fēndiàn	branch
哦	ò	oh
那里	nàli	there
样品	yàngpǐn	sample product
清楚	qīngchǔ	clear
这样	zhèyàng	this way
仓库	cāngkù	storage
过	guò	to pass (time, place); (also 'to spend'/'to celebrate')
麻烦	máfan	to bother, to trouble
等	děng	to wait

Language notes

jiào ràng qǐng
1.1 *Use of* 叫 , 让 *and* 请

So far you have come across two major functions of these words:

Function 1: Used at the beginning of commands and requests, usually calling for the action of a third person.

Jiào tā míng tiān lái
叫他明天来!   Ask him to come tomorrow!

Ràng lǎo shī kàn yí xià
让老师看一下!   Ask the teacher to have a look!

Qǐng tā jìn lai
请她进来!   Invite her in!

Function 2: Used to ask someone to do something. Can indicate the passive tense.

Mā ma jiào wǒ bié qù
妈妈**叫**我别去。   Mum asked me not to go. (I was asked by Mum not to go.)

Tā ràng wǒ zài zhè 'r děng
他**让**我在这儿等。   He asked me to wait here. (I was asked to wait here by him.)

Wǒ men qǐng lǎo shī lái wǒ men
我们**请**老师来我们
de jù huì   We invited the teacher to come
的聚会。   to our party.

méi
1.2 *Use of* 没 *for incomplete actions*

The negating word 没 **méi** or phrase 没有 **méi yǒu** (hasn't/ haven't) is used to indicate that an action is incomplete. It is used in front of the action verb and usually with the adverb 还 **hái** (still).

Tā hái méi dào jiā
他**还没**到家。   He *still hasn't* got home.

Wǒ hái méi tīng qīng
我**还没**听清。   I *still haven't* heard it clearly.

Tā méi gěi wǒ liú yán
她**没**给我留言。   She *hasn't* left me a message.

gěi
1.3 *Use of* 给 *as the preposition 'to', 'for'*

The word 给 **gěi** can be used as a verb, meaning 'to give'.

Tā gěi wǒ yì běn shū
他**给**我一本书。 He *gives* me a book.

Mā ma gěi wǒ sān shí kuài qián
妈妈**给**我三十块钱。 Mother *gives* me ¥30.

However, it is also commonly used as a preposition, meaning 'to' or 'for'. In this case, it is usually positioned directly after the subject of the sentence, before the verb, instead of at the end of the sentence as in English.

Tā gěi nǐ dǎ le diàn huà
他**给**你打了电话。 He made a call *to* you.

Wǒ gěi dì di mǎi le yì píng
我**给**弟弟买了一瓶 I bought a bottle of wine *for* my

pú tao jiǔ
葡萄酒。 younger brother.

huì de
1.4 *Use of* 会···的 *for certainty and assurance*

The structure 会 **huì** ··· 的 **de** is used when the speaker wants to express certainty. It's a way of offering assurance or making a strong statement or prediction.

Wǒ bú huì zǒu de
我不**会**走**的**。 I *won't* go.

Tā huì gào su nǐ de
他**会**告诉你**的**。 He *will* tell you.

Lǎo shī bú huì hē jiǔ de
老师不**会**喝酒**的**。 The teacher *won't* drink.

jiù
1.5 *Use of* 就 *for precise identification*

The adverb 就 **jiù** can be used to convey the precise identification of a person, location or time. It can be translated as 'right', 'exactly' or 'precisely'. Sometimes, it might not have a direct English translation but it still carries this meaning and is used for emphasis.

Tā jiù zài zhè ´r
他**就**在这儿。   He's *right* here.

Nǐ jiù shì Zhāng xiān sheng a
你**就**是张先生啊!   So you *are* Mr. Zhang!

Míng tiān jiù shì xīng qī tiān
明天**就**是星期天。   Tomorrow *is* Sunday.

Practice

5 Match the questions with the correct answers. One has already been done for you.

Nǐ yǒu shén me shì
1. 你有什么事?

Qǐng wèn tā shén me
2. 请问, 她什么
shí hou huí lai
时候回来?

Yào bu yào liú yán
3. 要不要留言?

Mǎ lì zài ma
4. 玛丽在吗?

Qǐng wèn nín shì nǎ wèi
5. 请问, 您是哪位?

Tā zài nǐ děng yí xià
a. 她在, 你等一下。

Wǒ shì tā de péng you
b. 我是他的朋友。

Kě néng xià wǔ sān diǎn
c. 可能下午三点。

Wǒ xiǎng wèn nǐ míng tiān
d. 我想问你明天
yǒu kòng ma
有空吗?

Má fan nǐ ràng tā gěi wǒ
e. 麻烦你让他给我
huí ge diàn huà
回个电话。

6 Listen to three phone messages and take notes for each of them.

Message	Who is calling?	For whom?	Regarding what?
1.			
2.			
3.			

7 Role play: Call a friend on the phone and imagine you encounter the following scenarios. Make up the conversation that would follow and act it out, either by yourself or with a partner. Write down what you could possibly say in Pinyin.

8 Your housemate can't get home as planned and leaves a series of instructions for you on your voicemail. What does he say? List the key points in English.

9 You were expecting a friend at your house at 3 o'clock, but now you can't be there. You need to leave a note for your housemate so that he will let your friend in, ask him to wait for you, and give him some of your magazines to read while he's waiting. Use the phrases below to create the note. There is a sample answer at the back of the book.

shuō hǎo le
说好了 (have arranged)

kě shì
可是

bù néng dào jiā
不能到家

má fan nǐ
麻烦你

qǐng tā jìn lai
请他进来 (to enter)

ràng tā zài jiā děng wǒ
让他在家等我

gěi tā kàn wǒ de zá zhì
给他看我的杂志 (magazine)

10 Underline the words in the following sentences that are used for emphasis, and then decide which of the two English translations is most accurate.

Wǒ huì dǎ diàn huà gěi tā de
1. **我会打电话给他的。**

    a. I will probably call him.
    b. I will definitely call him.

Tā bú huì bù lái de
2. **他不会不来的。**

    a. He will definitely come.
    b. He will not come.

Tā huì gào su nǐ de
3. 他会告诉你的。

    a. He will tell you.
    b. He might tell you.

Wǒ jiù bù shuō
4. 我就不说。

    a. I won't say.
    b. I can't say.

Tā jiù shì wǒ de lǎo shī
5. 他就是我的老师。

    a. He's my teacher, absolutely.
    b. He's my teacher.

Míng tiān jiù shì wǒ de shēng rì
6. 明天就是我的生日。

    a. Tomorrow is my birthday.
    b. Tomorrow is indeed my birthday.

2 You've got the wrong number!

Nǐ dǎ cuò le
你打错了!

Key expressions: **Problems on the telephone**

To talk about problems on the telephone:

Nǐ dǎ cuò le
你打错了!
You've got the wrong number!

Wǒ tīng bù qīng
我听不清。
I can't hear you clearly.

Diàn huà yì zhí zhàn xiàn
电话一直占线。
The line has been busy.

To check if there's a problem:

Méi shì 'r ba
没事儿吧?
Is everything ok?

Zěn me le
怎么了?
What's the matter?

To offer suggestions:

Nín zài shuō yí biàn   hǎo ma
您再说一遍，好吗？
Could you repeat that?

Nín dà diǎn shēng shuō   hǎo ma
您大点声说，好吗？
Could you speak louder?

Tīng de jiàn ma
听得见吗？
Can you hear me?

Wǒ guò yí huì 'r dǎ gěi nǐ
我过一会儿打给你。
I will call you back shortly.

---

11 Listen to three situations showing some common phone problems. After listening to each dialogue, see if you can summarize what the problem was (in Chinese).

a. Tom is calling to order some pizza

Tom:
Wèi   Wǒ dìng yí ge pǐ sà bǐng   liǎng píng kě lè
喂！ 我订一个匹萨饼，两瓶可乐。

A:
Shén me
什么？

Tom:
Wǒ dìng yí ge pǐ sà bǐng   liǎng píng kě lè
我订一个匹萨饼，两瓶可乐。

A:
Nǐ dǎ cuò le   Zhè shì sī rén diàn huà
你打错了。这是私人电话。

Tom:
Dǎ cuò le   bú huì ba   Shì   ma
打错了，不会吧？ 是 65587564 吗？

A:
Bú shì   wǒ zhè lǐ shì
不是，我这里是 65687564。

Tom:
Ò   zhēn duì bu qǐ   Dǎ rǎo le
哦，真对不起！ 打扰了！

A:
Méi guān xi
没关系。

b. Xiao Li calls Xiao Zhang to ask about the class reunion

Zhang: 喂！
_{Wèi}

Li: 喂！ 小张吗？
_{Wèi   XiǎoZhāng ma}

是我，小李。
_{Shì wǒ   Xiǎo Lǐ}

Zhang: 小李啊，有
_{Xiǎo Lǐ a   yǒu}

什么事儿吗？
_{shén me shì 'r ma}

Li: 我想问你晚上同学聚会是几点？
_{Wǒ xiǎng wèn nǐ wǎn shang tóng xué jù huì shì jǐ diǎn}

Zhang: 小李，你大点声说，好吗？我听不清。
_{Xiǎo Lǐ   nǐ dà diǎn shēng shuō   hǎo ma   Wǒ tīng bù qīng}

Li: 晚上同学聚会是几点？我忘了。
_{Wǎn shang tóng xué jù huì shì jǐ diǎn   Wǒ wàng le}

Zhang: 您再说一遍，好吗？这里信号不好。
_{Nín zài shuō yí biàn   hǎo ma   Zhè lǐ xìn hào bù hǎo}

Li: 我说晚上同学聚会是几点？听得见吗？
_{Wǒ shuō wǎn shang tóng xué jù huì shì jǐ diǎn   Tīng de jiàn ma}

Zhang: 真对不起，还是不行。这样吧，我过
_{Zhēn duì bu qǐ   hái shì bù xíng   Zhè yàng ba   wǒ guò}

一会儿打给你。
_{yí huì 'r dǎ gěi nǐ}

Li: 那好吧。我先挂了。
_{Nà hǎo ba   Wǒ xiān guà le}

c. Xiaoming's mother calls home

Xiaoming:
Wèi
喂!

Mother:
Wèi Xiǎomíng a jiā lǐ méi shì 'r ba
喂! 小明啊，家里没事儿吧?

Xiaoming:
Mā ma méi shì zěn me le
妈妈，没事，怎么了?

Mother:
Wǒ dǎ le hǎo jǐ ge diàn huà le yì zhí zhàn xiàn
我打了好几个电话了，一直占线。

Xiaoming:
Ò bù hǎo yì si Wǒ gāng hé yí ge tóng xué
哦，不好意思。我刚和一个同学
zài tǎo lùn zuò yè ne
在讨论作业呢。

Mother:
Shì zhè yàng a Hǎo yí huì 'r zài jiā lǐ jiàn
是这样啊! 好，一会儿在家里见。

New words and phrases: Problems on the telephone

错	cuò	wrong (also 'bad')
私人	sīrén	private
不会吧？	búhuìba?	It can't be!
打扰	dǎrǎo	to disturb
聚会	jùhuì	reunion; gathering; party
声	shēng	sound
清	qīng	clear
遍	biàn	time (referring to frequency)
听得见	tīngdejiàn	to be able to hear
信号	xìnhào	signal
挂	guà	to hang up
没事	méishì	fine; ok; all right
怎么了？	Zěnme le?	What's the matter? What's wrong?
好	hǎo	quite; rather (also 'good'; 'well', 'OK')
一直	yìzhí	all the time; always (also 'straight')
占线	zhànxiàn	occupied; busy (phone line)
不好意思	bùhǎoyìsi	sorry
讨论	tǎolùn	to discuss

是这样啊!	Shì zhèyàng a!	I see!
匹萨饼	pǐsàbǐng	pizza
没关系	méiguānxi	it doesn't matter; it's ok
并	bìng	in addition
为什么	wèishénme	why
四川北路	Sìchuān Běilù	North Sichuan Road (a street name)

Language notes

2.1 'Verb + 得 de / 不 bù + resultative complement' structure

The structure **verb + 得 de / 不 bù + resultative complement** is used to indicate whether or not a certain result can be attained or a certain status can be achieved.

kàn de jiàn
看得见
to be able to see

kàn bú jiàn
看不见
to not be able to see

tīng de qīng
听得清
to be able to hear clearly

tīng bù qīng
听不清
to not be able to hear clearly

xué de huì
学得会
to be able to learn/master

xué bú huì
学不会
to not be able to learn/master

huí de lái
回得来
to be able to come back

huí bù lái
回不来
to not be able to come back

2.2 *Use of* 了 _{le} ⋯ 了 _{le}

We've already talked about using 了 **le** after an action verb
to indicate its completion (see Unit 10), and 了 **le** is also used
to describe facts. If there's another 了 **le** at the end of the
sentence, then it has the function of summarizing or indicating
a change from a previous situation. Often, speakers can convey
some kind of emotion by using this structure, which makes it an
interesting feature of spoken Chinese.

Wǒ xué le wǔ nián Zhōngwén
我学了五年中文。
I studied Chinese for five years.

Wǒ xué le wǔ nián Zhōngwén le
我学了五年中文了。
I have studied Chinese for five years.
(This is the point the speaker has reached. It could indicate either
that it was a long time for the speaker or a sense of pride.)

Tā hē le sān bēi kā fēi
他喝了三杯咖啡。
He had three cups of coffee.

Tā hē le sān bēi kā fēi le
他喝了三杯咖啡了。
He has already had three cups of coffee.
(This is indicating that it's too much or he shouldn't have any
more.)

Wǒ děng le tā bàn xiǎo shí
我等了他半小时。
I waited for him for half an hour.

Wǒ děng le tā bàn xiǎo shí le
我等了他半小时了。
I've been waiting for him for half an hour.
(This is a complaint, indicating it's been a long time and the
speaker won't wait any longer.)

2.3 *Use of ' 在 + verb' for 'am/was doing'*
zài

To indicate that an action is ongoing at the present time, 在 **zài** is used in front of the verb.

Wǒ zài hē chá
我在喝茶。   I am drinking tea.

Nǐ zài zuò shén me
你在做什么?   What are you doing (now)?

Sometimes, the final particle 呢 **ne** is also used at the end of a sentence to indicate present ongoing situations.

Wǒ chī fàn ne
我吃饭呢!   I am eating (now)!

Tā zài dǎ diàn huà ne
他在打电话呢!   He's on the phone (now)!

The same structure can be used for the past continuous (i.e. a situation that was ongoing in the past) if a time expression is added.

Xià wǔ wǒ zài hē chá de shí hou   tā lái le
下午我在喝茶的时候, 他来了。
He arrived when I was having tea in the afternoon.

Zuó wǎn qī diǎn nǐ zài zuò shén me
昨晚七点你在做什么?
What were you doing last night at 7pm?

cì   biàn
2.4 *The difference between* 次 *and* 遍

Both of these words mean 'time', referring to the frequency of an action. The main difference is that 次 **cì** focuses more on experiences or less frequent actions, while 遍 **biàn** usually refers to more frequent or mechanical and repetitive actions.

Wǒ měi nián qù Zhōng guó liǎng cì
我每年去中国两次。   I go to China twice a year.

Zhè běn shū wǒ kàn le sān biàn
这本书我看了三遍。   I've read this book three times.

2.5 Indirect speech

Changing direct speech into indirect speech is straightforward in
Chinese; you just directly quote the indirect speech. There is no
need to change the tense of the quote.

Tā shuō   Wǒ míng tiān bù lái
他说："我明天不来"。
He said, "I won't come tomorrow."

Tā shuō tā míng tiān bù lái
他说他明天不来。
He said he wouldn't come tomorrow.

Tā gào su wǒ   Shàng ge xīng qī liù yǒu jù huì
她告诉我："上个星期六有聚会"。
She told me, "There was a party last Saturday."

Tā gào su wǒ shàng ge xīng qī liù yǒu jù huì
她告诉我上个星期六有聚会。
She told me there was a party last Saturday.

Note that the subject is not repeated in the quoted speech if it is
the same person who has just been mentioned.

Lǎo shī wèn wǒ   Nǐ shén me shí hou qù Zhōng guó
老师问我："你什么时候去中国？"
The teacher asked me, "When are you going to China?"

Lǎo shī wèn wǒ shén me shí hou qù Zhōng guó
老师问我什么时候去中国。
The teacher asked me when I'm going to China.

Instead of:

Lǎo shī wèn wǒ wǒ shén me shí hou qù Zhōng guó
老师问我我什么时候去中国。

Practice

12 Listen and complete the following telephone conversations.

a. A call to the hotel reception

Receptionist: _____, nín hǎo 您好，Běi jīng Fàn diàn 北京饭店。

Guest: _____, wǒ 我 _____ 113 fáng jiān 房间。
Wǒ yǒu míng tiān zǎo shang liù diǎn de huǒ chē 我有明天早上六点的火车，你 nǐ
_____ jiào xǐng wǒ 叫醒我？

Receptionist: _____。 Nín yào jǐ diǎn jiào nín 您要几点叫您？

Guest: _____。

Receptionist: Duì bu qǐ 对不起，_____。
Nín zài shuō yí biàn hǎo ma 您再说一遍，好吗？

Guest: Wǒ shuō míng tiān 我说明天 _____ jiào xǐng wǒ 叫醒我。

Receptionist: Hǎo de 好的，_____。 Hái yǒu bié de shì ma 还有别的事吗？

Guest: _____, xiè xie nǐ 谢谢你。

b. A call to a restaurant

Waiter:	Wèi Nǐ hǎo Shàng hǎi Cān tīng 喂！你好！上海餐厅。
Customer:	Wèi Nín hǎo Wǒ xiǎng yí ge zhuō zi 喂！您好！我想 _____ 一个桌子。
Waiter:	Hǎo 好，_____？
Customer:	wǎn shang _____ 晚上 _____。
Waiter:	Méi wèn tí Qǐng wèn 没问题。请问 _____？
Customer:	Sì wèi Wǒ xìng Zhāng jiào Zhāng Tiān 四位。我姓张，叫张天。
Waiter:	Hǎo de nín dìng le míng tiān wǎn shang 好的，_____，您订了明天晚上 sì ge rén de zhuō zi Xiè xie nín _____ 四个人的桌子。谢谢您 de yù dìng 的预定。_____！
Customer:	Xiè xie Zài jiàn 谢谢！再见！

c. A call to the train ticket office

Officer:	Wèi Shàng hǎi Huǒ chē zhàn Qǐng jiǎng 喂！上海火车站！请讲。
Customer:	Nǐ hǎo Yǒu qù Nán jīng de piào ma 你好。有 _____ 去南京的票吗？
Officer:	wǒ chá yí xià Hái yǒu piào _____，我查一下。还有票， nín yào jǐ diǎn de 您要几点的？

Customer: _____ shì xià wǔ liù diǎn
是下午六点。

Officer: Kě yǐ. Nín yào tè kuài _____ pǔ kuài?
可以。您要特快 _____ 普快?

Tè kuài _____, wǎnshang qī diǎn bàn dào
特快 _____，晚上七点半到

Nán jīng, pǔ kuài liǎng bǎi bā, _____ dào.
南京，普快两百八，_____ 到。

Customer: Wǒ dìng yì zhāng _____. Xiè xie
我订一张 _____。谢谢。

13 How do you say the following in Chinese?

1. You've got the wrong number.
2. I can't hear you clearly.
3. Is everything ok?
4. What's the call regarding?
5. Could you repeat that?
6. Could you speak louder?
7. I will call you back shortly.
8. This is a private number.

You'll find the answers in the Answers section.

14 Read the following short passage and then answer the questions:

Jīn tiān xià wǔ Liú Hóng qù mǎi dōng xi le Tā bú zài jiā
今天下午刘红去买东西了。她不在家

de shí hou tā de Yīng guó péng you Tāng mǔ gěi tā dǎ le diàn huà
的时候，她的英国朋友汤姆给她打了电话。

Liú Hóng de ér zi Xiǎomíng gào su Tāng mǔ Liú Hóng wǔ diǎn huí lai
刘红的儿子小明告诉汤姆，刘红五点回来。

Tāng mǔ má fan Xiǎomíng gào su Liú Hóng tā zhè ge zhōu mò dào Zhōng
汤姆麻烦小明告诉刘红，他这个周末到中

guó lǚ xíng xiǎng qǐng Liú Hóng de jiā rén yì qǐ chī fàn Tā shuō
国旅行，想请刘红的家人一起吃饭。他说

tā huì zài xīng qī liù xià wǔ dào Shàng hǎi tā de Zhōng guó shǒu jī
他会在星期六下午到上海，他的中国手机

hào mǎ shì Xiǎomíng gào su Tāng mǔ tā yí
号码是13898735738。小明告诉汤姆，他一

dìng huì gào su tā mā ma de   bìng zhù Tāng mǔ yí lù shùn fēng
定会告诉他妈妈的，并祝汤姆一路顺风。

Jīn tiān xià wǔ Liú Hóng zuò shén me qù le
1. 今天下午刘红做什么去了？

Shuí dǎ diàn huà gěi tā le
2. 谁打电话给她了？

Liú Hóng de ér zi Xiǎo míng zhī dao Liú Hóng shén me shí hou huí
3. 刘红的儿子小明知道刘红什么时候回

lai ma
来吗？

Nà rén wèi shén me dǎ diàn huà gěi Liú Hóng   Tā shuō le shén me
4. 那人为什么打电话给刘红？他说了什么？

15 You and your friend have arranged to go for dinner at a restaurant. It is the first time your friend has been to this restaurant and he calls you as he's having trouble finding his way. Try to complete the dialogue and then check the sample answers on the audio:

Wèi   shì wǒ   Xiǎo Wáng
Your friend: 喂，是我，小王。

You: Say hello and ask where he is.

Wǒ zài lù shang ne   Wǒ zhǎo bú dào cān tīng
Your friend: 我在路上呢！我找不到餐厅。
Nǐ zài nǎ 'r
你在哪儿？

You: Say you can't hear clearly. Ask him to speak louder.

Wǒ bù zhī dao cān tīng zài nǎ 'r   Nǐ zài nǎ 'r
Your friend: 我不知道餐厅在哪儿。你在哪儿？
Tīng de jiàn ma
听得见吗？

You: Say you can hear now. Say you are waiting for him in the restaurant. Ask which street he's on.

Your friend:	Wǒ zài Sì chuān Běi Lù shang 我在四川北路上。
You:	Ask if he can see a big hotel called the Tianxia Hotel.
Your friend:	Wǒ kàn de dào 我看得到。
You:	Ask him to turn left and go straight and the restaurant is on his right.
Your friend:	Wǒ xiǎng wǒ néng zhǎo de dào 我想我能找得到。
You:	Say ok and say you will wait for him.

Learning Chinese characters

Xué hàn zì
学汉字

Common radicals in Chinese characters (4)

⻊ "足" 'foot' character on its own, refers to actions with the feet or foot-related things

lù	tiào	tī	pǎo
路 (road)	跳 (to jump)	踢 (to kick)	跑 (to run)

辶 "走" 'walk' character on its own, refers to anything to do with distance or the action of walking

yuǎn	jìn	zhuī	jìn
远 (far)	近 (close)	追 (to chase)	进 (to enter)

门 "门" 'door' character on its own, refers to anything to do with the indoors or inside

wèn	jiān	bì
问 (to ask)	间 (room)	闭 (closed)

mèn
闷 (bored – your heart is locked in a room so you feel bored)

才 `手` 'hand' character on its own, refers to actions done with the hands in general

dǎ
打 (to hit)   lā
拉 (to pull)   tuī
推 (to push)   ná
拿 (to hold; to take)

饣 `食` 'food' character on its own, refers to food-related words

fàn
饭 (rice; meal)   è
饿 (hungry)   guǎn
馆 (restaurant)

bǎo
饱 (full (have eaten enough))

力 `力` 'power' character on its own, refers to strength or effort-related words

nán
男 (male; man)   dòng
动 (to move)   láo
劳 (labour)   jiā
加 (to add)

*Man –
the power in the field*

Write the characters in the text

16 Try writing the following characters in the stroke order indicated.

事 shì matter	一	㇇	一冖	一口	彐	写	写	事	
记 jì to take note	丶	讠	讠ㄱ	讠㇆	记				

错 cuò wrong	⺈	⻒	⺉	⺊	⻐	钅	针	钊	铓
	铓	错	错	错					
挂 guà to hang (up)	一	十	扌	护	扞	拝	拌	拝	挂
声 shēng sound	一	十	士	吉	吉	声	声		
清 qīng clear	丶	冫	氵	汀	汗	法	浩	泮	清
	清	清							
请 qǐng please	丶	讠	讠	讠	请	请	请	请	请
	请								
告诉 gàosu to tell	丿	丄	牛	生	牛	告	告		
	丶	讠	讠	讠	诉	诉	诉		
那 nà that	刁	刁	刁	那	那	那			
遍 biàn time (refers to frequency of actions)	丶	冫	宀	户	户	启	扁	扁	扁
	遍	遍	遍						

还 hái still	一	フ	不	不	不	还	还		
慢 màn slow	'	亻	忄	忄	忄	忄	忄	忄	悍
悍	悍	慢	慢	慢					

Making phone calls in China and some useful numbers

Whenever you answer the phone or call someone yourself, the first thing you say or hear is 喂 wèi. Usually Chinese people do not identify themselves when they answer the phone, so it's common for the caller to say who they are first. If it is a business call, then it is important and professional to say the name of your company and your job title.

The following are some useful telephone numbers to know while you're in China:

Ambulance	120	Fire	119
Police	110	Weather Forecast	121
Time	117	Directory Assistance	114
Phone problems	112		

China International country code	0086
Tourist Hotline in Beijing	010-65130828
Capital Airport	010-64563604
Beijing Railway Station	010-65128931
Beijing Taxi Corporation	010-68582661

The Directory Assistance number 114 is a free service. However, it will only find you a number for a company or organization, not a residential number. You can make long distance calls in telecom company offices or main post offices, or you can purchase an international phone card. For long distance calls within China, you need to know the area code of the city and dial that number before the local phone number.

Directions, hotels, hobbies and telephone conversations

Communicating in Chinese

Hàn yǔ jiāo liú
汉语交流

1 Match the appropriate responses to the following questions. The first one has been done for you.

Xiān sheng   nǐ qù nǎ 'r
1. 先生，你去哪儿？

Shén me shí hou dào Běi jīng
2. 什么时候到北京？

Qǐng wèn   nín guì xìng
3. 请问，您贵姓？

Fáng jiān lǐ dài kōng tiáo ma
4. 房间里带空调吗？

Nín zhù jǐ hào fáng jiān
5. 您住几号房间？

Nǐ xǐ huan kàn diàn yǐng ma
6. 你喜欢看电影吗？

Nǐ zuì xǐ huan shén me yùn dòng
7. 你最喜欢什么运动？

Wèi   Zhāng lǎo shī zài ma
8. 喂，张老师在吗？

Nǐ yào bu yào liú yán
9. 你要不要留言？

Wǒ xìng Wáng   jiào Wáng Tiān
a. 我姓王，叫王天。

Wǒ hěn xǐ huan
b. 我很喜欢。

Dāng rán dài
c. 当然带。

Qù Běi jīng Fàn diàn   xiè xie
d. 去北京饭店，谢谢。

Wǒ zuì xǐ huan yóu yǒng
e. 我最喜欢游泳。

Duì bu qǐ   tā bú zài
f. 对不起，她不在。

Bú yòng   xiè xie
g. 不用，谢谢。

Míng tiān xià wǔ sān diǎn dào
h. 明天下午三点到。

Wǒ zhù sì líng bā hào fáng jiān
i. 我住四零八号房间。

2 You want to go to Shanghai by train this Saturday around 3 p.m. At the ticket office, you check the details before booking. Fill in your part of the following conversation, and then listen to the dialogue on the recording to check your answers.

Assistant:
Nǐ hǎo   nǐ yào qù nǎ 'r
你好，你要去哪儿?

You: Say that you want to go to Shanghai.

Assistant:
Shén me shí hou zǒu
什么时候走?

You: Say around 3pm on Saturday.

Assistant:
Shí bā cì huǒ chē   xīng qī liù xià wǔ liǎngdiǎn sān
十八次火车，星期六下午两点三
kè chū fā   kě yǐ ma
刻出发，可以吗?

You: Say that's ok and ask how much it is.

Assistant:
Yī bǎi bā
一百八。

You: Say that you'll buy a ticket.

 3 Imagine you are going to Shanghai for a one-week holiday, arriving on 21 July and leaving on 28 July. You would like to book a single room. You would also like to know if breakfast is included and how to get to the hotel from People's Square. Have a conversation with the receptionist following the prompts on the audio. After the pause for you to speak, you'll hear a sample answer.

People's Square, Shanghai

4 Look at the following picture of a small town in China and write a few sentences about what you can see in this town.

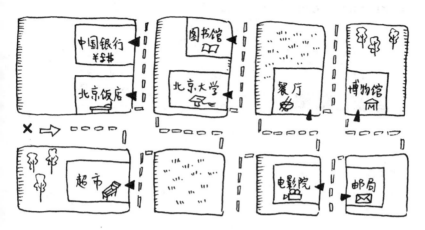

Start with:

Nà   li   yǒu yì   jiā   dà xué   dà xué de páng biān shì   tú   shū guǎn
那里有一家大学，大学的旁边是图书馆…

There are a few sample sentences to compare with your own in the Answers section.

5 Listen to a few dialogues about directions and answer the following questions about them:

Dialogue a
1. Where does the lady want to go?
2. Is it far?

Dialogue b
1. What bus goes to the hotel?
2. Where is the bus stop?

Dialogue c
1. Is there a library nearby?
2. Is the library to the left of a French restaurant?

6 Look at the following activities and for each one say whether you like it or dislike it (and how much). Interview a partner if you can.

7 How do you say the following in Chinese?

1. When will he be back?
2. Could you tell her to call me back?
3. May I ask who's calling?
4. Could you speak slower and I will note it down.
5. What is your telephone number?
6. I am sorry. I can't hear you. Can you speak louder?
7. You've got the wrong number.

8 Read the following sentences and then rearrange them so they make a proper story. The first sentence has been given to get you started.

_5_ ___ ___ ___ ___ ___ ___ ___ ___ ___

1.
Wǒ xiǎng wǒ shì wàng zài le fàn diàn de cān tīng
我想我是忘在了饭店的餐厅。

2.
Kě shì   cān tīng de jīng lǐ shuō méi yǒu kàn dào wǒ de bāo
可是，餐厅的经理说没有看到我的包，
wǒ hěn zháo jí
我很着急。

3.
Wǒ yào zǒu de nà tiān   wǒ de bāo bú jiàn le
我要走的那天，我的包不见了。

4.
Wǒ zhōng yú xiǎng dào wǒ kě néng bǎ bāo wàng zài chū zū chē shàng le
我终于想到我可能把包忘在出租车上了。

5.
Qù nián wǒ qù Měi guó kāi huì
去年我去美国开会 (to have a meeting/conference)，
zhù zài yì jiā fàn diàn
住在一家饭店。

6.
Jiù zài zhè ge shí hou   nà wèi chū zū chē sī   jī chū xiàn zài
就在这个时候，那位出租车司机出现在
le fàn diàn qián tái   shǒu lǐ hái ná zhe wǒ de bāo
了饭店前台，手里还拿着我的包。

7.
Bāo lǐ yǒu wǒ de hù zhào   fēi jī piào hé   rén mín bì
包里有我的护照，飞机票和2000人民币。

8.
Xìng hǎo cān tīng de jīng lǐ hěn rè xīn   jiào wǒ xiǎng xiang kě néng
幸好餐厅的经理很热心，叫我想想可能
bǎ bāo fàng   nǎ ′r le
把包放 (to put) 哪儿了。

9.
Cān tīng de jīng lǐ mǎ shàng dǎ diàn huà gěi chū zū chē gōng sī
餐厅的经理马上打电话给出租车公司。

10.
Wǒ shí fēn   gǎn xiè nà wèi chū zū
我十分 (extremely (lit. ten points)) 感谢那位出租
chē sī   jī hé cān tīng jīng lǐ de bāng zhù
车司机和餐厅经理的帮助！

Getting the pronunciation right

9 Listen and write the words in Pinyin with tones.

1. _____   2. _____   3. _____   4. _____   5. _____

6. _____   7. _____   8. _____   9. _____   10. _____

10 Listen and write the sentences in Pinyin with tones.

11 In Chinese, there are many idioms and they usually are based on real stories. Read the following story in Chinese about the idiom 自相矛盾 **zì xiāng máo dùn**. This refers to people who say or do things which are self-contradictory. Pay attention to all the aspects we've covered: sounds, tones and intonation, and then listen to the audio for comparison. You will find the translation of the story at the back of the book.

Cóngqián   yǒu ge mài bīng qì de rén   zài shì chǎng shang mài
从前，有个卖兵器的人，在市场上卖

máo hé dùn   Tā xiān jǔ qǐ dùn xiàng rén men shuō   Nǐ men kàn
矛和盾。他先举起盾向人们说："你们看，

wǒ de dùn shì shì shàng zuì jiān gù de   rèn hé fēng lì de dōng xi
我的盾是世上最坚固的，任何锋利的东西

dōu bù néng cì chuān tā
都不能刺穿它。"

Jiē zhe yòu jǔ qǐ tā de máo   xiàng rén men shuō   Nǐ men
接着又举起他的矛，向人们说："你们

zài kàn kan wǒ de máo   tā fēng lì wú bǐ   wú lùn duō me jiān
再看看我的矛，它锋利无比，无论多么坚

yìng de dùn   dōu dǎng bú zhù tā
硬的盾，都挡不住它！"

Wéi guān de rén tīng le tā de huà dōu jué de hěn hǎo xiào　　rén qún
围观的人听了他的话都觉得很好笑，人群

zhōng yǒu rén wèn　　　Nà ná nǐ de máo lái cì nǐ de dùn　　jié guǒ
中有人问："那拿你的矛来刺你的盾，结果

huì zěn me yàng
会怎么样？"

Mài bīng qì de rén tīng le zhāng kǒu jié shé　　wú cóng huí dá
卖兵器的人听了张口结舌，无从回答，

zhǐ hǎo ná zhe máo hé dùn zǒu le
只好拿着矛和盾走了。

Learning Chinese characters

Xué hàn zì
学汉字

12 Do you remember the meaning of these Chinese characters? And how many more characters can you write using them as radicals?

1. 人　　2. 女　　3. 火　　4. 言

5. 手　　6. 口　　7. 金

13 Match the following characters with their meanings. You haven't been introduced to any of these characters, but the radicals are there to help you.

1. 提　　2. 吞　　3. 浪　　4. 狼　　5. 饼

6. 惊　　7. 晓　　8. 腰　　9. 架　　10. 荷

a. shelf　　**b.** early morning　　**c.** to get scared; shocked
d. waist　　**e.** to carry　　**f.** wave (in the sea)　　**g.** wolf
h. to swallow　　**i.** pancake　　**j.** lotus

14 Which Chinese words can you recognize in the photos below?

1.

2.

3.

4.

5.

6.

7.

8.

Final thoughts

Congratulations! Now you have come to the end of this book and I hope you have enjoyed your journey learning Mandarin Chinese so far. I hope you feel that you have gained enough from this book to allow you take your knowledge of Mandarin Chinese to the next level.

There are many different ways in which you can further your study. If you would like to focus on listening and speaking Mandarin Chinese, then you may want to try the second level of *Colloquial Chinese* by Kan Qian (Routledge). There is a good online learning website called Chinese Pod (http://chinesepod.com/) that provides lessons for different levels. Travelling to China is always extremely helpful and exciting.

If you would like to continue learning Mandarin in a more systematic way so that you can read and write Chinese characters, then *New Practical Chinese Reader* by the Beijing Language and Culture University Press may be a good choice. It comes with CDs as well as DVDs for the dialogues in the book. It also offers practice on Chinese characters.

On our website at www.palgrave.com/modernlanguages/xiang you will find a whole host of suggested online resources including sites to improve conversation and character learning, online dictionaries and sites about Chinese culture. See page xviii for more details on this.

As with learning any language, the key to success is to read, write, speak and hear it on a regular basis.
In China, there is a famous saying
一口气吃不成胖子 **yì kǒuqì chī bù chéng pàngzi**, which means 'you can't get fat by only eating one meal'. So, one has to progress at a steady pace to reach the final destination. Finally, I wish you all the best and hope this book has offered you the foundation you need to master Mandarin Chinese.

Appendix

Pinyin sound combinations

Pīn yīn zǔ hé
拼音组合

In the following two charts, you will find all the possible Pinyin sound combinations in Mandarin Chinese. They can be heard voiced at www.palgrave.com/modernlanguages/xiang.

	a	o	e	-i	er	ai	ei	ao	ou	an	en	ang	eng	ong	ü	üe	uan	un
b	ba	bo				bai	bei	bao		ban	ben	bang	beng					
p	pa	po				pai	pei	pao	pou	pan	pen	pang	peng					
m	ma	mo	me			mai	mei	mao	mou	man	men	mang	meng					
f	fa	fo					fei		fou	fan	fen	fang	feng					
d	da		de			dai	dei	dao	dou	dan		dang	deng	dong				
t	ta		te			tai		tao	tou	tan		tang	teng	tong				
n	na		ne			nai	nei	nao	nou	nan	nen	nang	neng	nong	nü	nüe		
l	la		le			lai	lei	lao	lou	lan		lang	leng	long	lü	lüe		
g	ga		ge			gai	gei	gao	gou	gan	gen	gang	geng	gong				
k	ka		ke			kai	kei	kao	kou	kan	ken	kang	keng	kong				
h	ha		he			hai	hei	hao	hou	han	hen	hang	heng	hong				
j															ju	jue	juan	jun
q															qu	que	quan	qun
x															xu	xue	xuan	xun
zh	zha		zhe	zhi		zhai		zhao	zhou	zhan	zhen	zhang	zheng	zhong				
ch	cha		che	chi		chai		chao	chou	chan	chen	chang	cheng	chong				
sh	sha		she	shi		shai		shao	shou	shan	shen	shang	sheng					
r			re	ri				rao	rou	ran	ren	rang	reng	rong				
z	za		ze	zi		zai	zei	zao	zou	zan	zen	zang	zeng	zong				
c	ca		ce	ci		cai		cao	cou	can	cen	cang	ceng	cong				
s	sa		se	si		sai		sao	sou	san	sen	sang	seng	song				
y	ya		ye	yi				yao	you	yan		yang		yong	yu	yue	yuan	yun

	i	ia	ie	iao	iu	ian	in	iang	ing	iong	u	ua	uo	uai	ui	uan	un	uang	ueng
b	bi		bie	biao		bian	bin		bing		bu								
p	pi		pie	piao		pian	pin		ping		pu								
m	mi		mie	miao	miu	mian	min		ming		mu								
f											fu								
d	di		die	diao	diu	dian			ding		du		duo		dui	duan	dun		
t	ti		tie	tiao		tian			ting		tu		tuo		tui	tuan	tun		
n	ni		nie	niao	niu	nian	nin	niang	ning		nu		nuo			nuan			
l	li	lia	lie	liao	liu	lian	lin	liang	ling		lu		luo			luan	lun		
g											gu	gua	guo	guai	gui	guan	gun	guang	
k											ku	kua	kuo	kuai	kui	kuan	kun	kuang	
h											hu	hua	huo	huai	hui	huan	hun	huang	
j	ji	jia	jie	jiao	jiu	jian	jin	jiang	jing	jiong									
q	qi	qia	qie	qiao	qiu	qian	qin	qiang	qing	qiong									
x	xi	xia	xie	xiao	xiu	xian	xin	xiang	xing	xiong									
zh											zhu	zhua	zhuo	zhuai	zhui	zhuan	zhun	zhuang	
ch											chu	chua	chuo	chuai	chui	chuan	chun	chuang	
sh											shu	shua	shuo	shuai	shui	shuan	shun	shuang	
r											ru		ruo		rui	ruan	run		
z											zu		zuo		zui	zuan	zun		
c											cu		cuo		cui	cuan	cun		
s											su		suo		sui	suan	sun		
w											wu	wa	wo		wei	wan	wen	wang	weng

Answers to exercises

Unit 1

6 **1** evening **2** morning **3** afternoon **4** morning

9 **1** c **2** a **3** b

10 **1** 你好! **2** 老师 (, 您) 好! **3** 早上好!

(pinyin: Nǐ hǎo / Lǎo shī nín hǎo / Zǎo shang hǎo)

11 **1** afternoon **2** you (formal) **3** teacher

17 **1** c **2** f **3** e **4** a **5** d **6** b

20

、	一	你	我	他	好
一	二	夫	小	上	见
丿	三	王	张	老	晚
丶	四	明	天	再	们
丨	五	不	用	谢	早
ㄱ	六	同	学	师	您
ㄴ	七	问	中	也	化

Unit 2

2 **1** mu **2** fo **3** pi **4** pu **5** ba

3 **1** mǒ **2** fū **3** pá **4** bì **5** mē

9 **1** c Wángjīnglǐ hěn máng ma? **2** d Tā hěn lèi ma?
3 e Tāmen shì tóngxué ma? **4** b Liúlǎoshī yě hěn hǎo ma?
5 a Tā shì jīnglǐ ma?

10 **1** d **2** c **3** a **4** g **5** e **6** b **7** f

11 **1** Nǐ hǎo! **2** Wǒ hěn hǎo. **3** Xièxie. **4** Zàijiàn.

12 **1** T **2** F **3** T **4** T **5** T

16 Sample answer:

Nǐ hǎo ma   Nǐ jiào shén me   Nǐ shì nǎ li rén
你好吗？你叫什么？你是哪里人？
Nǐ shì Shàng hǎi rén ma   Nǐ zuò shén me gōng zuò
你是上海人吗？你做什么工作？
Nǐ gōng zuò máng ma
你工作忙吗？

17 **1** T **2** F **3** T **4** F

19 Sample answer:

Nǐ hǎo   Liú Hóng
You: 你好，刘红。

Nǐ hǎo   Hǎo jiǔ bú jiàn   nǐ hǎo ma
Liu Hong: 你好。好久不见，你好吗？

Wǒ hěn hǎo   nǐ ne
You: 我很好，你呢？

Wǒ yě hěn hǎo
Liu Hong: 我也很好。

Nǐ hǎo   wǒ jiào Mǎ lì
Friend: 你好，我叫玛丽。

Wǒ jiào Bǐ dé   Nǐ shì nǎ li rén
You: 我叫彼德。你是哪里人？

Friend:
Wǒ shì Fǎ guó rén   nǐ ne
我是法国人，你呢？

You:
Wǒ shì Měi guó rén   Hěn gāo xìng rèn shi nǐ
我是美国人。很高兴认识你。

Friend:
Wǒ yě hěn gāo xìng rèn shi nǐ
我也很高兴认识你。

You:
Zài jiàn
再见。

Liu Hong
& Friend:
Zài jiàn
再见。

20 1 a. C 2 b. D 3 e. B 4 c. A 5 d. E 6 g. F 7 f. G

21 1 Hello. How are you?
2 Hello. My name is David.
3 Hello. My name is Mary/Marie. I am a teacher.
4 Hello. My name is Liu Hong. I am a student. I am Chinese.
5 Hello. My name is Tom. I am a doctor. I am British.

Unit 3

2 1 ha 2 qu 3 ri 4 he 5 te

3 1 ná 2 rǔ 3 dā 4 xí 5 hè

8
Lǐ Míng   Liú Hóng   Lì li   Yún yun
1 李明   2 刘红   3 力力   4 云云

9
tài tai   ér zi   Běi jīng   ér zi   nǚ ér
1 太太   2 儿子   3 北京   4 儿子…女儿
gē ge   mèi mei
5 哥哥   6 妹妹

10 1 b 2 a 3 a 4 b 5 c

12
Wǒ bú shì Zhōng guó rén
1 我不是中国人。
Tā bú shì wǒ de ér zi
2 他不是我的儿子。

Tā men bú zhù zài Běi jīng
3 他们不住在北京。

Wǒ de bà ba bú zài Shàng hǎi gōng zuò
4 我的爸爸不在上海工作。

Tā bú jiào Mǎ lì
5 她不叫玛丽。

Wǒ méi yǒu gē ge
6 我没有哥哥。

Zhēn qiǎo
14 1 真巧!

Ràng wǒ lái jiè shào yí xià
2 让我来介绍一下。

Rèn shi nín hěn gāo xìng
3 认识您很高兴!

Zhè shì wǒ tài tai
4 这是我太太。

Nà shì shuí
5 那是谁？

15 Sample answers:

Nǐ de bà ba jiào shén me   Tā jiào
1 你的爸爸叫什么？他叫 John。

Tā shì nǎ li rén   Tā shì Měi guó rén
2 他是哪里人？他是美国人。

Nǐ de mā ma shì lǎo shī ma   Shì   tā shì lǎo shī
3 你的妈妈是老师吗？是，她是老师。/

Bú shì   tā shì yī shēng
不是，她是医生。

Nǐ de jiā dà ma   Dà   Bú dà
4 你的家大吗？大。/ 不大。

Nǐ yǒu jiě jie ma   Yǒu   wǒ yǒu liǎng ge jiě jie
5 你有姐姐吗？有，我有两个姐姐。/

Méi yǒu   wǒ yǒu yí ge dì di
没有，我有一个弟弟。

16a 2 Tā jiào shén me
她叫什么？

3 Nǐ men de lǎo shī shì nǎ li rén
你们的老师是哪里人？

4 Nǐ zhù zài nǎ li
你住在哪里？

5 Nǐ zuò shén me gōng zuò
你做什么工作？

17 1 c **2** h **3** f **4** a **5** g **6** b **7** d **8** e

18 a 1, 4, 8, 9, 14 **b** 2, 3, 6, 10, 11, 13, 15 **c** 5, 7, 12

19 1 Her name is Liu Hong. **2** She's a teacher.
3 Her father is Chinese. **4** No, she's a company manager.
5 Yes, she has one older brother. (Translation: Hello. My name
is Liu Hong. I am a teacher. My father is a doctor. He is Chinese.
My mother is British. She is a company manager. I have one
older brother and one younger sister. I love my family.)

21 Sample answer:

Nǐ hǎo wǒ xìng jiào Wǒ shì Yīng guó rén
你好，我姓 Smith，叫 John。我是英国人。
Wǒ shì xué shēng Wǒ jiā yǒu sì ge rén wǒ bà ba mā
我是学生。我家有四个人，我爸爸，妈
ma hé yí ge mèi mei Wǒ bà ba shì lǎo shī wǒ mā ma
妈和一个妹妹。我爸爸是老师，我妈妈
bù gōng zuò Wǒ de mèi mei yě shì xué shēng Wǒ ài tā men
不工作。我的妹妹也是学生。我爱他们。

Unit 4

2 1 hai **2** xiu **3** ri **4** wen **5** hui

3 1 wā **2** ruì **3** bái **4** qǐn **5** gěi

6b sì shí sì shí bā èr èr shí liù
四 4, 十 10, 四十八 48, 二 2, 二十六 26,
qī shí sān shí jiǔ
七十三 73, 十九 19

7 五 5, 十一 11, 四十三 43, 九十九 99,

wǔ   shí yī   sì shí sān   jiǔ shí jiǔ

二十八 28

èr shí bā

8 **a** 四百八十二

sì bǎi bā shí èr

b 一千九百九十

yì qiān jiǔ bǎi jiǔ shí

c 四千七百六十二

sì qiān qī bǎi liù shí èr

d 两万七千九百六十七

liǎng wàn qī qiān jiǔ bǎi liù shí qī

e 五十三万三千六百十二

wǔ shí sān wàn sān qiān liù bǎi shí èr

f 八百三十七万六千二百十四

bā bǎi sān shí qī wàn liù qiān èr bǎi shí sì

10 **a** 3 **b** 6 **c** 2 **d** 7 **e** 5 **f** 4 **g** 8 **h** 1

11 **1** 我有两个哥哥。

Wǒ yǒu liǎng ge gē ge

2 他有五幅画。

Tā yǒu wǔ fú huà

3 她的家有七个人。

Tā de jiā yǒu qī ge rén

4 我有两瓶啤酒。

Wǒ yǒu liǎng píng pí jiǔ

5 她有六双鞋。

Tā yǒu liù shuāng xié

6 我妈妈有一个妹妹。

Wǒ mā ma yǒu yí ge mèi mei

12 **1** He studies Chinese.
   2 Her room number is 208.
   3 He has one older sister and two younger brothers.
   4 She's 9 years old.
   5 His telephone number is 56689375.

14

	a.	b.	c.
Name	Wang Min	Bǐdé ('Peter')	Mǎlì ('Marie')
Nationality	Chinese	English	French
Age	20	34	60
Telephone no.	57762938	07932827822	948272981
No. of family members	3	5	4

15

Tā xué xí Zhōngwén
1 他学习中文。

Tā de jiā yǒu liù ge rén
2 他的家有六个人。

Tā de jiā zài Yīng guó
3 他的家在英国。

Tā de diàn huà hào mǎ shì
4 他的电话号码是 56689375。

Tā yǒu yí ge mèi mei
5 她有一个妹妹。

Tā de mèi mei jiǔ suì
6 她的妹妹九岁。

Zhāng Mǐn de xué yuàn hěn dà   yǒu   ge lǎo shī
7 张敏的学院很大，有 45 个老师，600

ge xué sheng
个学生。

Unit 1–4 Review

1 **1** Zǎoshang hǎo!   **2** Wǒ jiào (name).   **3** Búyòngxiè.
4 Zàijiàn!   **5** Wǒ shì Yīngguórén.   **6** Nǐ hǎo ma?

2 **1** b   **2** a   **3** c   **4** a   **5** a   **6** b

3 Sample answers:

A: Nǐ hǎo ma
你好吗?

B: Wǒ hěn hǎo
我很好。

A: Nǐ shì nǎ li rén
你是哪里人?

B: Wǒ shì Yīng guó rén
我是英国人。

A: Nǐ jiā yǒu jǐ ge rén
你家有几个人?

B: Wǒ jiā yǒu sì ge rén，wǒ bà ba，mā ma，
我家有四个人，我爸爸，妈妈，
jiě jie hé wǒ
姐姐和我。

A: Nǐ zuò shén me gōng zuò
你做什么工作?

B: Wǒ shì jīng lǐ
我是经理。

A: Nǐ de diàn huà hào mǎ shì duō shǎo
你的电话号码是多少?

B: Liù bā bā sān èr sì wǔ
六八八三二四五。

4

	Speaker 1	Speaker 2	Speaker 3
Name	Liu Ming	Zhang Jie	David
Nationality	Chinese	Chinese	British
City	Beijing	Shanghai	London
Age	33	27	49
Job	engineer	teacher	doctor
Telephone no.	4673524	59946383	3314659
No. of family members	3	4	4

5

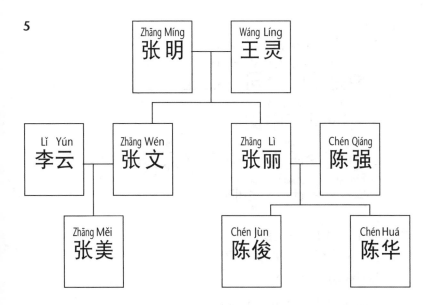

6 Xiǎo lì de fáng jiān lǐ yǒu
小丽的房间里有 (In Xiaoli's room)：**一杯**
yì bēi

kā fēi sì fú huà wǔ tiáo qún zi liù shuāng xié
咖啡；四幅画；五条裙子；六双鞋；

sān jiàn máo yī liǎng zhāng diàn yǐng piào liǎng píng kě lè
三件毛衣；两张电影票；两瓶可乐；

shí běn shū
十本书。

7 Nǐ hǎo Wǒ jiào Nǐ jiào shén me
1 **你好，我叫＿＿。你叫什么？**

Hǎo jiǔ bú jiàn Nǐ hǎo ma
2 **好久不见！你好吗？**

Hěn gāo xìng rèn shi nín
3 **很高兴认识您！**

Wǒ men qù hē kā fēi hǎo ma
4 **我们去喝咖啡，好吗？**

8 Zhè shì wǒ de mā ma
1 **这是我的妈妈。**

Tā bù máng
2 **他不忙。**

Ràng wǒ lái jiè shào yí xià
3 让我来介绍一下。

Tā shì wǒ men gōng sī de jīng lǐ
4 他是我们公司的经理。

Wǒ de jiā zài Zhōng guó
5 我的家在中国。

Zhōng wén xué yuàn yǒu sān shí ge lǎo shī   Xué yuàn yǒu
6 中文学院有三十个老师。or 学院有

sān shí ge Zhōng wén lǎo shī
三十个中文老师。

9   ba po me mi fu lü gai dui

hen li ru nü jie gou yan qin

kei ha shu bo xu xiu chi re

10   ban pie mi fei dou tuo ning la

ge ku heng jun qie xia pang ruan

yang wen tong qiong ji kao qian fo

11   1 pān   2 jǐn   3 kòu   4 dú   5 qiú   6 rìjì   7 guāguǒ
     8 hútu   9 xīnqí   10 nǚhái

12   1 dùn   2 niē   3 lòu   4 xiū   5 bǐ   6 kěxī   7 yúròu
     8 jīqì   9 tèbié   10 wùyè

13   (Check your answers with the character practice in the units.)

14   1 My father is well.
     2 Are you Chinese?
     3 My name is Peter.
     4 This is not my daughter.
     5 I live in Beijing.
     6 I have one younger sister. I don't any have younger brothers.

Unit 5

2   1 chǎi   2 zhuí   3 bāng   4 qìng   5 kēng

3   1 nǐhǎo   2 lǎoshī   3 bàba   4 péngyou   5 shéi

7　**1** 2004/11/17　二零零四年十一月十七号
èr líng líng sì nián shí yī yuè shí qī hào

2 1978/09/24　一九七八年九月二十四号
yī jiǔ qī bā nián jiǔ yuè èr shí sì hào

3 1999/01/31　一九九九年一月三十一号
yī jiǔ jiǔ jiǔ nián yī yuè sān shí yī hào

4 2020/07/29　二零二零年七月二十九号
èr líng èr líng nián qī yuè èr shí jiǔ hào

8　**1** b　**2** d　**3** f　**4** i　**5** e　**6** j　**7** a　**8** c　**9** h　**10** g

9　Sample answer:

You:　小王，今年我在中国过生日。
Xiǎo Wáng, jīn nián wǒ zài Zhōng guó guò shēng rì

Friend:　是吗? 你的生日是几月几号?
Shì ma　Nǐ de shēng rì shì jǐ yuè jǐ hào

You:　我的生日是三月九号。
Wǒ de shēng rì shì sān yuè jiǔ hào

Friend:　那是星期几?
Nà shì xīng qī jǐ

You:　星期六。你来我家吃生日蛋糕，
Xīng qī liù　Nǐ lái wǒ jiā chī shēng rì dàn gāo
好吗?
hǎo ma

Friend:　太好了，星期六我有时间，
Tài hǎo le　xīng qī liù wǒ yǒu shí jiān
我一定去。
wǒ yí dìng qù

You:　小王，你属什么?
Xiǎo Wáng, nǐ shǔ shén me

Friend:　我属马。
Wǒ shǔ mǎ

You:　啊，我也属马，真巧!
A　wǒ yě shǔ mǎ　zhēn qiǎo

11

Departure time	Country to visit	Arrival time
8 March	Britain	Wednesday
Saturday	Italy	Tuesday
20 March	Germany	21 March
24 March	France	

13b Sample answers:

Travel Agent:
Nǐ hǎo
你好！

You:
Nǐ hǎo
你好！

Travel Agent:
Nǐ dǎ suan qù nǎ li lǚ xíng
你打算去哪里旅行？

You:
Wǒ dǎ suan qù Běi jīng　Shàng hǎi hé Háng zhōu
我打算去北京，上海和杭州。

Travel Agent:
Nǐ dǎ suan shén me shí hou zǒu
你打算什么时候走？

You:
Sì yuè wǔ hào
四月五号。

Travel Agent:
Nǐ dǎ suan zhù jǐ tiān
你打算住几天？

You:
Liǎng ge xīng qī
两个星期。

Travel Agent:
Nǐ dǎ suan xiān qù nǎ li　zài qù nǎ li
你打算先去哪里，再去哪里？

You:
Wǒ dǎ suan xiān qù Shàng hǎi hé Háng zhōu
我打算先去上海和杭州，
zài qù Běi jīng
再去北京。

Travel Agent:
Hǎo de
好的。

14 **1** b **2** a **3** b **4** a **5** a **6** b

Unit 6

2   **1** càn   **2** zū   **3** piáo   **4** sǐ   **5** céng

3   **1** jīntiān   **2** sānyuè   **3** shēngrì   **4** míngnián   **5** xīngqīliù

7   **1** 3pm   下午三点
xià wǔ sān diǎn

    2 11:15am   上午十一点一刻
shàng wǔ shí yī diǎn yí kè

    3 8:30pm   晚上八点半
wǎn shang bā diǎn bàn

    4 17:35   十七点三十五分
shí qī diǎn sān shí wǔ fēn

    5 4:45pm   下午四点三刻
xià wǔ sì diǎn sān kè

    6 11:55   差五分十二点
chà wǔ fēn shí èr diǎn

8   **1** 1:55   **2** 20:15   **3** 4:30   **4** 16:20   **5** 6:05   **6** 8:45

11   **1** d   **2** e   **3** a   **4** b   **5** c   **6** f

13   **1** 李风星期一去喝咖啡。
Lǐ fēng xīng qī yī qù hē kā fēi

    2 他星期二下午和汤姆喝啤酒。
Tā xīng qī èr xià wǔ hé Tāng mǔ hē pí jiǔ

    3 他星期三去看电影，从晚上七点到九点。
Tā xīng qī sān qù kàn diàn yǐng cóng wǎn shàng qī diǎn dào jiǔ diǎn

    4 他星期四晚上十点祝朋友生日快乐。
Tā xīng qī sì wǎn shang shí diǎn zhù péng you shēng rì kuài lè

    5 他星期五晚上八点半在朋友家吃饭。
Tā xīng qī wǔ wǎn shang bā diǎn bàn zài péng you jiā chī fàn

    6 他星期六早上去公园，星期日下午去买东西。
Tā xīng qī liù zǎo shang qù gōng yuán xīng qī rì xià wǔ qù mǎi dōng xi

    7 不，他星期日去。
Bù tā xīng qī rì qù

16 **1** He suggested watching a film.
2 She needed to do shopping.
3 Sunday afternoon at 4 o'clock.

18 **1** 让我看一看 / 看一下。
    Ràng wǒ kàn yí kàn   kàn yí xià

2 让我想一想 / 想一下。
    Ràng wǒ xiǎng yì xiǎng   xiǎng yí xià

3 让她试一试 / 试一下。
    Ràng tā shì yí shì   shì yí xià

4 让我说一说 / 说一下我的工作。
    Ràng wǒ shuō yì shuō   shuō yí xià wǒ de gōng zuò

5 他想查一查 / 查一下时间。
    Tā xiǎng chá yì chá   chá yí xià shí jiān

20 **1** e **2** b **3** f **4** d **5** a

21

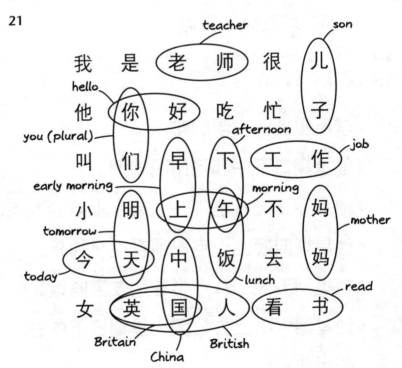

Unit 7

1   **1** mà   **2** fǔ   **3** bù   **4** mé   **5** pōu
      6 mǔ   **7** pá   **8** piān   **9** jǔn   **10** qù

2   **1** shíjiān   **2** qǐchuáng   **3** shuìjiào   **4** shénme shíhou   **5** kěyǐ

5a   **1** ￥68.20   **2** 20RMB   **3** ￥9.99   **4** 1.40RMB
      5 ￥2.50   **6** 25.62RMB

5b (20RMB) 二十块 (èr shí kuài)；(100RMB) 一百块 (yì bǎi kuài)；

(12.30RMB) 十二块三（毛）(shí èr kuài sān máo)；

(76.01RMB) 七十六块零一（分）(qī shí liù kuài líng yì fēn)；

(￥234.99) 二百三十四块九毛九（分）(èr bǎi sān shí sì kuài jiǔ máo jiǔ fēn)；

(￥1000) 一千块 (yì qiān kuài)；(￥23.40) 二十三块四（毛）(èr shí sān kuài sì máo)；

(￥45.88) 四十五块八毛八（分）(sì shí wǔ kuài bā máo bā fēn)

6 (4) 一杯咖啡两块五毛。(Yì bēi kā fēi liǎng kuài wǔ máo)；

(1) 一本书四十五块。(Yì běn shū sì shí wǔ kuài)；

(8) 一件毛衣一百五十。(Yí jiàn máo yī yì bǎi wǔ shí) (￥150)；

(6) 一张电影票八块三。(Yì zhāng diàn yǐng piào bā kuài sān) (￥8.3)；

(3) 一块蛋糕四块五毛。(Yí kuài dàn gāo sì kuài wǔ máo)；

(5) 一双鞋九十。(Yì shuāng xié jiǔ shí) (￥90)；

(7) 一瓶啤酒五块。(Yì píng pí jiǔ wǔ kuài) (￥5)；

(2) 一条裙子九百九十九块九毛九。(Yì tiáo qún zi jiǔ bǎi jiǔ shí jiǔ kuài jiǔ máo jiǔ)

8

1 Miàn bāo sān kuài yí ge
面包三块一个。

2 Yì zhāng yóu piào liǎng kuài
一张邮票两块。

3 Yì běn shū sān shí bā kuài sì máo
一本书三十八块四毛。

4 Yí ge hàn bǎo hé yì bēi kě lè yí gòng bā kuài èr
一个汉堡和一杯可乐，一共八块二。

9   a 1 T 2 T;   b 1 T 2 F;   c 1 T 2 F

10

1 Yì běn shū duō shǎo qián
一本书多少钱？

Yì běn shū sì shí kuài
一本书四十（块）。

2 Yì bēi kā fēi duō shǎo qián
一杯咖啡多少钱？

Yì bēi kā fēi shí kuài
一杯咖啡十块。

3 Yì bēi pí jiǔ duō shǎo qián
一杯啤酒多少钱？

Yì bēi pí jiǔ shí wǔ kuài
一杯啤酒十五块。

4 Yí jiàn máo yī duō shǎo qián
一件毛衣多少钱？

Yí jiàn máo yī liǎng bǎi sān shí kuài
一件毛衣两百三十块。

5 Yí ge hàn bǎo duō shǎo qián
一个汉堡多少钱？

Yí ge hàn bǎo jiǔ kuài jiǔ máo jiǔ
一个汉堡九块九毛九。

6 Yì píng kuàng quán shuǐ duō shǎo qián
一瓶矿泉水多少钱？

Yì píng kuàng quán shuǐ sān kuài wǔ
一瓶矿泉水三块五。

Yī tiáo qún zi duō shǎo qián
7 一条裙子多少钱？
Yī tiáo qún zi wǔ bǎi jiǔ shí jiǔ kuài jiǔ máo jiǔ
一条裙子五百九十九块九毛九。

Yí kuài dàn gāo duō shǎo qián
8 一块蛋糕多少钱？
Yí kuài dàn gāo qī kuài wǔ
一块蛋糕七块五。

Yì shuāng xié duō shǎo qián
9 一双鞋多少钱？
Yì shuāng xié sān bǎi liù shí kuài
一双鞋三百六十块。

Tài guì le
13 1 太贵了！

Sān bǎi kuài   zěn me yàng
2 三百块，怎么样？

Zài pián yi yì diǎn ba
3 再便宜一点吧！

Yì kǒu jià   wǔ shí kuài
4 一口价，五十块！

15 1 汉堡 hamburger
2 矿泉水 mineral water
3 面包 bread
4 可乐 coke
5 鞋 shoe
6 毛衣 sweater
7 啤酒 beer
8 蛋糕 cake

Unit 8

1 1 gè 2 nín 3 jiā 4 lā 5 rì
6 jiǔ 7 duì 8 hòu 9 gěi 10 liǎn

2 1 duōshǎo qián 2 guì 3 piányi 4 biéde 5 xiàcì

4 1 g 2 f 3 a 4 d 5 b 6 e 7 h 8 c

11 1 a bottle of beer 2 a hot chocolate and a piece of cake
3 a bottle of wine 4 a pot of tea and a ham sandwich

14 1 他要不要一杯咖啡?
Tā yào bu yào yì bēi kā fēi

2 她是不是美国人?
Tā shì bu shì Měi guó rén

3 我有没有三个妹妹?
Wǒ yǒu mei yǒu sān ge mèi mei

4 我们说不说中文?
Wǒ men shuō bu shuō Zhōng wén

5 我的啤酒加不加冰块?
Wǒ de pí jiǔ jiā bu jiā bīng kuài

6 他们家有没有中国茶?
Tā men jiā yǒu mei yǒu Zhōng guó chá

16 菜单 Menu
cài dān

冷盘 Cold Dishes (Starters)
lěng pán

烤鸭 Roasted Duck   20.00 元 / 份 20RMB
kǎo yā   yuán fèn per portion

冷豆腐 Cold Tofu   15.00 元 / 份 15RMB
lěng dòu fu   yuán fèn per portion

rè chǎo
热炒 Hot Dishes (Mains)

hóng shāo niú ròu   yuán   fèn
红烧牛肉 Beef with Soy Sauce   20.00 元 / 份 20RMB
                                         per portion

yú xiāng ròu sī   yuán   fèn
鱼香肉丝   20.00 元 / 份 20RMB
Fish Flavoured Shredded Pork   per portion

yáng ròu bāo   yuán   fèn
羊肉煲 Lamb Stew   25.00 元 / 份 25RMB
                                           per portion

táng cù yú   yuán   fèn
糖醋鱼 Sweet and Sour Fish   18.00 元 / 份 18RMB
                                           per portion

tāng
汤 Soup

hǎi xiān tāng   yuán   fèn
海鲜汤 Seafood Soup   2500 元 / 份 25RMB
                                           per portion

yǐn liào
饮料 Beverages

chá   yuán   hú
茶 Tea   3.00 元 / 壶 3RMB
                                           per pot

pí jiǔ   yuán   píng
啤酒 Beer   5.00 元 / 瓶 5RMB
                                           per bottle

kě lè   yuán   píng
可乐 Coke   3.50 元 / 瓶 3.5RMB
                                           per bottle

17   1 f   2 d   3 g   4 c   5 b   6 e   7 i   8 a   9 h

18   1 a   2 a   3 a   4 c   5 c

Unit 5–8 Review

1

Xiao Zhang:	Xiao Li:	Xiao Chen:
yesterday	tomorrow	today
58年04月12日	78年09月12日	81年03月07日
Wednesday	Sunday	Friday

2 **a** 1 T 2 F 3 T; **b** 1 T 2 F 3 F; **c** 1 T 2 F 3 F

3 Sample answer:

Wǒ měi tiān zǎo shang bā diǎn bàn qǐ chuáng   jiǔ diǎn yí kè qù shàng
我每天早上八点半起床，九点一刻去上
bān   Zhōng wǔ wǒ zài gōng sī chī wǔ fàn   Xià wǔ wǔ diǎn huí
班。中午我在公司吃午饭。下午五点回
jiā   Wǒ yì bān liù diǎn dào jiā   Cóng liù diǎn bàn dào qī diǎn
家，我一般六点到家。从六点半到七点
bàn wǒ zuò fàn   Wǎn shang wǒ bā diǎn chī wǎn fàn
半我做饭。晚上我八点吃晚饭。
Wǎn fàn hòu   wǒ yǒu shí qù kàn diàn yǐng   yǒu shí kàn diàn
晚饭后，我有时去看电影，有时看电
shì   yì bān shí yī diǎn shuì jiào   Zhōu mò de shí hou
视，一般十一点睡觉。周末的时候，
wǒ hé   wǒ de hǎo péng you cháng qù hē kā fēi hé mǎi dōng xi
我和我的好朋友常去喝咖啡和买东西。

4 1 ¥56.60 2 ¥18 3 ¥398 4 ¥250 5 ¥12.40 6 ¥23.50

5
Duō shǎo qián
1 多少钱？

Tài guì le
2 太贵了！

Bā shí wǔ kuài   zěn me yàng
3 八十五块，怎么样？

Wǒ yào le
4 我要了。

Gěi nǐ qián
5 给你钱。

Nǐ xiǎng yào mǎi shén me
6 你想要买什么?

Zài pián yi yì diǎn ba
7 再便宜一点吧!

6   Sample answers: For each order, you could start with

qǐng gěi wǒ   wǒ xiǎng yào   wǒ yào   lái
请给我, 我想要, 我要, 来,

or just say what you want directly.

yí fèn mǐ fàn   yí ge rén de mǐ fàn
1 一份米饭 / 一个人的米饭

yì bēi chéng zhī
2 一杯橙汁

yí ge tāng
3 一个汤

yì pán niú ròu
4 一盘牛肉

yì bēi rè qiǎo kè lì
5 一杯热巧克力

yí ge miàn bāo
6 一个面包

Míng tiān shí yī yuè sān hào
8   1 明天十一月三号。

Dà Wèi shì Yīng guó rén
2 大为是英国人。

Tā jīn nián èr shí bā suì
3 他今年二十八岁。

Jīn tiān xīng qī liù
4 今天星期六。

Wǒ   jīn tiān zǎo shang mǎi le yí ge dà dàn gāo hé yí jiàn
5 '我' 今天早上买了一个大蛋糕和一件
máo yī
毛衣。

Máo yī yǒu yì diǎn guì
6 毛衣有一点贵。

Tā men xià wǔ liǎngdiǎn bàn qù kàn diàn yǐng
7 他们下午两点半去看电影。

Bà ba mǎi le liǎngpíng pú tao jiǔ
8 爸爸买了两瓶葡萄酒。

Tā men wǎnshang zài jiā chī fàn   chī le shēng rì dàn gāo
9 他们晚上在家吃饭，吃了生日蛋糕。

Měi ge rén dōu hěn gāo xìng
10 每个人都很高兴。

9   lao bo he qi xun   jün wang ling ken lia
     hua kuo pie guo xian   feng jiao xiang qiong shuan
     zhong miu chuang

10   zhan cun zi se   shu cha nie lai   guai kang che jiong
     qin xia pi rong   ying wa tou mo   zhi ke qiu fang

11   1 zhǎng   2 qiāng   3 chuō   4 shù   5 xún
     6 shíjiān   7 guànhuài   8 huìyì   9 zhìshāng   10 yūnchuán

12   xuéxí qíngkuàng jiànkāng chénggōng xiǎngxiàng zànshí
     lǎoshī qiángpò zuànshí

13   1 T   2 F   3 F   4 F   5 T   6 T   7 F   8 F

14   Sample answer:

Xīng qī yī wǎnshang bā diǎn hé   chī wǎn fàn   Xīng qī èr
星期一晚上八点和 Tom 吃晚饭。星期二
xià wǔ sān diǎn hé   hē kā fēi   Xīng qī sān wǎnshang jiǔ
下午三点和 Lisa 喝咖啡。星期三晚上九
diǎn kàn diàn yǐng   Xīng qī wǔ xià bān hòu qù mǎi dōng xi   Xīng
点看电影。星期五下班后去买东西。星
qī liù qù gōng yuán   Xīng qī rì zhōng wǔ shí èr diǎn bàn hé
期六去公园。星期日中午十二点半和
chī wǔ fàn
Bob 吃午饭。

Unit 9

10 English: Train No. 81 is an express train so it is two hours faster than No. 51, and the ticket costs ¥50 more.

Chinese:
cì shì tè kuài suǒ yǐ bǐ cì pǔ kuài kuài
81 次是特快，所以比 51 次普快快
liǎng ge xiǎo shí piào jià yě guì wǔ shí kuài
两个小时，票价也贵五十块。

11 1
Wǒ xiǎng mǎi yì zhāng qù Shàng hǎi de huǒ chē piào
我想买一张去上海的火车票。

Huǒ chē jǐ diǎn chū fā
2 火车几点出发？

Huǒ chē jǐ diǎn dào
3 火车几点到？

Jǐ hào zhàn tái
4 几号站台？

Shí cì huǒ chē bǐ wǔ cì huǒ chē guì yì bǎi kuài
5 十次火车比五次火车贵一百块。

12a 1
Shī fù qù Cháng chéng Duō shǎo qián
师傅，去长城。多少钱？

Shī fù qù Yí hé yuán Duō shǎo qián
2 师傅，去颐和园。多少钱？

Shī fù qù Gù gōng Duō shǎo qián
3 师傅，去故宫。多少钱？

Shī fù qù Ào yùn cūn Duō shǎo qián
4 师傅，去奥运村。多少钱？

12b 1
Yì zhāng qù Cháng chéng de piào Qǐng wèn jǐ zhàn
一张去长城的票。请问，几站？

Yì zhāng qù Yí hé yuán de piào Qǐng wèn jǐ zhàn
2 一张去颐和园的票。请问，几站？

Yì zhāng qù Gù gōng de piào Qǐng wèn jǐ zhàn
3 一张去故宫的票。请问，几站？

Yì zhāng qù Ào yùn cūn de piào Qǐng wèn jǐ zhàn
4 一张去奥运村的票。请问，几站？

13 1 b 2 b 3 c 4 c 5 a

14

2 他星期一比星期五忙。他星期五比星
期一闲。

Tā xīng qī yī bǐ xīng qī wǔ máng　Tā xīng qī wǔ bǐ xīng
qī yī xián

3 这杯咖啡比那杯咖啡贵。那杯咖啡比
这杯咖啡便宜。

Zhè bēi kā fēi bǐ nà bēi kā fēi guì　Nà bēi kā fēi bǐ
zhè bēi kā fēi pián yi

4 这幅画比那幅画漂亮。那幅画比这幅
画难看。

Zhè fú huà bǐ nà fú huà piào liang　Nà fú huà bǐ zhè fú
huà nán kàn

5 他比他胖。他比他瘦。

Tā bǐ tā pàng　Tā bǐ tā shòu

6 她比她高。她比她矮。

Tā bǐ tā gāo　Tā bǐ tā ǎi

16

1 厕所在餐厅的左边。

Cè suǒ zài cān tīng de zuǒ bian

2 图书馆在办公楼的后面。

Tú shū guǎn zài bàn gōng lóu de hòu mian

3 超市在学校的对面。

Chāo shì zài xué xiào de duì miàn

4 电影院前面有一个饭店。

Diàn yǐng yuàn qián mian yǒu yí ge fàn diàn

5 我的家在博物馆的右边。

Wǒ de jiā zài bó wù guǎn de yòu bian

6 餐厅在办公楼的左边。

Cān tīng zài bàn gōng lóu de zuǒ bian

7 学校后面有一个公园。

Xué xiào hòu mian yǒu yí ge gōng yuán

8 饭店在超市的旁边。

Fàn diàn zài chāo shì de páng biān

Bó wù guǎn zài gōng yuán de duì miàn
9 博物馆在公园的对面。

Tú shū guǎn zài diàn yǐng yuàn de páng biān
10 图书馆在电影院的旁边。

chāo shì
17 超市 (supermarket) 2, C

Zhōng guó Yín háng
中国银行 (Bank of China) 4, A

tú shū guǎn
图书馆 (library) 1, B

Hé píng Diàn yǐng yuàn
和平电影院 (Peace Cinema) 3, D

18 Sample answers:

Wǎng yòu guǎi dào lù kǒu wǎng zuǒ guǎi dào dì èr ge lù
1 往右拐，到路口往左拐，到第二个路
kǒu wǎng yòu guǎi yóu jú jiù zài nǐ de zuǒ bian
口往右拐，邮局就在你的左边。

Wǎng yòu guǎi dào lù kǒu zài wǎng yòu guǎi dào lù kǒu wǎng
2 往右拐，到路口再往右拐，到路口往
zuǒ guǎi chāo shì jiù zài nǐ de yòu bian
左拐，超市就在你的右边。

Wǎng zuǒ guǎi dào lù kǒu zài wǎng zuǒ guǎi cān tīng jiù zài
3 往左拐，到路口再往左拐，餐厅就在
mǎ lù de duì miàn
马路的对面。

Wǎng yòu guǎi dào dì èr ge lù kǒu zài wǎng yòu guǎi
4 往右拐，到第二个路口再往右拐，
yì zhí zǒu tú shū guǎn jiù zài nǐ de zuǒ bian
一直走，图书馆就在你的左边，
mǎ lù de duì miàn
马路的对面。

Unit 10

5

Wǒ yào yì jiān dān rén fáng jiān dài wèi shēng jiān
1 我要一间单人房间，带卫生间。

Wǒ yào yì jiān shuāng rén fáng jiān dài wú xiàn shàng wǎng
2 我要一间双人房间，带无线上网。

Wǒ bú yào dān rén fáng jiān wǒ yào shuāng rén fáng jiān
3 我不要单人房间，我要双人房间。

Wǒ yào yì jiān shuāng rén fáng jiān dài kōng tiáo
4 我要一间双人房间带空调。

6 **1** Zhang Ming **2** a single room **3** three nights
4 307 **5** Yes, it does. **6** 7–10:30am

7 **1** b **2** a **3** b **4** b **5** c **6** b

8 Sample answers:

Wǒ yào yí ge dān rén fáng jiān dài wèi shēng jiān hé kōng tiáo
我要一个单人房间，带卫生间和空调。

Wǒ huì zhù wǔ tiān Wǒ de fáng jiān zài sì lóu Wǒ de fáng
我会住五天。我的房间在四楼。我的房

jiān bāo zǎo cān Wǒ zǎo shang bā diǎn bàn chī zǎo fàn
间包早餐。我早上八点半吃早饭。

9

Wǒ bǎ kā fēi hē le
2 我把咖啡喝了。

Mā ma huì bǎ zǎo fàn zuò le
3 妈妈会把早饭做了。

Wǒ bǎ hù zhào chá le yí xià
4 我把护照查了一下。

Tā bǎ wǒ men qǐng qù Zhōng guó le
5 他把我们请去中国了。

Tā bǎ yào shi gěi le wǒ
6 他把钥匙给了我。

Wáng xiān sheng bǎ dēng jì biǎo tián le
7 王先生把登记表填了。

11 **a** 2 **b** 7 **c** 1 **d** 6 **e** 3 **f** 4 **g** 5 **h** 8

12 1 我可以 / 能要一些咖啡吗？
Wǒ kě yǐ néng yào yì xiē kā fēi ma

2 你能不能 / 可不可以明天早上七点叫醒我？
Nǐ néng bu néng kě bu kě yǐ míng tiān zǎo shang qī diǎn jiào xǐng wǒ

3 我可以 / 能把行李寄存在这里吗？
Wǒ kě yǐ néng bǎ xíng li jì cún zài zhè lǐ ma

4 我可以 / 能在网上预定房间吗？
Wǒ kě yǐ néng zài wǎng shang yù dìng fáng jiā ma

5 我可以 / 能住一个星期吗？
Wǒ kě yǐ néng zhù yí ge xīng qī ma

6 我可以 / 能看一下房间吗？
Wǒ kě yǐ néng kàn yí xià fáng jiān ma

14 1 她住在了北京饭店。
Tā zhù zài le Běi jīng Fàn diàn

2 她先去了银行。
Tā xiān qù le yín háng

3 她刚回饭店，就发现她的包不见了。
Tā gāng huí fàn diàn jiù fā xiàn tā de bāo bú jiàn le

4 她的包里面有她的护照，300 美金和 1,000 人民币，还有一本通讯录和一个手机。
Tā de bāo lǐ miàn yǒu tā de hù zhào měi jīn hé rén mín bì hái yǒu yì běn tōng xùn lù hé yí ge shǒu jī

5 前台小姐很热心。
Qián tái xiǎo jiě hěn rè xīn

6 她可能把包忘在出租汽车上了。
Tā kě néng bǎ bāo wàng zài chū zū qì chē shàng le

7 出租车司机出现了，手里拿着她的包！
Chū zū chē sī jī chū xiàn le shǒu lǐ ná zhe tā de bāo

15 1 终于 zhōng yú   2 可能 kě néng   3 有…还有… yǒu … hái yǒu …

   4 …的时候 … de shí hou   5 马上 mǎ shàng   6 刚…，…就… gāng …, … jiù …

16 Sample answers:

2 他的房间是单人房间，带卫生间和
Tā de fáng jiān shì dān rén fáng jiān   dài wèi shēng jiān hé
空调。
kōng tiáo

3 那天，他在饭店餐厅吃饭。他把他的
Nà tiān   tā zài fàn diàn cān tīng chī fàn   Tā bǎ tā de
包忘在那里了。
bāo wàng zài nà li le

4 他的包里有他的护照，房间钥匙，
Tā de bāo lǐ yǒu tā de hù zhào   fáng jiān yào shi
500 块人民币。
kuài rén mín bì

5 他发现他的包不见了，非常着急。
Tā fā xiàn tā de bāo bú jiàn le   fēi cháng zháo jí

6 他去问前台，终于找到了他的包。
Tā qù wèn qián tái   zhōng yú zhǎo dào le tā de bāo

Unit 11

4 1 我喜欢喝咖啡。
Wǒ xǐ huan hē kā fēi

2 我不喜欢攀岩。
Wǒ bù xǐ huan pān yán

3 我更喜欢在网上聊天。
Wǒ gèng xǐ huan zài wǎng shang liáo tiān

4 我更不喜欢打篮球。
Wǒ gèng bù xǐ huan dǎ lán qiú

5 我最喜欢唱卡拉 OK。
Wǒ zuì xǐ huan chàng kǎ lā

Wǒ zuì bù xǐ huan bèng dí
6 我最不喜欢蹦迪。

5 a ☺   b ☺   c ☹   d ☹   e ☺
   f ☹   g ☹   h ☺☺   i ☹   j ☺☺
   k ☺   l ☹   m ☺   n ☺   o ☹☹

8 Xiao Wang:
   xǐ huan kàn diàn yǐng   bù xǐ huan bèng dí
   喜欢看电影，不喜欢蹦迪

   Xiao Zhang:
   xǐ huan kàn diàn yǐng   gèng xǐ huan chàng kǎ lā
   喜欢看电影，更喜欢唱卡拉 OK

   Xiao Li:
   zuì xǐ huan chàng kǎ lā   zuì bù xǐ huan
   最喜欢唱卡拉 OK，最不喜欢
   pān yán
   攀岩

   Xiao Liu:
   duì yóu yǒng yǒu xìng qù   duì chàng kǎ lā
   对游泳有兴趣，对唱卡拉 OK
   méi xìng qù
   没兴趣

9 Tā xǐ huan yóu yǒng   Tā gèng xǐ huan tī zú qiú   Tā zuì
   2 他喜欢游泳。他更喜欢踢足球。他最
   xǐ huan kàn shū
   喜欢看书。

   Zhè ge huā píng hěn guì   Zhè ge huā píng gèng guì   Zhè ge
   3 这个花瓶很贵。这个花瓶更贵。这个
   huā píng zuì guì
   花瓶最贵。

   Xīng qī yī tā hěn máng   Xīng qī èr tā gèng máng   Xīng qī
   4 星期一他很忙。星期二他更忙。星期
   sì tā zuì máng
   四他最忙。

11 duì   duì   duì   duì
    1 对   2 对   3 对   4 对
    bú duì   bú duì   duì
    5 不对   6 不对   7 对

12

2
Tā píng shí gōng zuò hěn máng
他平时工作很忙。

3
Tā jué de kàn shū jì yǒu yì si yòu fàngsōng   Tā jué de
她觉得看书既有意思又放松。/ 她觉得
kàn shū jì fàngsōng yòu yǒu yì si
看书既放松又有意思。

4
Tiān qì yì hǎo wǒ men jiù qù yě cān
天气一好我们就去野餐。

5
Tā měi ge xīng qī dōu hé péng you qù yí cì wǔ tīng
她每个星期都和朋友去一次舞厅。

13 Sample answer:

You:
Nǐ píng shí xǐ huan zuò shén me
你平时喜欢做什么？

Friend:
Wǒ xǐ huan yùn dòng yóu yǒng dǎ lán qiú wǒ dōu
我喜欢运动，游泳，打蓝球我都
xǐ huan Nǐ ne
喜欢。你呢？

You:
Wǒ yě xǐ huan yùn dòng wǒ xǐ huan tī zú qiú
我也喜欢运动，我喜欢踢足球，
wǒ gèng xǐ huan pān yán Kě shì wǒ píng shí
我更喜欢攀岩。可是，我平时
gōng zuò tài máng bù néng cháng qù pān yán
工作太忙，不能常去攀岩。

Friend:
Shì a wǒ gōng zuò lèi de shí hou wǒ zuì xǐ
是啊，我工作累的时候，我最喜
huan kàn shū hé tīng yīn yuè hěn fàngsōng
欢看书和听音乐，很放松。

You:
Zhōu mò de shí hou ne Nǐ xǐ huan zuò shén me
周末的时候呢？你喜欢做什么？

Friend:
Wǒ yǒu shí qù kàn diàn yǐng yǒu shí qù hé péng you
我有时去看电影，有时去和朋友
hē kā fēi Nǐ ne
喝咖啡。你呢？

You:
Wǒ bù xǐ huan hē kā fēi   wǒ zhǐ hē chá
我不喜欢喝咖啡，我只喝茶。
Zhōu mò   wǒ cháng qù gōng yuán   yě cháng qù mǎi
周末，我常去公园，也常去买
dōng xi   Ǒu ěr   wǒ qù hé péng you chàng kǎ lā
东西。偶尔，我去和朋友唱卡拉
wǒ de Zhōng guó péng you dōu hěn xǐ huan
OK，我的中国朋友都很喜欢。

Friend:
Wǒ yě xǐ huan   xià cì wǒ men yì qǐ qù
我也喜欢，下次我们一起去，
hǎo ma
好吗？

You:
Tài hǎo le
太好了！

14	Name	Activity	Every day	Once a week	Three times a week	Once every two weeks
	Li	watch movies		X		
		go for picnics				X
	Liu	sing karaoke		X		
	Wang	read	X			
	Chen	play basketball		X		
		play football				X

Unit 12

4a   1 F   2 T   3 F

4b   1 T   2 F   3 F   4 F   5 F

4c   1 F   2 T   3 T

5   1 d   2 c   3 e   4 a   5 b

6

Message	Who is calling?	For whom?	Regarding what?
1	Liu Hong's younger brother	Liu Hong	Leaves a message to call him back
2	Xiao Zhang	Xiao Ming	See a movie tomorrow night at 8pm
3	Fangfang	Fangfang's mother	Will be home late, so eat dinner, don't wait for her

8   Key points: He's too busy today and will probably get home at 9pm. He's sorry, he can't go to see a movie. He asks if you can buy some milk. If his mother rings, ask her to leave a message.

9   Sample answer:

Xiǎo míng   wǒ hé wǒ de yí ge péngyou shuō hǎo le jīn tiān xià
小明，我和我的一个朋友说好了今天下
wǔ sān diǎn tā lái wǒ jiā   kě shì wǒ sān diǎn bù néng dào
午三点他来我家，可是我三点不能到
jiā   Tā jiào Wáng Chén   Néng bu néng má fan nǐ qǐng tā jìn
家。他叫王辰。能不能麻烦你请他进
lai   ràng tā zài jiā děng wǒ   Nǐ kě yǐ gěi tā kàn wǒ de
来，让他在家等我。你可以给他看我的
zá zhì   Xiè xie
杂志。谢谢！

10

Wǒ huì dǎ diàn huà gěi tā de
1 我会打电话给他的。 b;

Tā bú huì bù lái de
2 他不会不来的。 a;

Tā huì gào su nǐ de
3 他会告诉你的。 a;

Wǒ jiù bù shuō
4 我就不说。 a;

Tā jiù shì wǒ de lǎo shī
5 他就是我的老师。a;

Míng tiān jiù shì wǒ de shēng rì
6 明天就是我的生日。 b;

11

dǎ cuò le
a 打错了 (wrong number)

xìn hào bù hǎo   tīng bù qīng
b 信号不好，听不清
(bad reception, couldn't hear clearly)

diàn huà yì zhí zhàn xiàn
c 电话一直占线 (line busy all the time)

12a

Wèi   nín hǎo   Běi jīng Fàn diàn
R: 喂，您好，北京饭店。

Wèi   wǒ shì   fáng jiān   Wǒ yǒu míng tiān zǎo shang
G: 喂，我是 113 房间。我有明天早上
liù diǎn de huǒ chē   nín néng bu néng jiào xǐng wǒ
六点的火车，您能不能叫醒我？

Dāng rán kě yǐ   Nín yào jǐ diǎn jiào nín
R: 当然可以。您要几点叫您？

Wǔ diǎn
G: 五点。

Duì bu qǐ   wǒ méi tīng qīng   Nín zài shuō yí biàn
R: 对不起，我没听清。您再说一遍，
hǎo ma
好吗？

G: Wǒ shuō míng tiān zǎo shang wǔ diǎn jiào xǐng wǒ
我说明天早上五点叫醒我。

R: Hǎo de   méi wèn tí   Hái yǒu bié de shì ma
好的，没问题。还有别的事吗？

G: Méi yǒu   xiè xie nǐ
没有，谢谢你。

12b W: Wèi   Nǐ hǎo   Shàng hǎi Cān tīng
喂！你好！上海餐厅。

C: Wèi   Nín hǎo   Wǒ xiǎng yù dìng yí ge zhuō zi
喂！您好！我想预定一个桌子。

W: Hǎo   shén me shí hou
好，什么时候？

C: Míng tiān wǎn shang qī diǎn bàn
明天晚上七点半。

W: Méi wèn tí   Qǐng wèn nǐ men jǐ wèi
没问题。请问你们几位？

C: Sì wèi   Wǒ xìng Zhāng   jiào Zhāng Tiān
四位。我姓张，叫张天。

W: Hǎo de   Zhāng xiān sheng   nín dìng le míng tiān wǎn shang
好的，张先生，您订了明天晚上
qī diǎn bàn sì ge rén de zhuō zi   Xiè xie nín de
七点半四个人的桌子。谢谢您的
yù dìng   Míng tiān jiàn
预定。明天见！

C: Xiè xie   Zài jiàn
谢谢！再见！

12c O: Wèi   Shàng hǎi huǒ chē zhàn   Qǐng jiǎng
喂！上海火车站！请讲。

C: Nǐ hǎo   Yǒu zhè ge xīng qī sān qù Nán jīng de
你好。有这个星期三去南京的
piào ma
票吗？

O:
Qǐng shāo děng   wǒ chá yí xià   Hái yǒu piào   nín yào
请稍等，我查一下。还有票，您要
jǐ diǎn de
几点的?

C:
Zuì hǎo shì xià wǔ liù diǎn
最好是下午六点。

O:
Kě yǐ   Nín yào tè kuài hái shì pǔ kuài   Tè kuài
可以。您要特快还是普快? 特快
sì bǎi kuài   wǎnshang qī diǎn bàn dào Nán jīng   pǔ kuài
四百块，晚上七点半到南京；普快
liǎng bǎi bā   wǎn shang shí yī diǎn dào
两百八，晚上十一点到。

C:
Wǒ dìng yì zhāng tè kuài piào   Xiè xie
我订一张特快票。谢谢。

13

1
Nǐ dǎ cuò le
你打错了。

2
Wǒ tīng bù qīng
我听不清。

3
Méi shì ba
没事吧?

4
Nǐ yǒu shén me shì
你有什么事?

5
Nín zài shuō yí biàn   hǎo ma
您再说一遍，好吗?

6
Nín dà diǎn shēng shuō   hǎo ma
您大点声说，好吗?

7
Wǒ guò yí huì 'r dǎ gěi nǐ
我过一会儿打给你。

8
Zhè shì sī rén diàn huà
这是私人电话。

14

1
Jīn tiān xià wǔ Liú Hóng qù mǎi dōng xi le
今天下午刘红去买东西了。

2
Tā de Yīng guó péng you Tāng mǔ dǎ diàn huà gěi tā le
她的英国朋友汤姆打电话给她了。

3
Tā zhī dao
他知道。

4
Tā shuō tā zhè ge zhōu mò dào Zhōng guó lǚ xíng   xiǎng qǐng Liú
他说他这个周末到中国旅行，想请刘
Hóng de jiā rén yì qǐ chī fàn   Tā shuō tā huì zài xīng qī
红的家人一起吃饭。他说他会在星期
liù xià wǔ dào Shàng hǎi   tā de Zhōng guó shǒu jī hào mǎ shì
六下午到上海，他的中国手机号码是
13898735738。

Unit 9–12 Review

1   1 d   2 h   3 a   4 c   5 i   6 b   7 e   8 f   9 g

4   Sample answer:

Nà li yǒu yì jiā dà xué, dà xué de pángbiān shì tú shū
那里有一家大学，大学的旁边是图书
guǎn。Cóng dà xué wǎng yòu guǎi, dào lù kǒu zài wǎng yòu guǎi,
馆。从大学往右拐，到路口再往右拐，
zǒu dào dì yī ge lù kǒu zuǒ guǎi, bú yuǎn jiù yǒu yí ge dà
走到第一个路口左拐，不远就有一个大
chāo shì, kě yǐ mǎi dào hěn duō dōng xi。Nà li yě yǒu yín
超市，可以买到很多东西。那里也有银
háng, fàn diàn, diàn yǐngyuàn hé yóu jú。Cóng diàn yǐng yuàn wǎng
行，饭店，电影院和邮局。从电影院往
zuǒ guǎi, dào lù kǒu, duì miàn yǒu yì jiā Fǎ guó cān tīng。
左拐，到路口，对面有一家法国餐厅。
Wǒ hěn xǐ huan chī nà li de cài。Cān tīng de dōngbian shì bó
我很喜欢吃那里的菜。餐厅的东边是博
wù guǎn。
物馆。

5a   1 Beijing University   2 No, it's not far.

5b   1 No. 30   2 It's on the opposite side of the road.

5c   1 Yes, there is.   2 No, it's to the right.

7
Tā shén me shí hou huí lai
1 他什么时候回来？
Má fan nǐ ràng tā gěi wǒ huí ge diàn huà
2 麻烦你让她给我回个电话。
Qǐngwèn, nín shì nǎ wèi
3 请问，您是哪位？
Qǐng nín shuōmàn yì diǎn, wǒ jì yí xià
4 请您说慢一点，我记一下。
Nǐ de diàn huà hào mǎ shì duō shǎo
5 你的电话号码是多少？

6 对不起，我听不清。您大点声说，
Duì bu qǐ　　wǒ tīng bù qīng　Nín dà diǎnshēngshuō
好吗?
hǎo ma

7 你打错了。
Nǐ dǎ cuò le

8 5, 3, 7, 1, 2, 8, 4, 9, 6, 10

9 **1** míngtiān **2** piányi **3** zhàntái **4** yìzhízǒu
5 hùzhào **6** yùdìng **7** shàngwǎng **8** xìnghǎo
9 xǐhuan **10** xìngqù

10 (The characters are for reference only.)

1 请问，附近有银行吗?
Qǐngwèn　　fù jìn yǒu yín háng ma

2 我想住五天。
Wǒ xiǎng zhù wǔ tiān

3 您的房间在八楼。
Nín de fáng jiān zài bā lóu

4 我最喜欢看书。
Wǒ zuì xǐ huan kàn shū

5 喂，李芳在吗?
Wèi　　　Lǐ Fāng zài ma

6 请他给我回个电话。
Qǐng tā gěi wǒ huí ge diàn huà

11 Translation: Once upon a time, there was a man who sold weapons, and he was selling a spear and a shield in the market. First, he raised his shield and said to the people: "Look, my shield is the hardest in the world. No matter how sharp a spear, it cannot penetrate this shield." Then, he raised his spear, and spoke to the people: "Look at my spear! It's so sharp! No matter how strong a shield, it cannot defend against my spear." The people around him found what he said very funny. One of them asked him: "So if you used your spear to poke your shield, what would the result be?" The guy who was selling the weapon was totally embarrassed and couldn't answer. So, he had to leave with his spear and shield.

12 Sample answers:

1 person: 你，们，作，做，他，信，住
(nǐ, men, zuò, zuò, tā, xìn, zhù)

2 female: 妈，妹，姐，奶，姥
(mā, mèi, jiě, nǎi, lǎo)

3 fire: 炒，烤，煲，烟
(chǎo, kǎo, bāo, yān)

4 speech: 说，认识，记
(shuō, rèn shi, jì)

5 hand: 拿，打，把，拉，找
(ná, dǎ, bǎ, lā, zhǎo)

6 mouth: 吃，喝，啊，吗，吧，听，喂，唱
(chī, hē, a, ma, ba, tīng, wèi, chàng)

7 metal: 钱，钟，铁，银
(qián, zhōng, tiě, yín)

13 1 e 2 h 3 f 4 g 5 i 6 c 7 b 8 d 9 a 10 j

14 You may recognize these characters:

1 女 'female'

2 饭店 'hotel'

3 出租车 'taxi'

4 路 'street'; 乐 'happy'; 南 'south'; 北 'north'

5 国 'country' and 银行 'bank'

6 您 the polite 'you'

7 口 'mouth'; the sign means 'entrance'

8 'tea', in one of the calligraphy styles

Chinese–English word list

a 啊 (exclamation:
  confirmation)

à 啊 (exclamation: sudden
  realization)

ǎi 矮 short

ài 爱 to love; love

Àodàlìyà 澳大利亚
  Australia

Àomén 澳门 Macau

Àoyùncūn 奥运村 Olympic
  village

bā 八 eight

bǎ 把 (grammar word)

bàba 爸爸 father

Bǎiwēipíjiǔ 百威啤酒
  Budweiser beer

bàn 半 half

bàngōnglóu 办公楼 office
  building

bāngzhù 帮助 help;
  assistance

bāo 包 1) to include
  2) bag (general term)

bāo 煲 (dishes cooked in a
  pot, like a stew)

bāshí 八十 eighty

Bāxī 巴西 Brazil

bāyuè 八月 August

bēi 杯 (measure word for cup,
  glass)

běi 北 north

Běijīng 北京 Beijing

běn 本 (measure word for
  books)

bèngdí 蹦迪 to go clubbing

bǐ 比 compared with

biàn 遍 time (refers to
  frequency)

biéde 别的 other (things)

bìng 并 in addition

bīngkuài 冰块 ice cube

Bōlán 波兰 Poland

bówùguǎn 博物馆 museum

bù 不 no; not

búcuò 不错 not bad; good

búguò 不过 however, but

bùhǎoyìsi 不好意思 sorry

Búhuìba? 不会吧？ It can't be!

bújiànbúsàn 不见不散 see you there (used to confirm a date)

bùle 不了 not really (used to decline an invitation)

bùxíng 不行 not possible; no way

Búyòngxiè! 不用谢 You're welcome!

C

càidān 菜单 menu
cāngkù 仓库 storage
cāntīng 餐厅 restaurant
cèsuǒ 厕所 toilet
chá 茶 tea
chá 查 to check
chà 差 to be short of
cháng 常 often
chǎng 场 (measure word for movies)
chàng 唱 to sing
chángcháng 常常 often
Chángchéng 长城 Great Wall
chǎo 吵 noisy
chǎo 炒 to stir fry
chāoshì 超市 supermarket
chē 车 bus; car; vehicle
chéngzhī 橙汁 orange juice

chī 吃 to eat
chōuyān 抽烟 to smoke
chūfā 出发 to depart
chūnjié 春节 Spring Festival (Chinese New Year)
chūqù 出去 to exit; to go outside
chūshēng 出生 to be born
chúshī 厨师 chef
chūxiàn 出现 to appear; to show
chūzūchē 出租车 taxi
cì 次 no. (only refers to trains)
cóng 从 from
cóng...dào... 从…到… from...to...
cuò 错 wrong; bad

D

dǎ 打 to hit; to punch
dà 大 large; big; old
dǎdiànhuà 打电话 to make a phone call
dài 带 to include; to have with
dàizǒu 带走 to take away
dǎlánqiú 打篮球 to play basketball
dàngāo 蛋糕 cake
dāngrán 当然 of course
dānrén 单人 single person
dào 到 to arrive
dǎrǎo 打扰 to disturb

dǎsuan 打算 to plan

dàtīng 大厅 lobby

Dàwèi 大卫 (a name) David

dàxué 大学 university

de 得 grammar word
(describes verbs)

Déguó 德国 Germany

děi 得 to have to; must

děng 等 to wait

dēngjìbiǎo 登记表
registration form

...de shíhou ···的时候
When...

diǎn 点 o'clock

diǎncài 点菜 to order

diànhuà 电话 telephone

diànhuàhàomǎ 电话号码
telephone number

diànnǎo 电脑 computer

diànshì 电视 TV

diàntī 电梯 lift/elevator

diǎnxīn 点心 snacks

diànyǐng 电影 film/movie

diànyǐngyuàn 电影院
cinema

dìdi 弟弟 younger brother

dì'èr 第二 second

dìfang 地方 place

dìng 订 to book; to confirm

dìtiě 地铁 underground,
subway

dìyī 第一 first

dōng 东 east

dōu 都 both, all

dòufu 豆腐 bean curd; tofu

duànliàn 锻炼 to do exercise

duānwǔjié 端午节 Dragon
Boat Festival

duì 对 correct; yes

duìbuqǐ 对不起 sorry

duìmiàn 对面 opposite

duō 多 1) how (question
word) 2) so; really

duōjiǔ 多久 how long (time)

duōshǎo 多少 how much/
how many

E

èr 二 two

értóngjié 儿童节 Children's
Day

érqiě 而且 in addition

èrshí 二十 twenty

èrshí'èr 二十二 twenty two

èrshísān 二十三 twenty
three

èrshíwàn 二十万 two
hundred thousand

èrshíyī 二十一 twenty one

èryuè 二月 February

érzi 儿子 son

F

Fǎguó 法国 France

fānchuán 帆船 sailing boat

fàndiàn 饭店 hotel

fàng 放 to put

fángjiān 房间 room

fàngsōng 放松 relaxing; relaxed

fāxiàn 发现 to discover

fēicháng 非常 extremely, very

fēijī 飞机 plane

fēn 分 1) minute 2) (a monetary unit in RMB) ¥0.01

fèn 份 (measure word for portions)

fēndiàn 分店 branch

Fēnlán 芬兰 Finland

fēnzhōng 分钟 minute (duration of time)

fú 幅 (measure word for paintings)

fùjìn 附近 nearby

fútèjiā 伏特加 vodka

fúwùyuán 服务员 waiter/ waitress

G

gāng...jiù... 刚 … 就… just...then...

gǎnxiè 感谢 to thank

gāo 高 tall

gàosu 告诉 to tell

gāoxìng 高兴 happy

gè 个 (measure word)

gēge 哥哥 older brother

gěi 给 to give; to

gēn 跟 to follow

gèng 更 more

gōngchéngshī 工程师 engineer

gōnggòngqìchē 公共汽车 bus

gōngsī 公司 company

gōngyuán 公园 park

gōngzuò 工作 job; to work

gòu 够 enough

guà 挂 to hang up

guǎi 拐 to turn

guàn 罐 a can of (measure word)

Guǎngzhōu 广州 Guangzhou (Canton)

Gùgōng 故宫 Forbidden City

guì 贵 expensive

Guìlín 桂林 (a city in Southern China)

guò 过 1) to spend, to celebrate 2) to pass (time, place)

guóqìngjié 国庆节 National Day

H

hái 还 1) still 2) also; in addition to

hǎixiān 海鲜 seafood

háizi 孩子 child, children

hànbǎo 汉堡 burger

Hánguó 韩国 South Korea

Hànsī 汉斯 (a name) Hans

hǎo 好 1) good; well 2) OK; all right 3) quite; rather

hào 号 day (to express dates)

hǎode 好的 OK; all right

hǎojiǔbújiàn 好久不见 long time no see

hǎowán 好玩 good fun; fun

hē 喝 to drink

hé 和 and

hěn 很 very

hépíng 和平 peace

hóng 红 red

hóngpútaojiǔ 红葡萄酒 red wine

hóngshāo 红烧 braised in soy sauce

hòu 后 after; afterwards

hòumian 后面 behind

Hóusài 候赛 (a name) José

hú 壶 a pot of (measure word)

huà 画 painting

huàjiā 画家 painter

huánjìng 环境 environment

huānyíngguānglín 欢迎 光临 (your presence is) welcome

huàn 换 to change

huāpíng 花瓶 vase

huí 回 to return

huì 会 1) meeting; conference 2) (grammar word – indicates future) 3) be able to

huílai 回来 to come back, to return

Huítóujiàn! 回头见! See you later!

huǒchē 火车 train

huǒchēzhàn 火车站 train station

huódòng 活动 activity

huǒtuǐ 火腿 ham

huòzhě 或者 or; alternatively

Hǔpáipíjiǔ 虎牌啤酒 Tiger beer

hùshi 护士 nurse

hùwài 户外 outdoor

hùzhào 护照 passport

J

jī 鸡 rooster; chicken

jǐ 几 how many

jì 记 to take note; to write down

jiā 加 to add

jiā 家 family, home

jiān 间 (measure word for rooms, buildings)

jiàn 见 to see

jiàn 件 (measure word for clothes on the top half of the body)

Jiānádà 加拿大 Canada

jiǎo 角 (a monetary unit in RMB) ¥0.10

jiào 叫 to call, to be called

jiàoshījié 教师节 Teacher's Day

jiàoshòu 教授 professor

jiàoxǐng 叫醒 to wake (somebody) up

jiārén 家人 family members

jiātíngzhǔfù 家庭主妇 housewife

jìcún 寄存 to deposit; to keep

Jǐ diǎn le? 几点了? What time is it?

jiějie 姐姐 older sister

jièshào 介绍 to introduce

jiézhàng 结帐 bill; check

jīngjù 京剧 Beijing opera

jīnglǐ 经理 manager

jīnnián 今年 this year

jīnróng 金融 finance

jīntiān 今天 today

jiǔ 酒 alcohol, alcohol drinks

jiǔ 九 nine

jiù 就 1) exactly; precisely 2) (grammar word: expresses emphasis) 3) just

jiǔshí 九十 ninety

jiǔyuè 九月 September

jì...yòu... 既···又··· not only... but also...

jìzhě 记者 journalist

juéde 觉得 to think; to feel

jùhuì 聚会 reunion; gathering; party

K

kǎbùqínuò 卡布奇诺 cappuccino

kāfēi 咖啡 coffee

kāihuì 开会 to have a meeting; to attend a conference

kǎlāOK 卡拉OK karaoke

kàn 看 1) to watch; to see 2) to read

kàndiànshì 看电视 to watch TV

kàndiànyǐng 看电影 to watch movies

kànjīngjù 看京剧 to watch Beijing opera

kànshū 看书 to read

kǎo 烤 to roast; roasted

kělè 可乐 Coke

kěnéng 可能 maybe; perhaps

kěshì 可是 but

kěyǐ 可以 can, could, be able to

kǒngpà 恐怕 to be afraid

kōngtiáo 空调 air conditioning

kuài 块 1) (a monetary unit in RMB) ¥1.00 (informal) 2) (measure word for piece, slice, etc.)

kuài 快 fast

kuàilè 快乐 happy

kuàngquánshuǐ 矿泉水 mineral water

L

lái 来 to come

làngfèi 浪费 to waste, waste

lánqiú 篮球 basketball

láodòngjié 劳动节 Labour Day

láojià 劳驾 excuse me

lǎolao 姥姥 mother's mother

lǎoshī 老师 teacher

lǎoyé 姥爷 mother's father

le 了 (grammar word)

lèi 累 tired

lěng 冷 cold

lěngpán 冷盘 cold dishes (usually served as starters)

lǐ 里 in, inside

Lǐ 李 (a Chinese surname)

liǎng 两 two (used in measuring quantity)

liǎngqiān 两千 two thousand

liǎngwàn 两万 twenty thousand

liáotiān 聊天 to chat

Lìli 力力 (a name, lit. strength)

líng 零 zero

liù 六 six

Liú 刘 (a Chinese surname)

Liú Hóng 刘红 (a Chinese name)

liùshí 六十 sixty

liúyán 留言 to leave a message

liùyuè 六月 June

Lóngjǐng 龙井 (a region in Hangzhou famous for its tea)

lóu 楼 1) building 2) floor, storey

lù 路 1) road, street 2) no. (only refers to buses)

lǜ 绿 green

lǜchá 绿茶 green tea

lùkǒu 路口 crossroad, junction

lúnchuán 轮船 ship

Lúndūn 伦敦 London

lǜshī 律师 lawyer

lǚxíng 旅行 to travel

M

mǎ 马 horse

ma 吗 (question particle)

máfan 麻烦 to bother; to trouble

mǎi 买 to buy

mài 卖 to sell

mǎidōngxi 买东西 to do shopping

Mǎlì 玛丽 (a name) Mary, Marie

mǎlù 马路 road; street

māma 妈妈 mother

màn 慢 slow

máng 忙 busy

máo 毛 (a monetary unit in RMB) ¥0.10 (informal)

máoyī 毛衣 sweater

mǎshàng 马上 at once, immediately

méi 没 not; no (only negates 'have/has')

měi 每 every

méiguānxi 没关系 it doesn't matter; it's OK

Měiguó 美国 the USA

měijīn 美金 US dollars

mèimei 妹妹 younger sister

méishì 没事 fine; OK, all right

měitiān 每天 every day

méiwèntí 没问题 no problem

miànbāo 面包 bread

mǐfàn 米饭 boiled rice

míngnián 明年 next year

míngtiān 明天 tomorrow

Míngtiān jiàn! 明天见! See you tomorrow!

mìshū 秘书 secretary

mòlìhuāchá 茉莉花茶 jasmine flower tea

mótuōchē 摩托车 motorbike

N

ná 拿 to take; to carry

nǎ or **něi** 哪 which

nà 那 1) that 2) in that case

nǎi 奶 milk

nǎinai 奶奶 father's mother

nǎiyóu 奶油 cream

nǎli 哪里 where

nàli 那里 there

nàme 那么 in that case, then

nán 男 male

nán 南 south

nánkàn 难看 ugly

Nánjīng 南京 (a city in China)

nǎ'r 哪儿 where

nàtiān 那天 on that day

nátiě 拿铁 latte

nǎxiē 哪些 which (plural)

ne 呢 (tag question particle)

néng 能 can; to be able to

nǐ 你 you

nián 年 year

nǐde 你的 your, yours

Nǐ hǎo! 你好! Hello!

Nǐ hǎo ma? 你好吗? How are you?

nǐmen 你们 you (plural)

nǐmende 你们的 your, yours (plural)

nín 您 you (polite, singular and plural)

Nǐ ne? 你呢? And you?

niúròu 牛肉 beef

nǚ 女 female

nǚ'ér 女儿 daughter

O

ò 哦 oh

ǒu'ěr 偶尔 occasionally

Ōuzhōu 欧洲 Europe

P

pán 盘 a plate of (measure word)

pàng 胖 fat

pángbiān 旁边 beside

pānyán 攀岩 to rock-climb

péngyou 朋友 friend

piányi 便宜 cheap

piào 票 ticket

piàojià 票价 ticket fee

piàoliang 漂亮 pretty; beautiful

píjiǔ 啤酒 beer

píng 瓶 bottle (measure word)

píngshí 平时 normally

pǐsàbǐng 匹萨饼 pizza

pǔkuài 普快 standard train

pútao 葡萄 grapes

pútaojiǔ 葡萄酒 wine

Q

qī 七 seven

qí 齐 complete; ready

qián 钱 money

qiánmian 前面 at the front

qiántái 前台 reception, front desk

qiǎokèlì 巧克力 chocolate

qìchē 汽车 car

qǐchuáng 起床 to get up

qīng 清 clear

qǐng 请 please

qīngchǔ 清楚 clear

Qīngdǎo 青岛 (a coastal city in China famous for its beer)

qǐngmànyòng 请慢用 please enjoy

qǐngwèn 请问 excuse me

qīshí 七十 seventy

qīyuè 七月 July

qù 去 to go

qūbié 区别 difference

qùnián 去年 last year

qúnzi 裙子 skirt

R

ràng 让 1) to let; to allow 2) to ask somebody to do something

ránhòu 然后 then, afterwards

rè 热 hot

rèchǎo 热炒 hot dishes (usually refers to main courses)

rén 人 person, people

rénmínbì 人民币 RMB, Chinese currency

Rénmín Guǎngchǎng 人民广场 People's Square

rènshi 认识 to get to know, to meet

rèxīn 热心 warm-hearted

Rìběn 日本 Japan

ròu 肉 meat

rúguǒ...jiù... 如果···就··· if ...then...

S

sān 三 three

sànbù 散步 to go for a walk

sānkè 三刻 three quarters

sānmíngzhì 三明治 sandwich

sānqiān 三千 three thousand

sānshí 三十 thirty

sānshíwàn 三十万 three hundred thousand

sānwàn 三万 thirty thousand

sānyuè 三月 March

shàngbān 上班 to (start) work

shàngcì 上次 last time; the previous time

Shànghǎi 上海 Shanghai

shāngrén 商人 businessman/woman

shàngwǔ 上午 morning

shāoděng 稍等 just a minute

shēng 声 sound

shēngrì 生日 birthday

shénme 什么 what

shénmeshíhou 什么时候 what time, when

shēntǐ 身体 body; health

shí 十 ten

shì 是 to be

shì 试 to try

shì 室 room

shì 事 matter; issue; thing

shíbā 十八 eighteen

shí'èr 十二 twelve

shí'èryuè 十二月 December

shífēn 十分 very much

shīfu 师傅 master

shíjiān 时间 time

shíjiǔ 十九 nineteen

shíliù 十六 sixteen

shíqī 十七 seventeen

shísān 十三 thirteen

shísì 十四 fourteen

shíwàn 十万 ten thousand

shíwǔ 十五 fifteen

shíyī 十一 eleven

shíyīyuè 十一月 November

shíyuè 十月 October

Shì zhèyàng a! 是这样啊! I see!

shōu 收 to receive; to accept

shǒu 手 hand

shòu 瘦 thin

shòuhuòyuán 售货员 shop assistant

shǒujī 手机 mobile

shōujù 收据 receipt

shū 书 book

shǔ 属 to be born in the year of (Chinese horoscope)

shuāng 双 (measure word for pairs)

shuāngrén 双人 two people/ couple

shúi *or* shéi 谁 who, whom

shuǐ 水 water

shuìjiào 睡觉 to sleep

shuō 说 to talk; to say

shūshu 叔叔 uncle (father's younger brother)

sì 四 four

Sìchuān Běilù 四川北路 North Sichuan Road (a street name)

sījī 司机 driver

sīrén 私人 private

sìqiān 四千 four thousand

sìshí 四十 forty

sìwàn 四万 forty thousand

sìyuè 四月 April

suì 岁 years old

suǒyǐ 所以 therefore

suǒyǒude 所有的 all

Sūshān 苏珊 (a name) Susan

T

tā 他 he; him

tā 她 she; her

tā 它 it

tāde 他的 his

tāde 她的 her; hers

tāde 它的 its

Tàiguó 泰国 Thailand

tài...le! 太 .. 了！ too...!

tàitai 太太 wife; Mrs

tāmen 他们 they; them

tāmen 她们 they; them (female)

tāmende 他们的 their(s)

tāmende 她们的 their(s) (female)

tāng 汤 soup

táng 糖 sugar

tángcù 糖醋 sweet and sour flavour

Tāngmǔ 汤姆 (a name) Tom

tǎolùn 讨论 to discuss

tèbié 特别 especially

tèkuài 特快 express train

tèsè 特色 specialty (refers to food, art, skills)

tī 踢 to kick

tián 填 to fill in (a form)

tiāngōng 天公 the gods

tiānqì 天气 weather

tiáo 条 (measure word for clothes on the lower half of the body)

tīng 听 to listen

tīngdejiàn 听得见 to be able to hear

tīngshuō 听说 to have heard that

tīngyīnyuè 听音乐 to listen to music

tīzúqiù 踢足球 to play football

tóngxuémen 同学们 classmates; class

tōngxùnlù 通讯录 address book

tuán 团 group; team

tuījiàn 推荐 to recommend

túshūguǎn 图书馆 library

W

wán('r) 玩（儿）to play

wán 完 to finish; to complete

wǎn 晚 late; to be late

wǎnfàn 晚饭 dinner

Wáng 王 (a Chinese surname)

wǎng 往 towards

wàng 忘 to forget

Wáng Míng 王明 (a Chinese name)

wǎngshang 网上 on the internet

wǎnshang 晚上 evening

wèi 喂 hello (on the phone)

wèi 位 person (polite measure word)

wèishēngjiān 卫生间 bathroom

wèishénme 为什么 why

wēishìjì 威士忌 whisky

wǒ 我 I; me

wǒde 我的 my; mine

wǒmen 我们 we; us

wǒmende 我们的 our; ours

wǔ 五 five

wǔfàn 午饭 lunch

wúliáo 无聊 boring

wǔshí 五十 fifty

wǔtīng 舞厅 disco; dance hall

wúxiànshàngwǎng 无线上网 wireless internet

wǔyuè 五月 May

X

xī 西 west

xiàbān 下班 to finish work

xiàchē 下车 to get off

xiàcì 下次 next time

xiàge 下个 next

xiān 先 first

xián 闲 free, not busy

xiàn 线 line

xiǎng 想 would like to; to want to

xiǎngdào 想到 to think of; to think about

Xiānggǎng 香港 Hong Kong

xiǎngyào 想要 would like

xiànjīn 现金 cash

xiānsheng 先生 husband; Mr

xiànzài 现在 now

xiān...zài... 先···再··· first...then...

xiǎo 小 little; small; young

xiǎojiě 小姐 Miss, young lady

xiǎoshí 小时 hour

xiàtiān 夏天 summer

xiàwǔ 下午 afternoon

Xībānyá 西班牙 Spain

xiē 些 some

xié 鞋 shoes

Xièxie! 谢谢! Thanks!

xǐhuan 喜欢 to like

Xīlà 希腊 Greece

xīn 新 new

xìng 姓 surname

xìnghǎo 幸好 fortunately

xíngli 行李 luggage

xínglipái 行李牌 luggage tag

xīngqī 星期 week

xīngqī'èr 星期二 Tuesday

xīngqīliù 星期六 Saturday

xīngqīrì 星期日 Sunday

xīngqīsān 星期三 Wednesday

xīngqīsì 星期四 Thursday

xīngqītiān 星期天 Sunday

xīngqīwǔ 星期五 Friday

xīngqīyī 星期一 Monday

xìnhào 信号 signal

xìnyòngkǎ 信用卡 credit card

xuédào 学到 to learn; to acquire

xuésheng 学生 student

xuéxí 学习 to study; study

xuéxiào 学校 school

xuéyuàn 学院 college; school

xūyào 需要 to need

Y

yā 鸭 duck

yǎnchū 演出 to perform

yángròu 羊肉 lamb

yàngpǐn 样品 sample product

yào 要 1) to want to 2) to need to; to have to 3) will

yàome 要么 or; either...or...

yàoshi 钥匙 key

yě 也 also; too

yěcān 野餐 to have a picnic

yéye 爷爷 father's father

yī 一 one

yìbǎi 一百 one hundred

yìbǎiwàn 一百万 one million

yìbān 一般 usually, in general

yícì 一次 once

Yìdàlì 意大利 Italy

yìdiǎn 一点 a little bit

yídìng 一定 definitely

yígòng 一共 altogether

Yíhéyuán 颐和园 Summer Palace

yī...jiù... 一···就··· as soon as

yíkè 一刻 a quarter

yìkǒujià 一口价 final price

yílùshùnfēng 一路顺风 to have a good journey

Yìndù 印度 India

Yīngguó 英国 Britain

yínháng 银行 bank

yǐnliào 饮料 beverage

yīnwèi 因为 because

yīnyuè 音乐 music

yìqǐ 一起 together

yìqiān 一千 one thousand

yīshēng 医生 doctor

yíxià 一下 (grammar word – refers to a brief action)

yíwàn 一万 ten thousand

yíyuè 一月 January

yìzhí 一直 1) straight 2) all the time; always

yòng 用 to use

yǒu 有 1) to have 2) there is; there are

yòu 右 right

yòubian 右边 right-hand side

yǒukòng 有空 to be free/ have time

yóupiào 邮票 stamp

yǒushí 有时 sometimes

yǒu xìngqù 有兴趣 to be interested in

yǒuyìsi 有意思 interesting

yóuyǒng 游泳 to swim; swimming

yóuyú 鱿鱼 squid

yú 鱼 fish

yuán 元 (a monetary unit in RMB) ¥1.00

yuǎn 远 far; far away

yuándàn 元旦 New Year

yuánxiāojié 元宵节 Lantern Festival

yùdìng 预定 to reserve; to book

yuè 月 month

yùndòng 运动 sports

Yúnyun 云云 (a name, lit. cloud)

yúxiāngròusī 鱼香肉丝 shredded pork with fish flavour

Z

zài 在 to be in/at/of (position)

zài 再 again

Zàijiàn! 再见! Goodbye!

zàishuō 再说 furthermore; moreover

zǎofàn 早饭 breakfast

zǎoshang 早上 (early) morning

Zǎoshang hǎo! 早上好! Good morning!

Zěnme le? 怎么了? What's the matter? What's wrong?

zěnmeyàng 怎么样 how; how about

zhàn 站 (bus) stop

zhāng 张 (measure word for flat objects)

Zhāng 张 (a Chinese surname)

zhàntái 站台 platform

zhànxiàn 占线 occupied; busy (phone line)

zhǎo 找 1) to look for 2) to give change back

zhǎodào 找到 to find

zháojí 着急 to be worried

zhè 这 this

zhèlǐ 这里 here

Zhēnqiǎo! 真巧! What a coincidence!

zhèyàng 这样 this way

zhǐ 只 only

zhīdao 知道 to know

zhǐhǎo 只好 to have to; to have no choice but to

zhīshi 知识 knowledge

zhíshùjié 植树节 Arbour day

zhíyuán 职员 clerk

zhōng 中 medium; middle

Zhōngguó 中国 China

zhōngqiūjié 中秋节 Moon Festival

Zhōngwén 中文 Chinese (language)

zhōngwǔ 中午 noon

zhōngyú 终于 finally, at the end

zhōumò 周末 weekend

zhù 住 to live; to stay

zhù 祝 to wish

zhuānyè 专业 major; specialism

zhuōzi 桌子 table

zhǔyi 主意 idea

zhùzài 住在 to live in/at

zìxíngchē 自行车 bicycle

zǒu 走 1) to leave 2) to walk

zuì 最 the most

zuìhǎo 最好 the best; ideally

zuìhòu 最后 finally, at the end

zuǒ 左 left

zuò 坐 to sit; to take (transport)

zuò 做 1) to do 2) to make

zuǒbian 左边 left-hand side

zuòfàn 做饭 to cook

zuòměi 作美 to make things easy

zuótiān 昨天 yesterday

zuòyè 作业 homework

zuǒyòu 左右 about, approximately

zúqiù 足球 football

Index

a 啊 as exclamation word 131
addresses 75
addressing people 9, 21, 30, 40
adjectives, formation of 155
adverbs, position of 176
ages 72
arrangements, making 128–30
'as soon as' **yī** 一 ... **jiù** 就 ...
   261
ba 吧 as exclamation word
   131
bǎ 把 structure 227
bargaining 150–3, 158
bǐ 比 comparative form 200
biàn 遍 287
birthdays 90–5, 112, 270
'both ... and ...' **jì** 既 ...
   yòu 又 ... 261
brief action
   verb + **yíxià** 一下 55
   verb + **yī** 一 + verb 132
bù 不 as negating word 49
can, to be able to 231–2
certainty and assurance
   huì 会 ... **de** 的 277
change of status using **le** 了
   119, 177

China Rail 219
Chinese characters
   history of 16–17
   how to form 18–19, 58, 109,
      133–4
   introduction iv, vi–vii
   learning v, 11
   radicals 215–6, 241–2,
      263–4, 293–4
   stroke order in writing 78–80
cì 次 287
common radicals 215–6,
   241–2, 263–4, 293–4
comparative form
   with **bǐ** 比 200
   with **gèng** 更 250
compass points 209
conditions, with **rúguǒ** 如果
   ... **jiù** 就 ... 'if ..., then ...'
   254
cóng 从 as preposition
   210–11
contrast adjectives 202–3
currency 140–2
daily routine 120–1
dào 到 as preposition 210–11
dào 到 : verb + **dào** 到 238

dǎsuan 打算 in simple future 104–5
dates 96
days of the week 90, 96
de 的
  as verbal attributive 199
  indicating possession 47–8
describing a situation 233
... **de shíhou** 的时候 for 'when ...', 'while ...' 237
difference between **cì** 次 and **biàn** 遍 287
directions 204–9
dōu: 'every ...' in **měi** 每 ... **dōu** 都 ... 259–60
drinks 161–6, 173, 183
duōshǎo 多少 'how many', 'how much' 103–4, 147
duration 100
eating out 170
emphasis **shì** 是 ... **de** 的 ... 97
entertainment 267
er 儿 in accent 209
'every ...' **měi** 每 ... **dōu** 都 ... 259–60
exclamation words **a** 啊 and **ba** 吧 131
family members 44–7
family values in China 61
festivals 91, 98–9, 138
finals 2
food 174–5, 183
Forbidden City 107, 201
frequency 122, 256, 260, 287–8

future, simple with **yào** 要, **huì** 会 and **dǎsuan** 打算 104–5
gāng 刚 ... **jiù** 就 ... 'just/not long after ..., and then ...' 237
gěi 给 as preposition 'to', 'for' 276–7
gender 33
gèng 更 as comparative 250
goodbye and thank you 13–15
Great Wall 107, 201
greetings 7–13, 24–6
guest–host setting 183
hand gestures for numbers 66
'he' and 'she' 43
hěn 很 'to be' 27
holidays and festivals 91, 98–9, 138
horoscopes 113
hotels Unit 10
huì 会 in simple future 104–5
huì 会 ... **de** 的 for certainty and assurance 277
identification, precise **jiù** 就 277–8
imperative 166–7, 211, 275–6
incomplete actions with **méi** 没 'hasn't/haven't done sth' 276
indirect speech 288
initials 3
interest, expressing 252–3
introducing
  a friend 52–4
  your family 43–7
  yourself 30

jǐ 几 'how many' 103–4, 147

jì 既 … yòu 又 … 'not only … but also …' 261

jiào 叫 275–6

jǐdiǎn 几点 'what time' (specifically) 123

jiù 就 for precise identification 277–8

jobs 25, 31–3

kěyǐ 可以 'may' 231–2

le 了 119, 177, 227–8

le 了 … le 了 286

leisure activities and hobbies Unit 11

liǎng 两 'two' for measuring amounts 65

likes and dislikes 248

location

 expressing 209–10

 hierarchy 30

 indicator zài 在 49–50

ma 吗 for yes/no questions 27

majiang 264, 267

making and answering phone calls 270–1

map of China 107

means of transport 194

measure words 67–9

méi 没

 as negating word 49

 incomplete actions 'hasn't/ haven't done sth' 276

měi 每 … dōu 都 … 'every …' 259–60

men 们 for the personal pronoun plural 12–13

menus 178

modification of tones 5–6

months of the year 91, 96

nǎ/něi 哪 'which' 103–4

nàjiù 那就 … ba 吧 177

nǎli 哪里 'where' 54–5

names 40

nationality 31–5

ne 呢 for tag questions 28

negating words bù 不 and méi 没 49

néng 能 231–2

New Year song 269–70

'no' 131, 167

'not only … but also …'

 jì 既 … yòu 又 … 261

nouns, formation of 154

numbers Unit 4, 64–5, 82

Olympic Village 201

passive tense, indication of 276

past continuous with zài 在 + verb 287

past with verb + le 了 119, 177, 227–8

permission, asking for 230–2, 275–6

personal information 71

personal pronoun plural men 们 12–13

phone calls Unit 12

phone numbers 72, 104, 296

Pinyin v, vi–vii, 1–2, 11

places of interest 107, 201

'please' using qǐng 请 166

plural nouns 69

poems 159–60, 247–8

position, expressing 209

possession using **de** 的 47–8

prepositions

cóng 从 and **dào** 到 210–11

gěi 给 'to', 'for' 276–7

present continuous with **zài** 在 + verb 287

prices 144–7

problems on the telephone 280–5

qǐng 请 'please' 166–7, 275–6

question particles

ma 吗 for yes/no questions 27

ne 呢 for tag questions 28

question words

'how' **zěnmeyàng** 怎么样 54–5

'how many' **jǐ** 几 103–4, 147

'how many', 'how much' **duōshǎo** 多少 103–4, 147

'what' **shénme** 什么 54–5

'what time' (specifically) **jǐdiǎn** 几点 123

'when' **shénme shíhou** 什么时候 103

'where' **nǎli** 哪里 54–5

'which' **nǎ/něi** 哪 103–4

'who' **shuí/shéi** 谁 54–5

radicals 215–6, 241–2, 263–4, 293–4

ràng 让 275–6

reasons, giving 256

requests 166–7, 230, 275–6

restaurants 170–5

resultative complement:

verb + **de** 得 / **bu** 不 + resultative complement 285

rúguǒ 如果 ...**jiù** 就 ... 'if..., then...' 254

shénme 什么 'what' 54–5

shénme shíhou 什么时候 'when' 103

shì 是 and **hěn** 很 'to be' 27

shì 是 ... **de** 的 ... for emphasis 97

shopping Unit 7

shuí/shéi 谁 'who' 54–5

signs 216, 304

simple future with **yào** 要, **huì** 会 and **dǎsuan** 打算 104–5

simple past with verb + **le** 了 119, 177, 227–8

slang expressions and sayings 221–2

sound combinations

complete 307–8

with the first tone 191–2

with the fourth tone 268–9

with the second tone 220–1

with the third tone 246–7

suggestions 128, 131–2, 153, 177

Summer Palace 201

superlative form with **zuì** 最 251

surnames 9, 30, 40

tài 太 ... **le** 了 construction 152

taiqi 267

telephone numbers 72, 104, 296

telling the time 116

time Unit 6

time expressions in sentences 123

time frequency 256

'to be' with 是 shì and 很 hěn 27

tones 3–6, 191–2, 220–1, 246–7, 268–9

tongue twisters 140, 192

tourist spots 107, 201

transport 193–8, 219

travel plans 100–2

travel in China 219

verb + not + verb for yes/no questions 167

verbal attributive with de 的 199

verbs, formation of 180

'when …'; 'while …' using … de shíhou 的时候 237

word formation 154–5, 180

yào 要 in simple future 104–5

'yes' 131, 167

yī — … jiù 就 … 'as soon as' 261

yī: verb + yī — + verb for brief action 132

yíxià: verb + yíxià 一下 for brief action 55

zài 在
  as location indicator 49–50
  + verb for present/past continuous 287

zěnmeyàng 怎么样 'how' 54–5

zhe: verb + zhe 着 238

zuì 最 for superlative form 251